Contemporary Judaic Fellowship
In Theory and In Practice

Contemporary Judaic Fellowship
In Theory and In Practice

Edited by
JACOB NEUSNER
Professor of Religious Studies
Brown University

KTAV PUBLISHING HOUSE, INC.
New York
1972

In memory of
Ruth Jezer Teitelbaum
כי מלאכיו יצוה לך לשמרך בכל דרכיך

CONTENTS

Part III

FELLOWSHIP AND ETHICS

Part IV

THE *HAVURAH* AS COMMUNE

1. *In Boston*

2. *In New York City*

3. *In Washington*

Part V

THE *HAVURAH* AS COMMUNITY

Part VI

CONCLUSION

PREFACE

Mr. William Scott Green kindly helped in editing the several papers. The editor also is indebted to Brown University for bearing the costs of the preparation of the manuscript. The several contributors are thanked for allowing their work to be reprinted and for advising the editor on the location of pertinent materials.

The work was well underway when the editor received word of the death of an old and cherished friend, one of the collaborators in the project, Ruthie Teitelbaum. In the last weeks of her life she had gathered the materials on the Denver *havurah* which are reprinted here. She and her husband, Dr. Daniel Thau Teitelbaum, helped to found that *havurah*, which, more authentically than any other, attempted to realize the original proposals of the editor. Ruthie touched many lives and enhanced them all. This book is dedicated to her memory not only because she is a contributor, but especially because it is about the hopeful search for community and the happy adventures of life she loved.

J.N.

Providence, Rhode Island

12 Kislev 5732
30 November 1971

FOREWORD

For more than a decade, public discussion in Jewry has focused upon fellowship and the problem of "community." That problem was seen to be the consequence of the failure of existing social forms to draw together isolated individuals in a common purpose and for personally meaningful activities. The Jewish discussion of that problem formed a small part of a much wider, considerably older inquiry into the nature and meaning of social relationships in modern urban life, on the "crisis" of the "radically isolated" individual, and on the difficulty in modern society of achieving satisfactory community-experience. In Protestant Christian circles, the renewal of the church through "small groups," and in Roman Catholic parishes, the development of the Pentecostal movement, represent correlative efforts to overcome the effects of the size and impersonality of religious institutions.

The discussions of fellowship in Judaism in time led in two directions. First, young people of the day began to form urban communes. Second, some adults experimented with the organization of small groups of committed people. Both made use of the same Hebrew term, *havurah*, originally translated by this writer as *fellowship*, although they applied it to quite different sorts of groups. The communes formed by the young seem analogous, in a general way, to the Dead Sea sect, the *yahad*, by contrast to the Pharisaic *havurah*. The former supplied the locus for the everyday life of the members, while the latter left its participants in the ordinary circumstances of the workaday world. Similarly, the youth-commune tends to create a very intense society, but it involves young people before they have embarked upon careers and taken up the responsibilities of raising a family, and it evidently does not retain their interest afterward. The small groups shaped by Reconstructionists, Jewish academicians, and others in the setting of adult life, in synagogues and under other larger organizational auspices, are bound together somewhat more loosely; their programs, however, are so planned that, if successful, the group continues, year in year out. To distinguish between these two forms of *havurot,* I have called the one *the havurah as commune,* the other, *the havurah as community.* This book is an effort to document the first thirteen years of the *havurah* in theory and in practice in American Judaism. Much, perhaps most, of the experience of Jewish fellowship lies outside the pages of this book, for important events and meaningful experiments were not commonly reduced to writing and preserved in the form of an essay which might be reprinted here. Still, the main outlines of thought on the subject are clear, and the record of the more important ventures is available.

Critics, indeed, have stressed the ephemeral character of the *havurot* in the form of communes, pointing out that their obvious links to the "youth-" or "counter-culture" of the late 1960s and early 1970s signify a short life span. The most trenchant observations come from Rabbi Wolfe Kelman, Executive Director of the Rabbinical Assembly, who underlines the connections between the commune-*havurot* and the Conservative movement in Judaism and rightly questions the sensationalism surrounding them (*Conservative Judaism,* Vol. 26, No. 1, 1971, p. 16):

> The leaders and founders of these dissenting groups with their rhetoric of anti-Establishment are primarily drawn from the ranks of Jewish Theological Seminary alumni and "dropouts." One wonders whether they develop their ambivalence about the Jewish tradition and the organized Jewish community after they enter the Seminary, or whether the Seminary tends, by its very nature, to attract a greater proportion of students with unresolved conflicts between reverence for traditional forms and institutions, and rebellion against them.

In any event, there is a growing vogue for Jewish Theological Seminary alumni to establish rabbinical schools, academies, and fellowships called *havurot*. For some reason, we rarely find Yeshiva and Hebrew Union College alumni in the leadership of these groups. Perhaps they are afflicted with fewer unresolved conflicts, or perhaps they find their schools providing less incentive to establish competing cells. The new Reconstructionist Seminary has a faculty that consists predominantly of Seminary alumni. A less conspicuous but older school is the Academy of Higher Jewish Learning, which began as a protest led by several Jewish Institute of Religion alumni after that school merged with Hebrew Union College. The Academy is now headed by a Seminary alumnus and has a faculty in which his colleagues predominate.

The most widely publicized radical group is the *Havurat Shalom*, founded by a group of young Conservative rabbis and a Reform Hillel director. It is presently located in Somerville, Massachusetts, and has attracted a group of students and teachers—an odd mixture of pacifists, educational innovators, and highly articulate dissenters from the institutional Synagogue. Synagogues produced the *havurah* members, and now they eagerly provide a platform for the latter's brutal critique of the progenitors and hosts. These encounters provide high visibility to the small membership of the Boston *havurah*, and the even tinier *havurah* in New York.

This observer tends to believe that the significance of the *havurot* has been highly exaggerated, partly by the need of some Jews to convince themselves that, like the Church, Judaism has also produced radical dissenters. I am inclined to suggest that this artificially inflated dimension of the youth culture will prove to be a passing fad remembered nostalgically by those who are easily seduced by slogans and fashions which promise instant eschatology, and by schools where students and teachers are interchangeable, love is God, and the greening of America is inevitable.

While I share Rabbi Kelman's prudent skepticism, I think it
worthwhile to consider how Jews managed to find a peculiarly
Jewish idiom in which to express a common cultural and
psychological phenomenon and so to fashion as "Jewish" one
epiphenomenon of what may end up merely a widespread fad,
or what may yet serve as a regenerative force in Judaism.

Let us consider, first of all, one way in which young Jews
formulated the problem of "community."

The Problem of "Community"

The problem of "community" was discussed at the
Conference on the Planning of the Future Jewish Community
held by the American Jewish Committee's Department of
Jewish Communal Affairs. The director, Steven F. Wind-
mueller, reports on the discussions as follows:

The first question that developed among the participants
centered on the problem of community. Many had
difficulty in coming to grips with the concept of community and in the relationships of community to individual
needs. As one young student suggested "My involvement is
part of my own struggle and is not related to the
community, rather the perpetuation of my own struggle."

Discussing the relationship between individualism and
communalism, one discussant concluded:

"What is clear is that no community is going to survive
which does not engage in involving individual human
beings on the deepest level. Any community that isn't
going to engage the deepest needs of its members is not
going to survive regardless of what the political
structures are."

With reference to the concept of man's relationship of
community, the representatives noted that young Jews had
a form of "engagement" with the Jewish community during
their adolescent years and that this initial contact with
organized Jewish Life has remained unexamined as a basis
for understanding attitudes and perceptions regarding
Jewish life on the part of young Jews.

"We have to recognize that the definition of an organic

Jew has to change; that American Jewry is constantly
developing new definitions."
In dealing with the development of new definitions, one of
the educators raised the following set of questions:
"What Jewish population are we talking about? If we are
talking about the future Jewish population are we saying
those of us who have an organic Jewish connection? Are
we talking about planning a Jewish community for those
people who have made some kind of personal peace with
their groping for Jewishness? That's one kind of
population. If we are going to discuss the Jewish
community for that kind of population, then we can
assume that kind of engagement, that kind of commitment. The other population is the broad mass of young
Jewish people, people who do not partake in community,
people whom you can't assume as having given a
commitment of any kind. Now if you are planning for the
Jewish community with that population in mind, then
you have to ask, what kinds of things facilitate that kind
of interception of the growing individual and his needs
and Jewish tradition? There are two levels. If you are
assuming as given some kind of Jewish commitment,
then you can move rapidly to political questions, tactical
questions, etc. If you are assuming a population for
whom you can't even assume an initial commitment to
Jewishness, and you are talking about planning a Jewish
community that is supposed to embrace all Jews, then
you are on the other level."
There was a general consensus that broad interpretation
and generalizations about Jewish life, and in particular
Jewish identity, would be a dangerous miscalculation.
Therefore, a selective agenda would be necessary in any
discussion of future Jewish community. Similarly the
discussion was to be guided by personalized or individual-
ized interests that the participants had. One young man
was consequently led to define the Jewish community as
"the sum total of problem areas that the Jewish people are
expressing."

In the final analysis, the discussion was to emphasize those items that were of primary importance to the Conference membership, because the Jewish agenda was indeed much broader and more sophisticated than the isolated subjects selected for discussion. One of the representatives present summarized this dilemma by suggesting

> "There are so many other areas with which we could deal, such as the funding of Jewish hospitals or the Jewish role in the Biafra crisis, but I for one would like to rap over Jewish problems in which the people here have a deep investment."

Clearly, the problem of "community" and various Jewish institutions and organizations have been confused. It is one thing to speak of "people who do not partake in community," and quite another to talk about "Jewish" hospitals or the "Jewish role" in the Biafra crisis. Considerable confusion in terminology seems to have characterized the discussion, which may reflect an underlying problem in formulating just what was bothering the younger generation. Consequently, anything proposed by anyone under thirty became evidence of "ferment" and any small, radical group given a Jewish or Hebrew name and a program was thought pertinent to the *havurah*-idea.

The Havurah *within the "Counter-Culture"*

We are not concerned here with every sort of youth-project of the past decade, but only with those defined as *havurot*, that both seem to have lasted more than a few months and involved more than a small clique. The Jewish student press, moreover, does not fall within our range of interest, nor do the activities of the North American Jewish Student Network and Press Service. Data on the Jewish wing of the international "youth-" or "counter-culture" may be found in the items collected by Geraldine Rosenfield, *What We Know about Young American Jews. An Annotated Bibliography* (N.Y.,

1970: American Jewish Committee). A *Digest of the Jewish Student Press* , covering about two dozen newspapers, is published by the Department of Jewish Communal Affairs of the American Jewish Committee and prepared by the Boston Chapter, under the chairmanship of Paulette J. Idelson. The phenomenon of the Jewish free university, a non-credit, wide-ranging set of adult education courses, often centered on university Hillel Foundations, likewise lies outside the range of our concern. These programs have developed in some numbers, but it is difficult to trace their growth or assess their impact, since they come and go, mutate and enter a second life, at a rapid pace. *A Guide to Jewish Student Groups 1971*, compiled and edited by Ann Rothstein (N.Y., 1971: North American Jewish Students' Network) includes, among two hundred organizations, the following, in existence as of March 1971, which might be, or develop into, *havurot: Fabrangen* (see below, pp. 185ff.); *Havurah* (New York) (see below, pp. 161ff.); *Havurat Shalom* Community Seminary (see below, pp. 149ff.); and the House of Love and Prayer, San Francisco, described as follows:

It's a house of love and prayer between two parks. Shlomo Carlebach is the inspiration and spiritual father of the House.

People wander in and stay for a day or two, a month, a year. Anyone can crash for couple of nights. Those who want to stay for a while, a couple weeks, a month, or more, talk to the committee of members of the House about why they'd like to stay.

Weekday individual and group prayers are decided on day to day. Everyone comes together for the evening meal. They wash each other's hands. They feed each other bread. In the evening there are classes. And later people come by with guitars to sing.

Scheduled classes take place three or four evenings a week. During the day people teach each other and teach themselves about Hebrew, Torah, Hassidism, *Kabbalah*. A more structured yeshiva is planned.

Friday night many people from the community gather with the people in the House. They sing and dance and chant and sway together. They tell Hassidic stories. They talk of the week's *sedra*. And then they eat together.

The people don't let *Shabbes* go until late. *Havdalah* has been said as late as 2 or 3 A.M. on Sunday.

The Jewish Residence House of the University of Pennsylvania is described as follows:

The J.R.H., a communal, "coop style" house of thirteen members, was formed in 1968. The purpose of such a house, from its initiation, was to provide an atmosphere conducive to traditional Jewish observance and scholarship, where committed Jewish students could live and study together, celebrate the Shabbat and festivals, and, hopefully, set an example of true halachic Jewish living for the campus community. The House is completely self-sustaining, with both undergraduate and graduate members from University of Pennsylvania and area colleges. Activities, most of which are open to all students, include a *Shabbat* dinner program, *Shiurim*, faculty dinner hours, temporary lodging for out-of-town students, holiday parties, and a library.

Jews for Urban Justice, begun in 1966, presents itself as "(1) creating a true collective community composed of people who feel it necessary to live in a communal, humanistic, Jewish life style; (2) continuing to organize the Jewish community towards radical political and social change."

All other groups listed in the *Guide* seem to be conventional in form and in program, e.g., Yeshiva College Student Council, various student Zionist societies, singing chorales and drama clubs, radical political groups, and the like. These cannot be regarded as *havurot*.

Havurot *in Hillel Foundations*

Hillel Foundations have explored the *havurah*-idea in many ways. Dr. Alfred Jospe reports (personal letter, November 19, 1971) that Hillel Foundations sponsor small *havurot* on many campuses, for instance, at Cornell, University of Arizona, and University of Texas. It is difficult to find documents or publishable essays on the experience of these *havurot*. One statement, "What is the Student Revolt All About?" by Gerald A. Goldman, published in the *Clearing House of Bnai Brith Hillel Foundations,* December, 1971, supplies an account of the theory of a *havurah* within the Hillel setting:

Students criticize us today for failing to promote a genuine Jewish community in America; for failing to involve them in decision-making, which would relieve them of a sense of helplessness at least in their lives as Jews; for failing to create significant forms of Jewish action, study and worship to lift Jewish life above the plastic and vicarious, that which is untrue to genuine human needs; and for failing to provide a place where persons can confirm their selfhood honestly. These are—each one of them—contemporary critiques of American society in general, and we would expect it to be this way. However, the excitement in challenge thrown to us by these critiques lies in the fact that they are (1) genuine to Jewish tradition, with its emphases on *ma'aseh, midrash,* and *tsibbur;* (2) essential if American Jewish life is to enjoy a place complementary to Jewish life in Israel; and (3) important to us if we are to fulfill ourselves as rabbis, teachers, and counselors.

Let us imagine the kind of Jewish community these students—or at least a vocal minority of them—are requesting:

First of all, it will be a community, and not a series of membership organizations, tangentially related and often in competition with one another. The most ideal of such communities is the *Havurah,* in which members live, eat, study, pray, and act together. Like the communes popular today, the *Havurah* affords the maximum in individual decision-making—an antidote to personal powerlessness; confirmation of selfhood as one whose worth is recognized by the group; the opportunity to create and experiment with new forms of Jewish action, study, worship, and life-styles (marriage, child-rearing, etc.). Its disadvantages are obvious: it can appeal only to a very few, and it runs the danger not only of internal collapse but also of Essene-like withdrawal from the larger Jewish community.

However, less extreme forms of Jewish community are possible. Following Rabbi Richard Levy's suggestions in the Spring '69 issue of *Judaism*, synagogues may divide into small action groups, not with "plastic" purposes, but with genuine tasks to be carried out in mini-communities. Instead of a ritual committee, for example, with its alienating formalism, there might be simply a *minyan* which worships together as a community. Its members, being limited in number and free to share their doubts and hopes with one another, can innovate new and better forms of worship—forms which bring congregants together instead of separating them, invite genuine expressions of human feeling, disappointment, grief, hope and trust, and, by abridging the distance between the pulpit and the congregation, free the rabbi from the role of a robed priest to that simply of teacher (thereby removing some of the psychological dangers inherent in the archaic priest-father role).

This mini-community might do more—perhaps initiate Sabbath dinners and celebrations at the homes of its members on a rotating basis, replacing the anonymity of contemporary Jewish Sabbath celebration with the genuine Jewish experience of peoplehood. *Shabbat* then wouldn't be from 8–10:30 P.M. on Friday evenings and 10 to 12 noon on Saturday mornings. There would be a nuclear community of Jews with whom one and his family may enjoy *Oneg* and *m'nuchah* from sundown to sundown. Imagine what such a modest development might mean for American Jewish life and for our work as rabbis!

As I hear the students, their pleas for a voice in the synagogue, to find relief from their feeling of helplessness, and their call for the opportunity to confirm themselves as individuals, as persons, in the synagogue are one and the same plea. Most contemporary synagogues are too large and too much in the control of persons whose age, financial position, and life-style freeze the options available to youthful innovations. Rabbi Levy referred to this phenomenon when he wrote—

"Most synagogues are organized according to a structure
paralleling a corporation, with officers and a board of
trustees. The entire structure of relationships within the
synagogue is one cause for the alienation of its
members."

This hyper-structuralism expresses itself everywhere in the
activities of the synagogue, especially in the obsessive
concern that everything "run smoothly." God forbid
someone should stand up when everyone else sits down at
services, or say something "too critical" of the rabbi, school
or services at a board meeting.

An air of paternalism hangs over the synagogue. The
rabbi decides what it means to be Jewish while the
president decides what it means to be solvent. And
everything is handed to paying members as a finished
product. This is from the rabbi's point of view an awesome
and ungrateful situation, which only serves to set him off
further from his people as "the professional Jew" rather
than as their guide and teacher as he would like to be.

What does this have to do with selfhood? Simply that if a
student is to be recognized as a person and not as a
well-greased cog in a formal service or formal lecture,
someone has to turn to him, ask him what he thinks, and
risk the foolishness or brilliance of his reply. As a person he
wants to do things for himself. He does not need a
programmer; he needs other persons to—in Zalman
Schachter's words—"Jew it with." As a person he insists
that the formal structure of worship, lectures, teas, etc., not
get in the way of his being with you and your being with
him.

Synagogue Experiments

Representative of the efforts of synagogues to experiment
with the *havurah*-idea is *Breet K'tanah* [sic!] a short-lived
small-group effort led by Rabbi Roland B. Gittlesohn of
Temple Israel, Boston. Rabbi Gittelsohn stressed concrete
commitment on the part of the *haverim*. Each was asked to

check twenty-one of the following items and so "to associate myself with you and my fellow-congregants in a *Breet K'tanah*":

I. *Worship*

I shall attend at least two Temple Israel Religious Services each month, either on Friday night or Saturday morning. On those Friday nights and Saturday mornings when I am not in Temple, I shall spend some time in prayer at home. I shall pray or meditate silently each night before sleep . . .

II. *Education*

I shall faithfully attend at least one Temple Israel Adult Education class this year.
On the appended list, I promise to read during the year not less than six books I have not previously read.
I pledge myself to subscribe to and read at least two of the magazines on the appended list . . .

III. *Identifiable Jewish Practice*

The *motzee* blessing will be recited at my dinner table every night.
I shall kindle candles and have *kiddush* recited each Friday night.
I shall either conduct or attend a *Seder* on Passover.
Either a full outdoor *sukkah* or a miniature *sukkah* within my home will be on view throughout *Sukkot* . . .

IV. *Ethical Inventory*

In attendance at Worship Services, I shall attempt honestly to evaluate my own ethical behavior in recent days.
Each night before falling asleep I shall reflect on the ethical aspects of my behavior that day.
I shall consciously think of the ethical ideals of Judaism before making any important decision in my business life and/or my relationships with my fellow men.
Some time during this year I shall make a conscious effort to be friendly to at least one person whom I have not liked in the past.

I shall increase this year the number of philanthropies to
which I have given in the past, as well as the amount I have
contributed.

I shall contribute this year as generously as possible to at
least two organizations I have not supported in the
past—one in the field of civil rights and one which works
for international peace.

I shall volunteer my time and effort to work this year on
behalf of at least one such organization.

By reading and/or personal experience, I shall attempt this
year to understand one racial or ethnic group which is now
strange to me.

The experiment seems not to have lasted long, at least not in
its original form. Rabbi Gittelsohn reports, "The group I
originally organized . . . was subsequently changed to the
Rabbi's *Havdalah* Hour. It amounts to much the same thing
except that individuals are no longer asked to make a
commitment toward the fulfillment of certain *mitzvot* in
order to join the group. We now meet one *Shabbat* afternoon
each month for a half-hour of conversation and refreshments,
followed by an hour-and-a-half of study or discussion, then
concluding with my own *Havdalah* service." Approximately
seventy members have affiliated with the *Havdalah* Hour, of
whom about forty to fifty attend regularly.

Other synagogue-based *havurot* have been difficult to
document. The editor circularized hundreds of rabbis,
through the Rabbinical Assembly and elsewhere, and received
not a single reply. What, if anything, has been done elsewhere
is thus not known.

The Reconstructionist Havurot

After this writer presented "Jewish Fellowship Today" as a
lecture at the meeting of the Reconstructionist movement in
May, 1961, the movement determined to make use of the
havurah-idea and adopted the name, *Federation of Reconstructionist Congregations and Fellowships.* The Federation
as of June, 1971, counts ten congregations and eleven *havurot*
which are listed as follows:

(1) Jewish Reconstructionist Society of Brooklyn; (2) Jewish Reconstructionist Group of Essex County; (3) Federation of Reconstructionist Fellowships (3 Fellowships), Denver, Colorado; (4) E. Lansing, Michigan; (5) Allentown, Pa.; (7) Somerville, N.J.; (8) Philadelphia, Pa.; (9) Philadelphia Friends of the Reconstructionist Rabbinical College; (10) Whittier, Calif.; (11) Palm Springs, Calif..

The report from Denver provides documents from a Reconstructionist *havurah* in action.

The Purpose of This Anthology

The editor has brought together writings on the theory and practice of the *havurah* in order to permit consideration of the early stages of the phenomenon. He hopes also to provide perspective for further efforts in exploring the *havurah's* regenerative potentialities. As noted, much that has happened has gone unreported. He cannot claim to record each and every experiment of the past thirteen years. The theoretical literature is easier to locate—for it took written form—but is equally thin. Much has been done, but much less has been critically and carefully thought through. And, alas, the thinkers, with noteworthy exceptions, have not been the doers, and the doers have not been the thinkers. That accounts for the striking disjuncture between the first three parts of selections and the next two.

The historical perspective is severely limited to materials from the first century. Left out are masses of evidence on *hevras* and other small groups devoted to religious purposes, characteristic of many periods and found in many locations in the history of Judaism. For example, Chaim Bermant, in *Troubled Eden: An Anatomy of British Jewry* (N.Y., 1970: Basic Books, Inc.), writes about the East European immigrants in London at the end of the nineteenth century:

> And the newcomers brought not only the languages . . . of Eastern Europe, they brought their own type of synagogues, the *Chevrot* (fraternities) . . .

These small groups, devoted to prayer, study, and other forms of piety, were intensely disliked by the older Jewish

community; Bermant quotes the *Jewish Chronicle* as follows:
> The *Chevrot* . . . originate partly in the aversion felt by
> our foreign poor to the religious manners and customs of
> English Jews . . . The sooner the immigrants to our shore
> learn to reconcile themselves to their new conditions of
> living, the better for themselves. Whatever tends to
> perpetuate the isolation of this element in the community
> must be dangerous to its welfare.

Bermant further cites a congregational rabbi:
> It is because Jews have lived within themselves in other
> countries on the *"Hebra"* principle that they have made the
> existence of Jews in those countries intolerable . . . the
> sooner the *"Hebra"* movement is crushed out of existence
> the sooner we will remove from our midst the only
> drawback to the advancement of Jews in this country.

Such sentiments indicate that the organization of Judaic
society into small groups for intensive religious life was both
far more commonplace than indicated in the essays in parts
I-III that follow, and considerably more controversial.

The earliest proposals, from Professor Petuchowski, Rabbi
Schachter, and this writer, are included despite their admitted
irrelevance to what actually was done later on. It seemed of
interest to compare the proposed experiment with what
followed. Neither the *havurah* as commune nor, with
noteworthy exceptions, the *havurah* as community made
much effort to consider either the historical precedents
adduced in the early proposals, or the efforts to define alternative *havurot* and the ethical and moral promise contained
in them.

Stephen C. Lerner's careful account of *havurah* as commune, within the "counter-culture" formed in the late 1960's,
presents the best report on the subject known to this writer.
Others, writing in newspapers and Jewish magazines, emphasized the colorful and dramatic, not to say sensational, and do
not merit reprinting, for they distort the facts by overemphasis
on what readers want to read—the praying and the piety; the
complexities and subtleties are left out. Rabbi Arthur Green,
Bill Novak, Alan Mintz, Paul Ruttkay, George E. Johnson, and

Robert Agus then provide memoires of their own thinking and experience. Rabbi Green's two papers —originally prepared for informal discussion in *Havurat Shalom*— represent his personal response to the experience of the early years. *Havurat Shalom* has continued not only to endure but to evolve; the group has changed both in personnel and in orientation, but the continuities and the evidence of a capacity for self-criticism and growth are impressive. The *Havurah* in New York City—despite its slightly pretentious title, for it might more accurately have called itself a small *havurah* that sometimes meets in an apartment on a street in the Upper West Side of Manhattan—is represented by a report on the first year. Alongside is Alan Mintz's rich account of his own thought and experience within that group. Mintz speaks for himself, but he exemplifies the best thinking among the commune-oriented *haverim*.

The *havurah* as community was, if anything, even more difficult to document. Much of the literature consists of intensely personal accounts—confessions—of how people rediscovered "their Judaism" or returned to modes of traditional life. While such reversioners found others with whom to form small groups, these groups seem, in the main, to have consisted of little more than like-minded friends. The papers by Professor Daniel Elazar and Mr. George Driesen, and the documents compiled by the late Mrs. Ruth Jezer Teitelbaum, however, do provide evidence of what was worked out by *havurot* as communities of adult families. Strikingly, the groups discussed by Professor Elazar and Mr. Driesen do not continue in their original framework at all, so the *havurah* as community would seem still less stable than the *havurah* as a mode of the common "counter-culture." The Denver *havurot* form an important exception. They are committed, however, not only to the formation of communities but also to a specific and well-defined theological position, that of Reconstructionism. So they would seem to represent something quite different from the academic *havurah* and the study-circle. Professor Leonard Fein's and Rabbi Gendler's thinking about the *havurah* and the synagogue, both structured and unstructured, appears to correspond in theory to the Reconstructionist *havurot* in practice.

Bill Novak contributes the conclusion. He looks backward, forward, and inward. His seems to the editor to be the clearest voice, and his is among the best minds devoted to the *havurah* as commune; he exhibits wide sympathies and a temperate, judicious appreciation for the works of others, even those who have thought and done differently from himself.

The editor has not attempted to standardize transliterations or other matters of style. The authors speak in their own way, and have taken responsibility for correcting proofs of their respective articles. Not all of the papers were written for publication; many of the contributions in parts IV and V were not intended for publication at all. They therefore exhibit an informality of expression and thought characteristic of ideas in the process of formation, rather than the discipline of fully worked out theories or programs. It seemed worthwhile to include them as important evidence on an interesting phase in the formation of *havurot*, even though in form they may not exhibit the care their authors would normally have given. The paper by Bill Novak was commissioned for this volume. Several other contributions, in particular those by Robert Agus and Arthur Green, were originally written for private circulation. The Denver materials were not meant for publication at all and are included primarily as illustration of the activities of those *havurot*.

Toward the Renaissance of Community in

Contemporary Judaism?

I have few illusions about either the importance or the success of the early proposals and experiments. The theoretical statements, if read at all, seem to have yielded little more than some slogans and empty, verbal symbols—a program based on rather vague impressions of something heard about in some obscure place. The practical experiments have produced promising groups, both *havurah*-communes and *havurah*-communities, but these involve no considerable part of the available constituency and are not likely to.

Perhaps both the thinkers and the doers have deluded themselves by the pretentious thought that, while really going nowhere in particular, they may move toward the renaissance of community in contemporary American Judaism. But I think not. For, despite the limited and often ephemeral—sometimes even deplorable—results of the early stages of development, the *haverim* do address themselves to a considerable problem. If not for everyone, then at least for themselves, if not for life, at least for a time, they do solve that problem. This seems to me the incontrovertible conclusion to be adduced from the evidence before us. We do not stand where we did in the late 1950s and the early 1960s. We have worked out viable social alternatives for the religious life of Judaism. The massive, expensive, impersonal synagogue, organization, or institution now is not the only way for Jews to achieve common purposes. While for some the new alternatives were either unnecessary or uninteresting, for others they provided moments of deep communion within a profoundly Judaic society. Admittedly, the *havurah*-communes and the *havurah*-communities did not complete the task. But they did not desist from it.

ACKNOWLEDGEMENTS

The editor gratefully acknowledges permission granted by the following to reprint essays and papers in this book:

The Reconstructionist, for Jakob J. Petuchowski, "Toward a Modern Brotherhood"; Daniel J. Elazar, "An Academic *Havurah*"; and George Driesen, "A Satisfying Form of Jewish Experience." © 1960, 1962, and 1966, respectively, by Jewish Reconstructionist Foundation;

Judaism, for Zalman M. Schachter, "Toward an Order of B'nai Or.' A Program for a Jewish Liturgical Brotherhood." © 1964 by American Jewish Congress;

Conservative Judaism, for Stephen C. Lerner, "The Havurot." © 1970 by Rabbinical Assembly;

Arthur Green, for "*Havurat Shalom:* A Proposal," and "Some Liturgical Notes from *Havurat Shalom.*" © 1972 by Arthur Green;

Response, for "The *Havurah* in New York City. Some Notes on the First Year," by Bill Novak; and "A Proposal for the Unstructured Synagogue," by Everett Gendler. © 1970 and 1971, respectively, by *Response;*

Alan L. Mintz, for "Along the Path to Religious Community," by Alan L. Mintz, in *The New Jews,* edited by James A. Sleeper and Alan L. Mintz, and *Midstream,* Vol. 16, No. 3, 1970. © 1971 by Alan L. Mintz and James A. Sleeper;

Journal of the Central Conference of American Rabbis, for "The Making of a Jewish Counter-Culture," by Bill Novak. © 1970 by Central Conference of American Rabbis;

Union of American Hebrew Congregations, for "The Need for Community in Synagogue Life," by Leonard J. Fein. © 1971 by Union of American Hebrew Congregations;

The Colorado Reconstructionist Federation, for "From the Denver *Havurot*," materials compiled by Ruth Jezer Teitelbaum. © 1972 by the Colorado Reconstructionist Federation;

Robert Agus and Paul Ruttkay, for "Proposal for *Fabrangen*," © 1972 by Robert Agus and Paul Ruttkay;

George E. Johnson, for "Fabrangen: A Coming Together," © 1972 by George E. Johnson;

Bill Novak, for "My Experience of a *Havurah*," © 1972 by Bill Novak.

In addition the editor gratefully acknowledges permission granted by Vallentine, Mitchell & Co., Ltd., London, to reprint his essays, which appeared as follows: *Fellowship in Judaism. The First Century and Today* (London, 1963: Valentine, Mitchell & Co., Ltd.), pp. 11–30, 60–74; and *Judaism in the Secular Age. Essays on Fellowship, Community, and Freedom* (London, 1970: Valentine, Mitchell & Co., Ltd.; and New York, 1970: Ktav Publishing House, Inc.), pp. 83–116. Both © Jacob Neusner, 1963 and 1970, respectively.

PART ONE

A HISTORICAL
PERSPECTIVE

I

QUMRAN AND JERUSALEM:

TWO TYPES OF JEWISH FELLOWSHIP IN ANCIENT TIMES

Jacob Neusner

The modern world knows two forms of Utopianism, social and revolutionary. The social Utopian would restore society to its ancient ideal, proposing to reconstruct the city out of its own stone and mortar. The revolutionary Utopian would build a new society on the ruins of the old, destroying in order to create. These two Utopian forms recall the efforts of "moral men" in an earlier "immoral society," that of Jewish Palestine during the Second Commonwealth. In the centuries before the start of the Christian Era, these men drew apart from the common life to discover social forms capable of embodying religious ideals.

The central issue of the Jewish Commonwealth was how to transform biblical precept into daily practice. It was, therefore, religious rather than humanitarian Utopianism that moved men to dream of a better world: how to translate the vision of lawgiver and prophet into the workaday situation of a later and lesser age. Biblical Judaism had taught that the pious man ought to love those who love God, and to abhor those who despise Him. "Blessed is the man who walks not in the counsel of the wicked, nor stands in the way of sinners, nor sits in the seat of scoffers . . ." (Psalms 1:1). Conversely the pious man says, "I am a companion of all who fear Thee and of those who keep Thy precepts" (Psalms 119:63). The Psalmist's choice of the word companion (haver) connotes more than merely friend, but rather fellow-worshipper, one who is an associate in a common sacred task. Indeed the word recalls an earlier pagan and pre-Mosaic meaning, "to tie together by magic charm, knot, or spell." In the Second Commonwealth there were many such "charmed circles," groups of companions who came together to form fellowships of the faithful. These communes took two forms. That founded at Qumran represented revolutionary Utopianism,

1

and those founded in Jerusalem and elsewhere, social
Utopianism. This paradigm may offer some insight into the
sociology of Judaism at a crucial moment in Jewish history.

The wilderness communes were drawn by the vision of the
wilderness, the setting for Israel's holiest drama, and recalled
the compelling words of Jeremiah: "I remember the devotion
of your youth, your love as a bride, how you followed me in
the wilderness, in an unsown land" (Jeremiah 2: 2). In the
sun-parched hills, the members of the commune thought to
make a new beginning, to create a sanctuary of purity in the
land they thought to be profaned. These communes, of which
there were many, saw themselves morally secure only behind
the barrier of rough terrain and within a high wall of
discipline. The Qumran group escaped from sinful men in
order to found a better and holier society: "This is the
regulation for the men of the community who devote
themselves to turn away from every evil and to hold fast to
everything which He has commanded as His pleasure: they
shall separate themselves from the assembly of men of deceit,
they shall be a community, with Torah study."[1] The Psalmist
of Qumran likewise expressed this attitude:

> The nearer I draw to Thee
> The more I am filled with zeal
> Against all that do wickedness.
> For they that draw near to Thee
> Cannot see Thy commandments defied . . .
> So for mine part, I will admit
> No comrade into fellowship with men,
> Save by the measure of his understanding . . .
>
> Only as Thou drawest a man unto Thee
> Will I draw him unto myself,
> And as Thou keepest him afar,
> So too will I abhor him.
>
> I will not enter into communion
> With them that turn their back upon Thy covenant.[2]

The members of the wilderness communes whom Philo called Essenes likewise avoided the cities "because of the iniquities which have become inveterate among city dwellers, for they know that their company would have a deadly effect upon their own souls."[3] The wilderness communes brought together very good Jews, fully normative, if somewhat abnormal in their devotion to the Torah and to both its moral and its ritual precepts.[4] They followed the main lines of Jewish law as meticulously as the men in the synagogues whom they abandoned in their flight. They did indeed have their peculiar emphases, both in theology and in ritual, but this marked them apart as a heterodoxy, not a heresy. The men of Qumran were zealous, too deeply committed to the sacred to believe and behave according to the common faith. Escape to the wilderness provided a way to purer, holier life than the men of the cities promised ever to live.

The alternative was the road to Utopia chosen by some of the Pharisees of Jerusalem. They founded religious communes within the common society of the villages and towns, and lived the holy life among profane and ordinary men. This was the way of the Pharisaic fellowship (called Havurah), which brought together some of the larger numbers of Jews who identified themselves with the Pharisaic viewpoint (It is emphasized that not all Pharisees were demonstrably members of the Pharisaic fellowship at any time, although all members of the fellowship were probably Pharisees, adhering to their interpretation of Judaism.) In the words of Josephus, "they are able greatly to persuade the body of the people, and whatsoever they do about divine worship. . . they perform according to their direction, insomuch that the cities give great attestations to them on account of their entire virtuous conduct, both in the actions of their lives and their discourses also."[5] The Pharisaic sages taught their followers, "Do not separate yourself from the community,"[6] but on the contrary, they lived among the masses, teaching and admonishing, seeking to bring all men closer to their Father in heaven. They sought out the heart of the people, and were willing, according to the Gospel, to "traverse sea and land to make a single proselyte" (Matt. 23:15). Thus they exercised formidable influence over the mind of Jewish Palestine.

At the same time, however, the Pharisaic fellows distinguished themselves from the common people by observing even the most neglected details of the Torah, the laws of ritual purity and by giving tithes and heave offerings as set forth in Scripture. In doing so, they cast up a barrier between themselves and the outsider (called in the sources *Am-Ha-aretz*), for an outsider was for many reasons a potential source of ritual defilement. Even in the towns and villages, therefore, the Havurah formed a separate society. Two biblical precepts contended in the Pharisaic ethics: first, that all Israel is to be a kingdom of priests and a holy people (and this was understood to mean at the very least a people ritually pure and holy), and second, that every individual Jew everywhere was himself to be as ritually fit as a priest to perform the sacrificial act in the Temple. The Pharisees believed in the sanctity of all Israel, and passionately affirmed the obligation of every Jew to his King. Obsessed with the vision of life and society sanctified in every detail by the commandments of the Torah, they observed and taught the Jewish people to carry out even those laws which were both troublesome and generally ignored.

Although the masses of the people regarded the acts of careful tithing and ritual purification as far beyond the proper task of a Jew, the fellows were not prepared to give up the struggle. They founded their associations in the villages and towns, among the people but not of them. These associations were not organizations in the pattern of Qumran, and had neither officers nor formal constitution, but were rather groups of people who recognized one another as part of the same fellowship of observant and pious men. They taught their eccentricities of observance by example, ever aware not to imitate their students. Thus they sought at once to transform and to transcend society, to "live Utopia" in an unredeemed world. They elaborated laws to govern the infinite specific situations presented by a ritually pure life among defiled men. In such a way the fellows resolved the tension between the precept that demanded sanctification of all Israel, on the one hand, and of every Jew, on the other.

All the communes went far beyond the measure of the Law. Some, and among them the associations described by Philo and Josephus as Essenes, by the Qumran documents as the Many, and by the Zadokite Fragments as the Congregation, thought to find a way to God in the solitude of the wilderness. What sets the Pharisaic fellowship apart is the search for the Godly community within the society of men.

In ancient times the commune was a widespread form of social organization for religion. It was common to the Pythagorean schools of Hellenistic Egypt and to the Nabataean kingdom to the south of the Dead Sea. Jewish Palestine itself provided rich analogues to the Pharisaic order. Many of the sects, particularly the Essenes and the Qumran group, shared with the Pharisees common institutional forms. Indeed Josephus characterizes the social form of Judaism as a series of self-sufficient sects, and the similarities between the Qumran association and the groups known in Josephus and Philo as Essenes and Pharisees have impelled scholars to identify the Qumran literature with one or another known group. The specific forms of the Pharisaic fellowship were determined, however, by the particular obsession of the associates: food.

The Bible had commanded Jews to return to God through the priests and Levites some part of the gifts of the land. Traditions ascribed to Abraham, and later to Saul, the practice of eating even the remaining unconsecrated produce in a state of ritual purity. Tradition likewise ascribed to Solomon the practice of washing hands before a meal as an act of ritual purification. Thus every Jew was obligated to eat his "secular" (unconsecrated) produce in the purity which characterized the Temple priest in his holy office. This concern was entirely natural in the ancient world, where ritual purity was the common concern of pagan temple, mystery cult, and even of the philosophical schools of the Pythagoreans. In very early days, the Pharisaic fellowship took on specific form and precise definition from the effort to observe the difficult religious obligations of tithing and ritual purity. Even by the first century the schools of Hillel and Shamai disputed certain details in the rule of the fellowship, indicating both a fixed tradition and sufficient interval in which to forget some details. The purpose of the fellowship from the first was to carry out the obligations incumbent on all men.

The Qumran community shared this obsession with ritual defilement, regarding even the Temple as irreparably unclean. They established themselves in the wilderness and elaborated rules by which others might reach their sanctity through a year of probation, a vote of the members, and a second, novitiatory year. The Essenes likewise admitted a newcomer into their fellowship by stages. Josephus records: "A candidate anxious to join their sect is not immediately admitted. For one year, during which he remains outside the fraternity, they prescribe for him their own rule of life . . . . Having given proof of his temperance during this probationary period, he is brought into closer touch with the rule, and is allowed to share in the purer kind of holy water, but is not yet received into the meeting of the community . . . " After this exhibition of endurance his character is tested for two years more, and only then if found worthy is he enrolled in the society. But before he may touch the common food, he is made to swear tremendous oaths . . . ."[7]

The Pharisees received into their fellowship any Jew who undertook to nourish his body in a manner appropriate to the sanctity of his soul. Not all followers of the Pharisees accepted the rule of the fellowship. There were many kinds of Pharisee, as both the Talmud and the Gospels recognize, and there were even sages who were considered outsiders in relationship to the fellowship. A slave might become an associate without his master. The specific rules of affiliation were exhaustive and beyond them there were no distinctions between members and outsiders. The testimony of outsiders was accepted in regard to the Kashrut (legal fitness) of food, but not in regard to its ritual purity. Thus they were presumed to adhere to the dietary laws, like all good Jews, even though they stood outside the fellowship.[8]

Transcending family, caste, and class distinctions, the fellowship established a new policy within the old society of city and village, a community based upon the willingness of the individual to assume obligations imposed upon him by an ancient and unrepudiated commandment. This disruption in the social order recalls the Gospel saying, "I have come not to bring peace but a sword . . . for I have come to set a man against his father and a daughter against her mother" (Matt. 10:34-37). The fellowship represented a considerable complication in the urban order. The city could contend with men who separated themselves from the common life in exclusive, alien communes in the wilderness. Reciprocal indifference may have governed the day-to-day contact between the new society at Qumran and the old. Even the Essenes in their villages and neighborhoods in the towns apparently faced inward towards their commune. On the other hand, the Pharisaic association posed a peculiar problem for the general society. At many intimate and some crucial relationships in daily life, the fellow was guided by a complicated rule that made social intercourse intricate and delicate. The wilderness heterodoxies formed new polities built on the ruins of the old, and the individual moved from one exhaustive, clearly defined and exclusive pattern of human relationships into another equally comprehensive and unambiguous situation. The act of the self-conscious, private individual began and ended with the act of affiliation to the new order. For the Pharisaic associate, on the other hand, entry into the new polity was only the first step on a path towards individualism and disintegration of customary social patterns.[9]

A new member of the Havurah discovered that his relationships with outsiders had become fundamentally transformed. He could no longer associate with any man freely and carelessly. In certain ways his social intercourse completely changed in character, and in every way he had to rearrange his habits of daily life into a new and complex structure.

Obedience to the rule of the order meant that special concern for the sanctity of food entered into hitherto simple social relationships. The implications of the rule were thus translated in very great detail into everyday terms. The rules called for new adjustments in the life of the fellow, multiplying the problems bound up in living with men indifferent to obligations he considered sacred. The obvious solution to these problems was to retreat to neighborhoods dominated by the commune, or to escape entirely from the common, defiled society. This option was, however, precisely what the fellowship rejected at the start.

The particular emphasis on ritual purity and tithing indicates that the Havurah was fundamentally a society for strict observance of laws of ritual cleanliness and holy offerings. This was, indeed, all it might have been. Membership in the association could be achieved only through adherence to a pattern of actions which demonstrated devotion to neglected commandments and traditions of Judaism. In urban society, deeds alone truly marked the man rather than any commitment of faith or intellect. The social relations in the city, brief and random at best, could not manifest any profound virtue of mind or heart. They could, however, serve as a tentative measure of a man's willingness to serve God in ways held particularly significant. The fellowships were open to hypocrites, it is true, and the Gospels and Rabbinic sources give evidence that a faith expressed only through deeds might represent in the end only a meaningless pattern of naked gestures. Such a perplexity troubled the Pharisaic fellows and their heirs.

In the wilderness commune, on the other hand, the total personality of an individual became relevant. "When he enters into the covenant . . . then they shall examine their spiritual qualities in the community, in their mutual relationship, according to everybody's insight and actions . . . They shall register them in the order, one before the other, according to his insight and his doings . . . "[10] In Qumran the commune examined a man about "his intelligence and his actions . . . " Likewise the Zadokite Community examined newcomers, each "about his actions and his understanding and his strength and his property . . ."[11] In the close life of the wilderness commune, all these things were relevant and important. In the towns and villages only deeds spoke compellingly about a man.

The prosaic literature of Pharisaic law represented, therefore, the comprehensive articulation of all that could ever characterize such a fellowship. Unlike the wilderness associations, the Havurah could have no other standard but how a man carried out his religious obligations throughout the subtle patterns of daily life. The associates in the intellectual classes, sitting in the academies, schools, and courts of Palestinian Jewry, did in truth reveal the almost unlimited intellectual dimension of their order and its cause. The following story indicates, however, their unrelenting emphasis on the act as the final measure of the man:

> Akabya ben Mahaleleel testified to four opinions. His colleagues answered, Akabya, retract these four opinions that thou hast given, and we shall make thee Father of the Court in Israel. He said to them: Better that I be called a fool all my days than that I be made a godless man before God even for an hour; for they shall not say of me, He retracted for the sake of office . . . In the hour that he died, he said to his son, My son, retract the four opinions which I gave. His son answered, Why didst not thou retract? He answered, I heard them from a majority, and they also heard their opinions from a majority. I continued steadfast to the tradition that I heard, and so did they. But thou hast heard a decision both from an individual and from the majority. It is better to leave the opinion of the individual and to hold the opinion of the majority. His son answered, Father, commend me to thy fellow sages. He said, I commend thee not. He answered, Perchance thou hast found in me some cause for complaint. Akabya answered, No, but thine own deeds will bring thee near, or thine own deeds will remove thee far [from the fellowship].[12]

The fellows of the academic sages in the streets and fields of

the land likewise wove a fabric of actions that represented the
effort to build God's kingdom on earth.

The Qumran community chose a revolutionary path to
Utopia. The men who fled to the Judean desert abandoned all
hope of restoring society or of rebuilding it on its imperfect
foundation. At Qumran they established their order, defined
its rule, and prepared the way for others to join them. In all
this they demonstrated from their city on the hill above the
Dead Sea that God was truly sovereign on earth. Their rule
was simple, neither elaborated nor complicated by a
repudiated past. The men of Qumran struck out to build their
new city upon the ruins of the old.

The Pharisaic fellowship made a moral decision to endure
the "iniquities inveterate among city dwellers" so that men
far from God's way might return to it through precept and
example. The associates consecrated themselves to keep the
neglected ordinances governing tithes and ritual purity. They
too defined the rule of their order, educated men in the
manner of keeping it, and determined a sequence of concerns
by which an outsider might come by degrees to enter into
fellowship. The infinite implications of the rule for day-to-day
affairs were spelled out, and the precise, detailed information
so gained made it possible for the associates to keep the faith
in the company of men who did not. It was, in fact, law which
made possible the Pharisaic choice of a social way to Utopia.

The dilemma of the Pharisaic fellowship, and the manner of
its resolution, continue to speak out of the troubling question
of Hillel:

> If I am not for myself, then who will be for me?
> But being only for myself, what am I?
> And if not now, when?[13]

[1] *Manual of Discipline,* V, 1, 2.

[2] Thanksgiving Scroll, XIV, 14-22, pass. Tr. Theodore Gaster, *The Dead Sea Scrolls,* (N.Y., 1956) p. 188-190.

[3] Philo, *De Quod Probus Liber Sit,* XII, 76.

[4] Cf. S. Lieberman, "Light on the Cave Scrolls from Rabbinic Sources," *Proceedings of the American Academy for Jewish Research,* XX, 395-404.

[5] Josephus, *Antiquities,* XVIII, 1, 3.

[6] Avot, 2: 5.

[7] Josephus, *Jewish War,* II, viii, 7.

[8] Mishnah and Tosefta Demai, Chs. 2 and 3. Cf. S. Lieberman, *Tosefta Kipshutah, ad. loc.* Cf. also Talmud Bavli, Bekhorot 30b-31a.

[9] Cf. Mishnah Demai 2: 2, 3; Tosefta Demai 2: 2, 3, 10, 11; and Lieberman, *op. cit. ad. loc.* Cf. also S. Lieberman, "Discipline in the so-called Dead Sea Manual of Discipline," *Journal of Biblical Literature,* LXXI, 4 (1952), 199-206.

[10] *Manual of Discipline* V, 20-21.

[11] Zadokite Fragments 13: 11, ed. Ch. Rabin, *The Zadokite Fragments,* (Oxford 1954), p. 66.

[12] Mishnah Eduyot, 5: 6-7.

[13] Avot 1: 14.

II

FELLOWSHIP THROUGH LAW

THE ANCIENT HAVURAH

Jacob Neusner

The Havurah (fellowship) was, as I have said, a religious society founded in the villages and towns of Jewish Palestine during the Second Commonwealth in order to foster observance of the laws of tithing and ritual purity.[1] The sources on the fellowship are preserved in rabbinic literature, and the Havurah has therefore been associated with the Pharisees; one must, nonetheless, retain the distinction between the Havurah and the whole Pharisaic sect, since there is no evidence that all Pharisees were members of a fellowship.

Membership represented a status recognized by other members and not a formal affiliation with an organized society. The *haver* (member) of such a fellowship undertook to carry out, even in the company of non-observant men, those ritual laws which were generally neglected. Thus he taught their observance by example and precept. At the same time, the members distinguished themselves from the common society by their strict adherence to ritual laws which separated them in crucial relationships of daily life. Members cast up a barrier between themselves and the outsider, *am ha-aretz*, who was by definition a source of ritual defilement.[2] The laws concerning food demanded more than what many men accepted as their proper religious obligation. The mass of farmers were careful to give heave-offering (*terumah gedolah*), but they did not always hand over the other agricultural dues to the priest and Levite.[3] Hence meticulously observant men

13

had to take care to separate all necessary tithes and offerings.[4] Likewise the associates held that even secular food (hullin) had to be eaten in a state of ritual purity, and the masses of men did not do so.[5] Nonetheless, the Pharisaic traditions ascribed to the ancients the practice of eating even common food in a state of priestly purity, [6] and the commandments to tithe were biblically enjoined. This was, therefore, a natural concern for pious men.[7]

The member was a Jew who undertook to give all tithes and other sacred offerings from his foods and who undertook to preserve both for himself and others the ritual purity of his foods. Anyone might make such a commitment, man, woman, or child.[8] The fellowship cut across family ties. Wives might become members without their husbands, and children without their parents, though if a child was born into a family known to adhere to the rule, he was assumed to be observant until he indicated otherwise.[9] There were no caste distinctions, for some members of the priestly and Levitical castes were associates and others were not.[10] Furthermore not all Pharisees were adherents of the order; many kinds of men claimed to be Pharisees, and at both early and later periods, some sages were considered outsiders in relation to the fellowship.[11] A slave might become an associate and his master remain an outsider, and vice versa.[12] The specific rules of membership were exhaustive; whoever adhered to them became a member; beyond them, there were no distinctions between members and outsiders, and all outsiders were considered reliable on questions of ritual fitness of foods, even though they were not reliable to give evidence as to their ritual purity.[13]

Becoming a member of the order caused a revolution, therefore, in the life of the new member. Personal relationships had to be reconstructed, and new patterns of behavior determined according to the specific regulations of the fellowship. The first obligation, for the outsider who entered into the status of "reliability" was to give all required tithes and heave-offerings. The second, for the "initiate," was to guard the ritual purity of these holy offerings, and in addition, to eat even secular produce in a state of ritual purity. In the third and final stage, the novice had to keep even those common foods he did not consume from ritual contamination, both at home and in commerce. A person entered the order by means of a formal undertaking, given unconditionally.[14] A newcomer might, however, proceed stage by stage to accept the obligations of a member, and he might at any point choose to go no further. He remained, in such a case, in his present status, and was not expelled from membership entirely. Such flexibility followed from the very purpose of the fellowship: to encourage Jews to fulfil neglected religious duties. At each stage, the newcomer reached a level of observance higher than before; if, therefore, he chose to remain only partially affiliated, this did not conflict with the purpose of the fellowship.

The primary sources on the process of entering the fellowship are as follows:

Mishnah Demai 2:2

He that undertakes to be reliable must give tithe from what he eats and from what he sells and buys, and he may not be the guest of an outsider. R. Judah says, Even he that is the guest of an outsider may still be reckoned trustworthy. They replied, He would not be reliable in what concerns himself, how then could he be trustworthy in what concerns others?

Mishnah Demai 2:3

He that undertakes to be a member may not sell to an outsider [foodstuff that is] wet or dry, nor buy from him [foodstuff that is] wet; and he may not be the guest of an outsider, nor may he receive him as a guest in his own garment.

Tosefta Demai 2:2

He that imposes upon himself four things is accepted to be a member: not to give heave-offering or tithes to an outsider; not to prepare his pure food in the house of an outsider; and to eat even ordinary food in purity. . . .

Tosefta Demai 2: 10–12.

And he is accepted first with regard to "wings" and is afterwards accepted for purities. If he only imposes upon himself the obligations concerning the "wings" (cleanness of hands) he is accepted; if he imposes upon himself the obligations concerning pure food, but not concerning "wings," he is not considered reliable even for pure food.

Until when is a man accepted? The school of Shamai say, For liquids, thirty days; for clothing, twelve months. The school of Hillel say, for either, thirty days.

The problem of defining the stages of affiliation is thus not simple. The Mishnah and Tosefta Demai give two different definitions, and the additional comments in the Tosefta require explanation. From Tosefta Demai 2: 11 and 2: 12, it is clear that there were several stages of entry into the fellowship.[15] An outsider had to conduct himself according to the rule of the fellowship, and afterwards was received for "wings" and purities. He was nonetheless kept in the status of a novice with regard to liquids until after thirty days, and became a full member after twelve months (according to the school of Shamai). Professor Lieberman cites R. Jonah, who explains the difference between the definition of the Mishnah and that of the Tosefta by suggesting that the Tosefta deals with conditions to be fulfilled before one can be admitted, while the Mishnah deals with obligations incumbent on the established member.[16] It seems, rather, that the definitions of both texts deal with stages of affiliation before full membership. I suggest, following R. Jonah, that the Tosefta deals with the earliest stage, which would be an initiatory period; and the Mishnah deals with a later stage, which would be a novitiate. The description of the two stages of membership in Tosefta Demai 2: 11 and 2: 12 could, consequently, represent a broad definition of all the major concerns of the neophyte, and the Tosefta Demai 2: 2 and Mishnah Demai 2: 3 represent specific details incumbent on the newcomer. The sources relate, apparently, as follows:

Tosefta Demai 2: 10	Tosefta Demai 2.2
Purities	Not to give *terumah* and tithes to an outsider.
Purities	And not to prepare purities for and near an outsider.
Wings	And that he eat his common food in ritual purity and take upon himself to be trustworthy, tithing what he eats, etc.
Tosefta Demai 2.11	Mishnah Demai 2.3.
Liquids	He does not sell an outsider wet or dry foods. And he does not acquire from him wet foods.
Garments	He does not accept the hospitality of an outsider. And does not receive him in his home in his (the outsider's) garment.

If this paradigm is a correct arrangement of the sources,[17] the stages of affiliating to the fellowship become clear. At the first stage of affiliation, the newcomer undertook to be reliable to give tithe from what he ate as well as from what he sold and purchased (from others for resale).[18] At the second level a reliable person entered the stage of initiation, in which he began to keep the laws of eating food in ritual purity.[19] Thus he began his affiliation by showing particular concern for ritual offerings, and for the purity of the food the initiate ate and prepared for himself. At the third stage, the novitiate, the newcomer undertook to guard the ritual purity of food under any circumstances; thus he could not sell any foodstuff (wet or dry), for in either case the outsider would contaminate the food by his touch, nor could he purchase from him food that is wet, and thus contaminated (moist produce was susceptible to uncleanness and dry produce was not), nor could he receive the outsider as a guest, on account of his contaminated garment. Following the period of reliability, the initiatory period was divided into two parts. First, the man became an initiate for "wings," that is, for the cleanness of his hands when he ate. Afterwards he obligated himself regarding "purities," that is, to preserve the sanctity of consecrated produce, withholding it from a priest or Levite who was an outsider, and who would probably consume the offerings in a state of impurity. In the novitiate, likewise, two periods punctuated entry into the fellowship. At first, the novice had to preserve his garments and liquid foods from ritual impurity, not allowing impurity to come upon any food in his possession or under his authority, by refraining from commerce in produce with outsiders, and by not purchasing from an outsider food that had been made ritually susceptible to uncleanness. At the same time, he had to take care to keep his garments from defilement, so that they might not contaminate his food; and he had to take care that the garments of outsiders did not touch his foodstuffs or defile them in any way. This novitiate lasted for thirty days in regard to both liquids and garments, according to the school of Hillel, or for thirty days in regard to liquids and twelve months in regard to garments, according to the school of Shamai. At the end of the three periods, of reliability, initiation, and the novitiate, the associate was considered dependable in all matters of tithes, of the ritual purity of his own food, of food he sold, and of his garments. Thus the following stages become apparent:

1. Reliability—(1) concern for tithing.
2. Initiation—(1) concern for tithing, and (2) for ritual purity of the initiate's own food; (2A) first for the cleanness of hands, and (2B) later for the cleanness of ritually sacred foods.

3. Novitiate—(1) concern for tithing, (2) for ritual purity of the novice's own food, and (3) for food in his domain; and (4) (possibly) later, for the purity of his garment.

Some people conducted themselves privately according to the rule of the fellowship, particularly giving tithes meticulously. In such a case, a man was received immediately into the initiatory stage and instructed how to become a fully accredited member. If not, he was instructed, and only afterwards received into the initiatory stage.[20]

A later dispute may be illumined by this sequence of affiliation. During the latter half of the second century C.E., Rabbi Meir and Rabbi Judah disputed on whether a person in the status of reliability for tithes might accept the hospitality of an outsider and remain reliable. Rabbi Meir did not consider such hospitality permissible, apparently on account of the candidate's eating untithed food. Rabbi Judah answered, according to the same assumption, "In all the days of householding, people never hesitated to eat in one another's homes, and even so, the produce in their own homes was properly tithed." If, however, it was entirely possible for an individual to set aside tithes from the food which an outsider served him, and this is stated explicitly, then it is difficult to comprehend Rabbi Meir's tradition, prohibiting someone in the fellowship from accepting an outsider's hospitality. Apparently Rabbi Meir and Rabbi Judah held ancient traditions on the sequence of affiliation. Rabbi Meir's source forbade such hospitality, and Rabbi Judah's tradition was that such a prohibition against an outsider's hospitality did not apply at this stage (but rather at the later, novitiate level). Hence Rabbi Judah was correct, according to the sources, in disputing Rabbi Meir's contention that the hospitality of an outsider was forbidden to a reliable person; such hospitality was indeed prohibited to the novice, but on account of ritual contamination, not on account of tithes.[21] Indeed, it is explicitly stated that this prohibition did apply to the full member.[22]

After the destruction of the Temple, the fellowship apparently changed considerably; by the end of the second

century C.E. the rule of the order ceased to be defined in its
original terms at all. One discovers an elaboration of the
conditions for becoming a fellow, "R. Judah says, 'He may not
rear small cattle [a conservation measure], nor be profuse in
vows of levity, nor contract corpse uncleanness, nor minister
in the banquet hall.' They said to him, 'These things never
came within the rule.'" This was correct, for the original
articles of the fellowship did not cover such matters.[23]

A man who undertook to enter the fellowship had to do so
before three members, although his dependents might declare
their adherence before him. If he left the fellowship, he had to
reassume these obligations upon return, if he might return at
all. According to one opinion, if he violated his oath secretly,
he was never eligible to reaffiliate, for he was a hypocrite.
According to another, if he violated his oath secretly, then
only by his own admission had he become suspect, and since a
man's testimony against himself is discounted, he may indeed
return in repentance; but if he violated his oath publicly, and
others gave evidence against him, he might not re-enter the
fellowship under any circumstances, as it is written (Jeremiah
3: 14), "Return, O faithless children . . ."[24] Furthermore a tax
farmer was expelled from the moment he took his seals of
office, although when he ceased to collect taxes, he could
rejoin the association through a new, formal undertaking.[25]

The new member of the fellowship could no longer
associate with any man freely and carelessly. In many ways he
had to rearrange his habits of living into a new and complex
pattern. The legal literature of the rabbinic period preserved
many details of the relationship between members and
outsiders. Obedience to the rule of the order meant that
concern for the sanctity of foods entered into hitherto simple
social relationships, and the implications of this rule were
translated, in minute detail, into everyday affairs. One
principle governed every relationship: absolutely no compromise between the rule of the fellowship and the demands of
the workaday world. The only exception, "for the sake of
peace," was actually a mere leniency, and not a compromise
at all.[26] At each of the three stages, the rule multiplied the

problems bound up in living with men who were indifferent to obligations the member considered sacred. The fellowship chose to articulate the rule of the order, and to elaborate it to guide the member through the infinite, specific situations of daily life. These laws represented precise statements of the measure of the law, no more, no less. Such elaboration of law has been viewed with little sympathy by modern scholars, "Nothing was left to the free personality, everything was placed under the bondage of the letter . . . A healthy moral life could not flourish under such a burden. Action was nowhere the result of inward motive, all was, on the contrary, weighed and measured. Life was a continual torment to the earnest man, who felt at every moment that he was in danger of transgressing the law."[27] This body of law was, however, fundamentally descriptive and enormously helpful. It was useful for people who adopted the rule of the fellowship, a rule they held as ancient and as sacred as the Ten Commandments, to know what to do and what not to do in the commonplace and homely situations of daily life. Having agreed, for example, to preserve the ritual purity of foodstuffs, the associate needed to know to what extent he was obligated to keep food only partially within his domain out of the hands of an outsider, in a common inheritance or in a joint agricultural or commercial enterprise. The formidable growth of law was a necessary consequence of the urban, unsegregated character of the fellowship. In the city and in the company of unobservant men, the potential range of problems to be solved by the fellowship rule was infinite. With precise and detailed information for guidance, the member might keep both his place in society and his sacred resolve.[28]

The fundamentally uncompromising[29] articulation of law became manifest in social, commercial, agricultural, and personal relationships.[30]

The member had, for example, to keep his cooking utensils out of possible contact with an outsider, who would render them unclean for several reasons.[31] Hence if he lived in the same courtyard with an outsider, he could not leave his vessels in the yard. He could not leave his pots or dishes in the

domain or control of an outsider at any time.[32] On the other
hand, an outsider was not suspect of touching the property of
a member if he entered his domain without permission; he
was presumptively careful not to contaminate the dwelling of
a member.[33] If the member married the daughter of an
outsider or purchased his slave, he had to adjure the
newcomer to the rule of the order; if, on the other hand, his
daughter or slave entered the domain of an outsider, the
member was assumed to remain observant until proven
otherwise. In any case the undertaking had to be renewed.[34] A
man might enter the fellowship without his wife; if he was
reliable (for tithes) and his wife was not, then associates might
purchase food from him, but might not accept his hospitality,
for he was as one who lives "in the same basket with a
snake." If his wife was reliable and he was not, then associates
might accept his hospitality but not purchase food from
him.[35]

Family relationships were no less complex. In matters of
inheritance, the associate might make no exchange of food
with an outsider who shared his inheritance; but he might
say, "Take the wheat there, and I shall take this wheat here,"
leaving to the outsider food that was either ritually unclean or
susceptible to impurity, and keeping the ritually clean food
for himself. He might not be the direct cause of an outsider's
receiving food.[36] The son of a member might visit the
non-observant members of his parents' families, so long as the
outsiders did not give him unclean food. If they did, he would
defile his own home, and hence might not visit his relatives
any longer. Hospitality was difficult; if, for instance, a man
left an outsider within the house awake, and found him
awake, or asleep and found him asleep, or awake and found
him asleep, the house remained clean [the possibility that the
outsider moved about and contaminated the house is
discounted], but if he left him asleep and found him awake,
the house is unclean, according to Rabbi Meir, or that part of
the house is unclean which he could touch by stretching out
his hand, according to the sages.[37] Apparently the outsider
was considered normally careful not to defile the house of the

associate, as was seen above, for here again it would not be possible to allow him to remain alone in a member's home at all. A fellow of the order could not in any case accept the hospitality of an outsider, or receive him into his own home unless he put on ritually clean garments.[38] While a member could not prepare for an outsider any kind of food, and vice versa, an outsider might still watch the pot of a member; he might not add spices. Wives of members and of outsiders might prepare food together under conditions of extreme caution.[39] In any case, the word of an outsider on the ritual purity of food or on its condition with regard to tithes and heave-offerings was accepted when he spoke en passant or in his innocence.[40] An outsider might not act as the agent of a fellow, or vice versa, in any matter to do with foodstuffs, although the outsider might act as agent of the member to purchase dry stuffs when the act was clearly specified in advance ("Buy me cabbages from the corner store and from no one else").[41] If a member left his produce in the care of an outsider, the food remained in its presumptive state of tithes and heave-offerings, but it was rendered unclean if it was moist. If an outsider entered an associate's house, "such time as the member can see them that go in and out, only foodstuffs and liquids and open earthenware vessels become unclean, but if the householder could not see them that go in and out, even though the outsider could not move himself or was tied up, all becomes unclean."[42]

Commercial relations were similarly transformed. It was difficult for a member of the fellowship to sell foodstuffs, for his only customers could be other members (but there is no evidence that members refrained from such commerce entirely). A farmer, for example, might sell olives only to another associate, according to the opinion of the Shamaites, and although the school of Hillel permits him to sell to a reliable person, still the scrupulous members of the latter school followed the opinion of the school of Shamai. There were other limitations on what foods the member might sell to outsiders under any circumstances; on the other hand, members might bring their grain to an unaffiliated miller, since grain was dry-milled. They might also employ outsiders in their foodshops, since their rules were presumably obeyed; and if an associate was in partnership with an outsider, other members might still purchase food at the shop and assume that the member had removed the proper tithes. If the associate took a field as sharecropper, he had to give tithes for his landlord, deducting them from the latter's share; under certain circumstances, the associate-landlord had to tithe the crops of his non-observant tenants from his own share. Finally, a journeyman-member might study a craft with an unaffiliated master and vice versa; in the latter case, the journeyman was considered observant of all rules of the fellowship during his working hours, but if he wanted to enter the order, he had to give a formal undertaking.[43]

Just as a member of the fellowship could not give priestly or Levitical dues to an outsider, so he could not present his first-fruits to an outsider, or repay to an unaffiliated priest any fines or recompense due to the priesthood for misuse of priestly produce. The associate had to pay fines to a priest of the fellowship, and the latter compensated the unaffiliated priest for the produce he had lost. If the consecrated produce of priests was mixed together, then the associate had to purchase the share of the outsider (unlike the situation of joint inheritance). The garments of an outsider could not, of course, come into contact with consecrated food; if they did, the priest had to burn the produce.[44]

While these laws indicate the configuration of rules which guided the fellowship, they do not by any means exhaust the vast legal literature relevant directly or indirectly to the life of the members.[45] Membership in the fellowship was achieved through a pattern of actions which demonstrated the initiate's devotion to certain neglected Jewish traditions. Dedicated to keep the ordinances on tithing and the purity of foods, the associates defined the rule of their fellowship, educated newcomers in the manner to keep it, and determined a sequence of obligations by which an outsider might learn by degrees to enter into the full observance of the Jewish faith. With neither a formal organization nor a sovereign authority to enforce a man's undertaking, the members of the fellowship followed the teaching of Shammai, "Say little and do much!"[46]

NOTES AND REFERENCES

[1] J. Baumgarten, "Qumran Studies," *Journal of Biblical Literature,* LXXVII, 3, 249-257, states, "All in all it seems quite difficult to make out of the havurah anything more than a society for the strict observance of ritual cleanliness." I have found no evidence to contradict Dr. Baumgarten's judgment. On the contrary, there is no indication that all Pharisees were members of a fellowship, although all members were Pharisees and accepted their views on Jewish law. There is, furthermore, no indication in the sources I have examined that the fellowship was an organized society at all, with officers or a formal governing body. A person became a member by stating his intention to keep the rules of the fellowship before three old members; he entered into the framework of obligations membership imposed. Membership thus entailed nothing more than a recognized status.

[2] Buechler's thesis (A. Buechler, *Der Galiläische Am Ha-Ares des Zweiten Jahrhunderts,* Vienna, 1906) that the laws of ritual purity and strict tithing applied primarily to members of the priestly cast achieved some popularity among historians of this period. This thesis has been demolished by G. Allon in his essay, cited in detail below, "The Application of the Laws on Ritual Purity" (cf. G. Allon, *Researches in the History of Israel,* Tel Aviv, 1957, I, 148-177). Buechler thought that the extension of these laws to the common people took place in the second century C.E.; because of the rabbis' bitterness at the Hadrianic persecutions, they devised these laws to separate the Jewish people once for all from the gentile world. Allon discusses and refutes this thesis as well.

[3] The common people apparently recognized the biblical injunction to give heave-offering (cf. TB Sotah 48a), but were not careful to separate other offerings.

[4] Significantly, the laws concerning the Pharisaic fellowship were inserted in the tractate on "doubtful produce" *(demai)*, the doubt being whether produce has been fully and properly tithed. The observance of these laws involved separating first-tithe and heave-offering of the tithe, as well as second-tithe, to be eaten in Jerusalem, and poor-man's tithe (these last were given alternately, in the seven-year cycle, years one, two, four and five were for second-tithe, three and six for poor-man's tithe). On the enactment of the laws of "doubtful produce," cf. Sotah 48a (Mishnah Ma'aser Sheni, 5:15); H. Albeck, *Seder Zeraim* (Tel Aviv, 1957), 69-70; and especially, S. Lieberman, *Hellenism in Jewish Palestine* (New York, 1950), p. 143, note 28.

[5] All men ought to remain ritually pure, according to rabbinic sources.

Cf. Allon, op. cit., pp. 169-176. Ritual purity was a widespread obsession. Cf. *inter alia*, the following: Philo, *De Specialibus Legibus*, III, 205; Josephus, *Contra Apion*, 2: 26; *Antiquities* III, xi, 3; cf. especially W. Brandt, *Juedische Reinheitslehre und ihre Beschreibung in den Evangelien* (Giessen, 1910), pp. 1-55; and also J. Harrison, *Prolegomena to the Study of Greek Religion* (Cambridge, 1903), pp. 24-29; M. Nilsson, *History of Greek Religion* (2nd ed., Oxford), pp. 84-85, 218-220. Buechler states (in "Levitical Impurity of the Gentile in Palestine before the year 70," *Jewish Quarterly Review*, n.s. XVII, 80-81), "They assumed that Levitical impurity of the gentile affected only the priest on duty [in the Temple] and the ordinary Jew only when he was ritually pure for a visit to the Temple and for participation in a sacrificial meal. The private associations between Jew and gentile were in no way restricted, and commercial and other relations were not affected by the Levitical purity ascribed to the gentile." On p. 48 of the same article, Buechler asks, "Is there any, even the slightest indication in rabbinic literature that the touch of a gentile caused a defilement, and that such a defilement was taken into account by the strictest Jew not an Essene in Temple times?" One such indication at least will be found in Mishnah Avodah Zarah 4: 9. The reason for the prohibition is obviously that the Jew will assist the gentile in the process by which grapes become susceptible to contamination and the gentile will forthwith—by touch—contaminate them! (Buechler would argue that this applies only to the priest, but no evidence supports this view.) Cf. also Tosefta Makshirin 3: 7. Allon discusses this *Mishnah* . . . and states that the sages regarded ritual purity as the obligation of every Jew; since many did not keep the laws of purity, the sages "found it necessary . . . to seek out the company [of observant men] and to set themselves apart by means of a formal act of undertaking, to fulfil meticulously these laws." Cf. also TB Hullin 2: 6; and the dispute of the schools of Hillel and Shamai, TB Berakhot 8: 2, 3, in which all parties agree that it is forbidden to render foods unclean during a meal, disagreeing on the best means to prevent impurity.

⁶ Abraham ate his secular food in ritual purity, TB Baba Mesi'a 87a; Bereshit Rabbah, ch. 44. For Saul, cf. Midrash Tehilim, ps. 7, ed. Buber, p. 32a; Pesikta de R. Kahana, ed. Buber, 78; Pesikta Rabbati, ch. 15 ed. Friedman, p. 68a. For a complete discussion of this question, cf. Buechler, op. cit., pp. 119–124, and Allon, op. cit., pp. 158–169, esp. p. 159, note 52.

⁷ Cf. for example the view of Philo, *De Specialibus Legibus*, III, 205.

⁸ Cf. Tosefta Demai 2: 2–3: 10, pass., S. Lieberman, *Tosefta Kipshutah* (N.Y., 1955), *ad loc*. Specific citations follow.

⁹ The fellows cut across family lines, cf. Tos. Dem. 2: 15, 16, 17, 3: 5, 9.

¹⁰ The distinction between member priests and Levites and others is implicit in Mishnah Demai 2: 2, 3 and Tos. Demai 2: 2, 3. There is no apparent economic distinction either; at least, according to Tos. Demai 2: 19, a journeyman apprentice is a member and his craftsman-teacher is not (and vice versa); cf. also Tos. Demai 2: 15, 3: 5, 3: 9.

¹¹ Seven kinds of Pharisees are listed in Sotah 22a (TP Sotah 5: 7; cf. TP Berakhot 9: 7). Cf. also Tos. Demai 2: 17, the opinion of Abba Shaul, and the parallel passage in Bekhorot 30a; and Professor Lieberman's comment, *op. cit., ad loc*. Cf. also TP Demai 2: 3 and Professor Lieberman's comment and

emendation to the passage, *Tarbiz*, XX, 110-111: A sage in Babylon tells some women to be cautious in approaching him, for he is in the status of an outsider in relationship to ritual purities; cf. also L. Finkelstein, *Introduction to the Treatises Abot and Abot of Rabbi Nathan* (New York, 1950) p. 243.

[12] Tos. Demai 3: 36, 3: 9; TP Demai 2: 2 *inter alia.*

[13] TP Demai 2: 3. This is a point often misunderstood in secondary works on this period.

[14] Tos. Demai 2: 3, Berkhorot 30a. Cf. Lieberman, *op. cit.*, p. 211, note 9. Cf. also Tos. Dem 2: 13, TP Dem. 2: 3; Bekhorot 30b on the formal undertaking. The undertaking is a kind of vow or oath, cf. Lieberman, *op. cit.* p. 217. For the possibility of accepting only the first obligation of membership, cf. Tos. Dem. 2: 3, 5, II.

[15] Lieberman, *op. cit.*, p. 216, para. 37.

[16] Cf. also Rabin, *op.cit.*, p. 12, note 7.

[17] According to this interpretation of the several sources, wings, purities, liquids, and garments in Tos. Demai 2: II, 12, have specific meanings as detailed below. The following evidence supports this explanation:

Wings means "washing of hands" according to Professor Lieberman and earlier commentators. Cf. Lieberman, *op. cit.*, pp. 215-216; Bekhorot 30a and Rashi *ad loc.;* the 'Arukh HaShalem, explains this unusual usage by reference to Kelim 17: 14, Tos. Kel. B.M. 7: 5; TP Nazir 4: 10 (TB Nazir 46b).

Purities comprehends both concern for the ritual purity of food that the initiate eats (i.e., that he will not prepare pure foodstuffs near an outsider), but also concern for preserving the purity of consecrated food. For a similar ambiguity, cf. M. Oholot 18: 2, Bekhorot 3: 2, 3: 13. This latter connotation is preserved in TP Demai 2: 2 by Rav Mana, who equates "purities" with "tithes." Furthermore, Kossovsky (*Concordance to the Tosefta*, Jerusalem, 1939) states that "purities" in the Tosefta connotes anything which is done or preserved in ritual purity; for the detailed meaning of "purities" in the TP passage cited, cf. Lieberman, *op. cit.*, p. 215.

Liquids in Tractate Makshirin connotes "that which renders dry produce susceptible to become impure," precisely the meaning assigned here. Cf. *inter alia* Makshirin I: I, 6: 4, and Albeck, *Seder Tohorot* (Tel Aviv, 1959), p. 411. The word MSKH as used in Leviticus 11: 34 was interpreted by the rabbis to mean a liquid (one of seven) capable of rendering dry produce susceptible to impurity; hence liquids in Tos. Demai 2: 11 connotes concern not to bring a liquid into contact with dry produce. Parallel usages are in Pesahim 17b, Terumot 2: 2, etc. Liquids likewise implies, and as its primary meaning, concern to protect the purity of liquids.

Garments means, according to Rashi (Bekhorot 30b-31a; cf. also Lieberman, *op. cit., ad loc.*) that the novice must learn to keep his garment in the state of purity appropriate to an associate. Cf. Mishnah Hagigah, ch. 2 at the end; for an instance of such concern, cf. Tos. Tohorot 5: 16. If the novice accepts the hospitality of an outsider, he will render his garment unclean by virtue of the uncleanness of the chairs; when the outsider is dressed in his own garments, he is a source of impurity, for his garments can render an object unclean when it is carried (cf. Hagigah 2: 7). The general term garments in Tos. Demai 2: 2 apparently connotes these two specific details. Cf. also Mishnah Tohorot, 4: 5.

For another explanation of the difference between the two definitions, cf. L. Finkelstein, *The Pharisees* (Philadelphia, 1938), II, p. 662.

[18] Tos. Demai 2: 3, Mishnah Demai 2: 2. In the matter of tithes, the reliable person must not only keep the laws himself, but he must keep others from transgressing as well. In the second stage, the initiate must keep only his own food in a state of ritual purity. The novice, however, must be careful for others as well.

[19] Tos. Demai 2: 2, following Professor Lieberman's emendation. Cf. Lieberman, *op. cit.*, p. 210, notes 4 and 5.

[20] On private conformity to the rule, cf. Lieberman, *op. cit.*, p. 214. I only propose this interpretation as most sensible, for if the newcomer was immediately received into the final stage of membership in the order, how was he to carry out the complicated observance of ritual purity "as he goes along?" He could, on the other hand, certainly give the necessary tithes and heave-offerings without further instruction. Hence I propose that the initial reception was into the stage of reliability, and he was instructed, "as he goes along", in the responsibilities of the initiate.

[21] I have found no support for this hypothesis.

[22] Mishnah Demai 2: 3.

[23] For evidence of this change in the nature of the fellowship, cf. Sotah 9: 15; Tos. Shabbat I: 7; Bekhorot 30b. Lieberman, *op. cit.*, p. 216, para. 40, states, "According to the tradition of the Babylonian Talmud, Abba Shaul hands on an ancient law, but afterwards, when the Temple was destroyed, the standards of ritual purity (observed by the priests) were raised, so as not to place credence in any man, even a sage." Professor Lieberman cites Maimonides, *The Book of Cleanness, Laws of Commonwealth* (Tel Aviv, 1953), III, 119; and the extensive variations in the definition of the fellow, Bekhorot 47b.

Rabbi Judah's definition is emended by J.N. Epstein, *Introductions to Tannaitic Literature* (Jerusalem–Tel Aviv, 1957 to read as presented here; cf. Rabin, *op. cit.*, p. 12, note 9. Rabin's treatment of the rule of the novitiate varies considerably from the view presented here. Rabin, *op. cit.*, 18-20.

[24] Cf. Bekhorot 31a; Tos. Demai 2: 9, and Lieberman, op. cit., *ad loc.* TP Demai 2: 3; TB Avodah Zarah 7a, and the comment of the Tosafot there. I follow Professor Lieberman's comment, *op. cit.*, p. 214, paras. 28-29.

[25] Tos. Demai 3: 9; TB Bekorot 31a; TP Demai 2: 3; Lieberman, *op. cit.*, p. 224, paras. 15-17.

[26] Mishnah Gittin 5: 9 (parallel in Shevi'it 5: 9; TB Gittin 61a).

[27] E. Schuerer, *History of the Jewish People in the Time of Jesus Christ* (Edinburgh, 1894), II, pp. 102, 106-107, 124. For other viewpoints on the *Halakhah* in general, cf. R. Herford, *The Pharisees* (London, 1924); G.F. Moore, *Judaism* (Cambridge, 1954), Finkelstein, *op. cit.*

[28] Finkelstein, *op. cit.*, I, 74-75, and the same author's article in the *Harvard Theological Review*, XXII, 209-210.

[29] This is not to imply that the Pharisaic viewpoint was extreme. On the contrary, the tendency was, on the whole, moderate, given the range of possibilites that presented themselves to the sages. Cf. for many examples, Tractate Kelim, pass., and the *Code of Maimonides, Book of Cleanness*

(Book Ten), tr. H. Danby (Yale Judaic Series, Vol. VIII; N.H., 1954), particularly the preface of Professor Julian Obermann (pp. v-xiv), and the introduction by Canon Danby (pp. xxxiii-xlv); also the commentary Eliyahu Rabbah to the Sixth Division of the the Mishnah by the Gaon Rabbi Elijah of Vilna, in Danby, *The Mishnah* (Oxford, 1933), pp. 800-804; and cf. also the comment of Allon, *op. cit.*, p. 176, who suggests that the following pattern is discernible in the disputes on ritual purity: the Sadducees demanded the strictest possible interpretation of the laws of ritual purity, but limited the application of these laws to the priests in the Temple itself; the Essenes likewise interpreted the laws very strictly, and applied them to every situation in daily life; but separated themselves into communes of observant men and women; among the Pharisees, the tendency to apply the laws of purity to daily life conflicted with the impulse to limit severely the laws of purity. Allon continues, "There were two basic principles guiding the Pharisees; one, to make the law congruent to the needs of the living, and the other, to extend the principle of sanctity to every man (not only the priests) and to every place (not only the Temple). The second principle obligated the sages to teach Israel to observe ritual purity, and to demand complete separation [from uncleanness]. However, life demanded the limitation of these laws, for it is not possible, or at least very inconvenient, to keep them. Therefore . . . the traditions, such as washing hands before a meal, which were not difficult to keep, or which were particularly crucial, such as the prohibitions concerning women in the menstrual period, were carried out." For a discussion of the implications of the laws of purity in economic life, cf. L. Ginzberg, *Jewish Law and Lore* (Philadelphia, 1955), pp. 79-84, 109, 113, 120-122; S. Zeitlin, *History of the Second Jewish Commonwealth, Prolegomena* (Philadelphia, 1933). Professor Zeitlin discusses the modification of the laws of purity for the sake of convenience, and concludes, "The Pharisees from time to time modified the *halakot* in order to make the law accord with the requirements and demands of life."

The entire question of the sociological application of the laws of ritual purity has by no means been exhausted. It would be worthwhile, for one thing, to know in detail and through a study of texts (*contra* Schuerer) what these laws actually meant in the daily life of the Palestinian Jew during the several major epochs of the *Halakhah* in the Second Commonwealth and afterwards; and for another, what were the principles that governed the articulation and elaboration of the laws of purity.

[30] This is merely a brief summary of certain social relationships affected by the fellowship and its rule. A complete survey would entail not only a study of the specific laws which deal with the relationship of member and outsider, but also a consideration of each of the laws of ritual purity and impurity.

[31] Midrash-uncleanness, Maddaf-uncleanness, etc. Cf. Toh. 8: 2, and Maimonides, *Book of Uncleanness, ad loc.* .

[32] Tohorot 8: I, 2, 3.

[33] *Ibid.*, 8: 5.

[34] Tos. Demai 2: 16, 17 parallel TB Avodah Zarah 39a; Tos. Avodah Zarah 3:9; Bekhorot 30b. Cf. Lieberman, *op. cit., ad loc.*

[35] Tos. Demai 3: 9; cf. TP Demai 2: 2. For the expression "dwell with

with a serpent," cf. TB Ketuvot 71a. For problems of an associate who worked as a house servant of an outsider, cf. Tos. Demai 3-6; TP Demai 2:2. The servant had to see to tithing the food, and if it was known that the waiter was a member, then the affiliated guests might assume that the food had been tithed. But it is most important to note that a member might in fact work for an outsider, and even serve food to his table.

[36] Mishnah Demai 6:8, 9.

[37] Tos. Demai 2:15, 3:5 (parallel TB Yevamot 114a). If the child ate unclean food at the relative's he could render his own home unclean. Cf. Tohorot 2:2.

[38] Tos. Demai 2:2, 3.

[39] Tos. Maaserot 3:13; Tos. Demai 4:29, 3:1, 2:2, 4:31, 32. Tos. Demai 4:27 (compare 2:2). Mishnah Taharot 7:4.

[40] Tos. Demai 2:24; Maaserot 5:2; Mishnah Makshirin 6:3. Cf. also Tos. Demai 5:5; Mishnah Demai, 4:6.

[41] Tos. Demai 2:20, 2:21, 2:22, 3:2. Compare 4:26, 5:3, 8:1. Mishnah Demai 6:22; Tos. Demai 8:1.

[42] Tos. Demai 4:22, 28; Mishnah Taharot 7:5. Cf. also ibid. 7:I, 2; 8:1, 2.

[43] Mishnah Demai 6:6; Tos. Demai 2:3 (Mishnah Demai 2:2). Cf. Tos. Demai 3:15. Other sources include the following: Tos. Demai 2:18—19, 3:5, 8 9; Mishnah Demai 3:4, 6:1, 8. Cf. also Mishnah Terumot 3:4, Maaserot 3:13, 7:12.

[44] Bikkurim 3:12; Tos. Demai 3:I, 2, 3, 5; Mishnah Demai 2:2, 3; Tos. Terumot 7:4; TP Terumot 6:I; Mishnah Taharot 4:5.

[45] For other references, cf. the following, *inter alia*, in the TB: Berakhot 36b, 40b, 47b; Shabbat 13a, 32a; Erubin 37a, b; Pesahim 4a, b; Yoma 8b; Moed Katan 22b, 26b-27a; Hagigah 18b, 22a, 23a, 24b, 25a, 26a; Kiddushin 33b; 56a, b; Sotah 49a, b; Sanhedrin 8b, 40a, 72b, 90b; Avodah Zarah 7a, b, 39a, 41b, 42a, 64b, 70b; Makkot 6b (parallel Sanhedrin 8b), 9b; Shevuot 16a; Niddah 6b, 15b, 33b; Kelim 9:2 (parallel Eduyot I:14); Oholot 5:5 (cf. Hagigah 3:4, Parah 5:I); Makshirin 6:3; Zabim 3:2, Tohorot 7:4.

On the question of whether the fellowship had some kind of communal meal, cf. Pesahim 113b, and the discussion of Rabin, *op. cit.*, p. 32; Rabin cites Mishnah Sanhedrin 8:2, and the statement of A. Geiger in "Sadducaer und Pharisaer" (*Jüd. Zeitschrift*, 1868, p. 25). Rabin says, "Nothing in the context of Tosefta Demai suggests that the *haburah* held common meals, but we must remember that the word can also be employed in a general way for a group holding a common meal in connexion with some religious occasion . . . With all due reserve I think that the new evidence of the scrolls gives grounds for reviving Geiger's theory that the common meals formed an essential part of *haburah* life and influenced various features of Pharisee practice . . ." The relationship of the fellowship to the *havurah shel mitzvah* is not yet clear; the fellowship discussed here may be simply one example of such societies or status-groups formed to carry out particular religious obligations.

[46] Avot.

PART TWO

THE EARLIEST PROPOSALS

III

TOWARD A MODERN BROTHERHOOD

Jakob J. Petuchowski

"Thou hast chosen us from all peoples, Thou hast loved us and hast found pleasure in us, Thou hast exalted us above all nations, and Thou hast sanctified us by Thy commandments." In these few words, which occur in the liturgy of every festival, the Jew, throughout the ages, has given expression to a complex of ideas which represented the whole *raison d'etre* of his life as a Jew. It is a *complex* of ideas in more than one sense. The ideas co-joined here are what they are precisely because they exist in this particular combination. It is a case of the whole being more than the sum of its parts. Each idea in and by itself would already represent a kind of distortion. We are moving here in the realm which Max Kadushin called "Organic Thinking." with our misgivings about breaking up the complex clearly borne in mind, it will be necessary for our purposes to consider each part of this complex in its own right. First of all, there is the "Thou"—not just a philosophical abstraction, but a personal God Who 18642- B.C.E.), can be addressed in prayer, precisely because He is a *personal* God, a God Who has dealings with the children of men. Then there is the "us"—the group, the people; to be precise, the People of Israel. And that is no ordinary people, but a people "loved" and "chosen" by God—a *chosen* people. Finally, we have the idea that this

Jakob J. Petuchowski is Professor of Rabbinics and Jewish Theology at Hebrew Union College–Jewish Institute of Religion, Cincinnati, Ohio.

chosen people has been sanctified by divine commandments;
and we may add to our list of ingredients of this complex the
level of *sanctity* (or better still: *kedushah*), and the concept of
commandment (or better still: *mitzvah*).

And just as a reminder that we really cannot break up the
complex, and consider the individual components by themselves, we merely have to visualize the utter nonsense which
would ensue were we to speak of the divine commandment
without the "election," or of the "election" without the
divine commandment.

This much, then, is clear: The Jew in the past approached
his God as a member of the chosen people. He performed his
Jewish obligations because they added the dimension of
sanctity, which is the "constitution" of this chosen people.
And both the "constitution" and the "chosenness" were real
to him because the personal God had willed them to be so;
and the personal God, Who was also the God of History ("Our
God and God of our fathers") was the Supreme Reality.

It follows, therefore, that, when the Jew in the past
submitted to the regimen of Torah Law, it was not so much a
case of his being personally committed to this or that aspect
of it, but simply of his being a member of a people which had
committed itself to the Torah as its constitution. The ideal
set-up for this kind of life would, of course, be the corporate
life, the polity which knows of no distinction between
Church and State. And, judging by such biblical chapters as
Exodus 19 (magnificently interpreted by Martin Buber in his
book on Moses), this was exactly the divine purpose in leading
the Children of Israel out of Egypt, through the desert, and
into the Promised Land. And this is the very setting in which
alone the legislation of the Torah can be understood—with,
what appears to the modern Westerner as, its curious mixture
of moral and ritual provisions. The sanctity of the sanctuary
was as much a concern of the body politic as was the
administration of criminal law; and the distinctiveness of the
Jewish garb could be mentioned in one breath with the duty of
loving one's neighbor.

Now, all of this can be, and has been, explained historically.

Religion, it has been said, has, in its primitive stages, little concern for the individual. It is a matter for the group as a whole. Only as religion grows in sophistication, so it is claimed, does it manifest an interest in the salvation of the individual *qua* individual. And then this paradigm is illustrated with a reference to prophets like Ezekiel, the post-Exilic Psalms, and—more often than not—the teachings of Jesus of Nazareth, who, needless to say, is said to represent the "highest" type of religion.

But there are always two possibilities; and no committed Jew could possibly agree that the concept of "a kingdom of priests and a holy nation" represents a "lower" type of religion than that which glories in the "saved individual." Happily there are even some Christians who would agree with us. For example, Dr. James Parkes, an Anglican clergyman, believes in the *equal validity* of the two covenants which God made with mankind—the covenant of Sinai, when God called the "holy community," and the covenant of Calvary which God made with the "saved individual." Both covenants are equally authentic, both are equally important in the divine economy.[1]

Be that as it may. This much has been clearly seen by Parkes: that Judaism stands or falls with the concept of the "holy community." This is so true that, long after Jeremiah and Ezekiel and the Psalmists had manifested their interest in the individual, Maimonides, in the 12th century C.E., could include the following statement in his codification of Jewish Law: "He who withdraws from the ways of the community, even though he does not commit any transgressions, but merely separates himself from the congregation of Israel, and performs the commandments not in their midst, . . . such a one has no share in the World-to-Come."[2]

How effectively the ideal of the "holy community" was translated into reality in the days of the First Temple is a matter of considerable doubt. The Bible itself knows of all too many kings who "did what was evil in the eyes of the Lord." But, we know that, at the beginning of the Second Commonwealth, a covenant was signed by the returning exiles, in which the people committed itself to abide by the Law of Moses. And this covenant was accompanied by a solemn oath in which, according to the late Dr. Lauterbach, future generations were to see *the* source of authority behind the observance of the Torah. Later disagreements had reference not to the *source* of that authority, but to the scope to which it extended.[3]

It is with the destruction of Temple and State in the year 70 C.E. that we would expect a breakdown of the constitution of the theocratic Jewish State, and—since that "constitution" and the Torah were identical—it would not have been surprising if the reign of Torah Law had come to an end there and then. This, however, is *not* what happened!

As Professor Hans Joachim Schoeps points out: "It is generally agreed that we have the Pharisaic theologians of the time to thank for the fact that this rupture of the historical tradition did not prove fatal and put an end to Jewish history altogether. It was the sages of Jabneh, of Lydda, of Caesarea, and Bene-Brak, who were the first to develop the concept of the 'as if' into an enduring principle of Jewish history. The Theocracy no longer existed, but its constitution remained in force as if it did. The Temple no longer existed, but Jews the world over bowed in prayer in its direction as if it did. . . .

"This disregard of the actual facts, this abstracting of Judaism from every reality of the here and now, was a phenomenal accomplishment. It did indeed 'save' Judaism —that is to say, by means of the 'as if,' Judaism was adapted to exile and was removed to the plane of the timeless. The faith of the Jews proved more real than reality and overcame it. The sages of Jabneh assumed, as the most self-evident thing in the world, that the royal decrees of God the King as set forth in the constitution of the Covenant (the Torah) were as valid in their day as before. Hence they strove, by putting up 'a fence around the Torah,' to preserve Judaism in isolation from time and space. . . . This was a greater feat than Alexander's conquests or the empire of the Caesars. For it effected a paradoxical retroactive annulment of historical fact: the Jewish state turned out not to have fallen at all in the year 70, but was preserved in its laws, and lived on, metamorphosed, in the ghetto."[4]

The picture drawn by Professor Schoeps is true to the broad outlines of the remarkable phenomenon it is meant to depict. It is not, however, quite true to some of the details. The Rabbis, for example, did not delude themselves—or anyone else—into thinking that the conditions after 70 were identical with those before the Destruction. Their legislation differentiates between laws dependent for their observance upon the soil of the Land of Israel, and laws not so dependent.[5] Recognition was furthermore given to the fact of Jews' living under Gentile jurisdiction—so that the non-Jewish civil law was declared to be religiously binding on the Jew.[6]

What is more, the inability of the Jewish courts to inflict capital punishment on offenders in religious and ritual matters made it possible for all kinds of religious deviationists to continue to live within—and to harrass—the faithful community. There were the *minim* and the *apikorsim*, the *meshumadim* and the *mumarim*—all disregarding and rebelling against various aspects of Jewish belief and practice, without, at the same time, being removed from the scene.[7] The existence of these deviationists, on the one hand, and the lure of the outside world, on the other—whether pagan, Christian, or later, Moslem—meant, of course, that those Jews who remained faithful to the Torah tradition did so in the full knowledge of the alternatives. This, in turn, implies that the Jewish way of life was not simply accepted by the individual just because it was "traditional," and because of his environment. Rather did it mean the full commitment of the *individual* Jew. It is within this context that we have to understand such rabbinic statements as the one about "each Jew having to regard himself as though he personally had been redeemed from Egypt,"[8] or as the frequent reiteration that the Revelation at Sinai must be as topical to the Jew as if it had happened to him "today."[9] Above all, the daily recitation of the *Shema* was regarded as an act of individual commitment, *kabbalat 'ol malkhut shamayim*, "the acceptance of the yoke of the Kingdom of Heaven" on the part of the Jew who recited it. Moreover, it was taught that this acceptance of God's rule had to precede the acceptance of the commandments.[10]

It seems to us, therefore, that there was less of a "disregard of the actual facts" than Schoeps would have us believe. The Jewish way of life, as one Rabbi put it, had to be acquired anew by each individual, because it was not simply an "inheritance."[11]

But, in general outlines, the picture drawn by Schoeps is undoubtedly correct. Particularly as time went on, and the ghetto environment became more and more self-contained, while the traditional modes of behavior were raised to the level of divine commandments, there must have been a closer relation to pre-Destruction Jerusalem than to the contemporary outside world. Much of the *problematik* of Jewish observance, which arose with the Emancipation and the opening of the ghetto gates, simply was not anticipated as long as the fiction of "as if" could be maintained.

Nor, under the circumstances, should we underestimate the power of the environment and the relative ease of conformity. We are dealing here with what the late Dr. Leo Baeck called *Milieufrömmigkeit*, the "piety of the environment." Where everybody else observes the Sabbath by refraining from work, you would not want to disregard the Sabbath. Where everybody else is cooking her meals in accordance with the traditional dietary laws, it would not often occur to you to do otherwise.

But there is danger in this "piety of the environment." It may dissolve into nothing the moment you leave that environment. Such indeed was the case with the thousands from Eastern Europe who, as their ship approached the Statue of Liberty in New York harbor, threw overboard their *tefillin* bags together with their loyalty to the inherited way of life. But what happened in the case of the American immigrants was but typical of what happened to the post-Emancipation Jew in general. With the crumbling of the ghetto walls, this Jew was emancipated from more than mere political disabilities. He also emancipated himself from the Jewish past, which he so much identified with that hateful environment.

In an attempt to save Judaism by separating it from its erstwhile environment, Reform Judaism was born. It endeavored to create what Leo Baeck called *Individual-Frömmigkeit*, the "piety of the individual." Henceforth it should be possible for a man to be a Jew even if he did not live in a Jewish environment. This called for personal conviction and individual commitment. It also called for the recognition of the transitoriness of the *forms* in which Judaism was embedded in the past, and the independence of the "essence" of Judaism from any given form—though not necessarily from the necessity of having forms in general.

The *Halakhah* was a thing of the past. It applied in any case, as Samuel Holdheim endeavored to prove in detail—and on the basis of talmudic maxims themselves—only to the theocratic Jewish State. But, with the disappearance of the State, God Himself manifested His Will that the old "constitution" be abolished. The "autonomy of the Rabbis," their role as administrators of Jewish Law, was now an anachronism. Torah was *Lehre* (Teaching), not *Gesetz* (Law).

Yet the determination of what the "essence" of Judaism really was has remained a moot point from the very beginning. In spite of occasional attempts in the Middle Ages to determine the dogmatic content of Judaism, attempts which never resulted in universal acceptance, there has been an unending debate during the last 150 years on whether Judaism is amenable to dogmatic formulations in the first place.[12] And as for the "essence" itself, that took on Hegelian, Schlegelian, or Kantian colorations, depending upon the philosophical *Weltanschauung* of him who undertook its distillation.

In the meantime, matters that were taken for granted in the Jewish past, with or without a dogmatic formulation, had become highly problematical for the modern Jew in search of his "individual piety." The supposed scientific demonstration that Moses could not have written the Pentateuch was understood, with what logic it has never been shown, as a clear proof that God did not reveal the Torah! And as for God Himself, the "God of Abraham, Isaac, and Jacob" gradually made way for the Absolute, for the "Guarantor of our Ethics," and, finally, for an apotheosis of our own social strivings. Nor could the "scandal" of Israel's "election" long withstand the levelling qualities of modern liberal and democratic thought.

In short, of the whole complex of ideas with which we began this presentation—the personal God, the chosen people, the dimension of sanctity, and the divine commandment—nothing remained but the dimension of sanctity, albeit identified now with bourgeois morality and social meliorism, and the people itself, *minus* its "chosenness." And the "people" was now to be reduced to "pious individuals."

But, in the long run, and notwithstanding some notable exceptions, the creation of the "pious individual" is a task in which Reform Judaism did *not* succeed. On the contrary, whereas Reform Judaism originally envisaged a Jewish piety without a Jewish environment, what, in point of fact, has come about is the Jewish environment without a Jewish piety. When we speak of "sociological Judaism" today, there is no reason to exclude from this definition those gatherings of Jews which are known as Reform Temples—or even that particular organization which proclaims loudest of all that the Jews are a group of religious individuals, and not a people.

This phenomenon can be, and has been, accounted for in terms of "waves of immigration," the rise of anti-Semitism, guilt feelings for what happened in Europe, and whatever else you like. Similar explanations can be, and have been, offered for the Exodus from Egypt, or for the survival of the Jew through the millennia. Such explanations may not be wrong. But, for the believing Jew, they are incomplete. They leave God out of the picture. Perhaps our latter-day "sociological Judaism," coming after fifteen decades of feverish assimilation attempts, is likewise a "finger of God" pointing in the right direction, and away from the road to theological anarchy and nihilism whither the products of early Reform Judaism were tending.

I must add that I personally have no great liking for the "sociological Judaism." It is something crass and materialistic. It is pagan and basically "un-Jewish." But so were the Children of Israel before they came to Sinai! I cannot gainsay the fact that even this kind of Judaism is instrumental in making the modern Jew aware of his Jewish destiny. And more often than not in our past a recognition of Jewish destiny has led to a reawakening of devotion to the *God* of Jewish destiny. And if, as we have tried to indicate earlier, the "holy community" is the vehicle through which God's Sinaitic Covenant is to be realized, then the sense of community, even without the initial perception of the sphere of the holy, may not be an altogether false start.

As it is, it has come about under the impact of "sociological Judaism" that demands have been voiced for greater "warmth" in the Reform worship service, for more rituals in the temple, and for more home ceremonies. Let it be clearly understood, however, that pageantry, however beautiful, is not yet a divine commandment, a *mitzvah*—unless it is felt to have something to do with one's personal relation to God. And any number of "customs and ceremonies," found by statistical inquiry to be practised by such-and-such a percentage of Reform Jews will yet fall short of being *Halakhah* unless and until the divine "thou shalt!" vouches for their authenticity and their compelling nature.

This divine "thou shalt!" however, is something which no human agency can mediate any longer. This much men like Samuel Holdheim have clearly seen. We lack the presupposition—the "autonomy of the Rabbis"—which would facilitate a life under *Halakhah* as it was understood in the Jewish past. A stress on the "piety of the individual" is now inescapable—even though the original espousal of this cause has led to an anarchy which we have had reason to regret.

It is the *individual,* who, spurred on by a contemplation of Jewish destiny and of his own "Jewishness," will have to develop a positive relationship to the documents of the Jewish past. It is the *individual* who will have to discover the Word of God in the sources which purport to contain it. And he will have to do so irrespective of the literary history of the ancient Hebrews. By this we mean that ascribing the authorship of the Pentateuch to a number of human writers and compilers—instead of to the one Moses known to Tradition—does not by any means settle the question whether or not the Torah is the record of Israel's experience of divine Revelation. Nor that other question either: whether or not the Torah contains specific injunctions which God wants *me* to carry out.

It will be quite generally conceded that the validity of the commandment to love our neighbor is not dependent upon its supposed "Mosaic" authorship. Conceivably, then, my adherence to what the Torah has to say about Sabbath observance or dietary restrictions can be just as independent of problems of literary history. But it will *not* be independent of my serious and worshipful study. It will *not* be independent of my endeavor to find in the Torah the Will of God for *me*. It will *not* be independent of my searchings of conscience, and of my fumbling attempts at observance.

But it will have to be "all my own work." As a modern Jewish individual in search of God's *mitzvah* to *me*, I can no more be bound by wholesale and hyper-critical rejection of Jewish traditions (such as the *Pittsburgh Platform*, for one) than I can subscribe to wholesale and uncritical acceptance of the totality of the *Shulhan Arukh*. And, although I shall describe myself as a "Reform Jew" because of the state of mind in which I confront the totality of the Tradition, I shall have to refrain very carefully from prejudicing the issue by labeling various customs and ceremonies as either "Orthodox" or "Reform."

Such is the "piety of the individual" which is called for in an age when a *Halakhah* promulgated by authority, and enforced by the environment, is neither possible nor, perhaps, desirable. And just because it is the "piety of the *individual*," this piety will be marked by a considerable degree of subjectivity. One individual's observance of the Sabbath, for instance, is unlikely to be identical with that of another individual. But this is the price which will have to be paid for that kind of piety. It is, after all, nothing but an honest facing up to the fact—pointed out long ago by Franz Rosenzweig —that what we have in common nowadays is the "landscape," and no longer the common road which wound its way from the close of the Talmud to the dawn of the Emancipation. The best we can do today is to work at our individual roads in the common "landscape." Perhaps the future will again know of a common road, or, more likely, of a common system of roads.[13]

This, however, in and by itself, is *not* the complete solution to our problem. What is to prevent this kind of individualism and subjectivity from turning into the complete anarchy and nihilism which resulted from an earlier start in that direction? And what about the "holy community," which, as we have seen, is basic to God's Covenant with Israel? It is obvious, therefore, that some balance will have to be struck between that which the individual *qua* individual discovers as God's Will for him, and that which is needed to bind the scattered individuals together into one group, to be precise, which is the historic People of Israel in space and in time.

Let us illustrate what we mean by a down-to-earth example:

A Jewish individual has worked at, and mastered, the art of prayer. He has found spiritual solace and inspiration in communion with God. He has even made a regular habit of prayer; he has discovered in prayer a *mitzvah,* something that God wants him to do. But it is prayer in the vernacular. This Jew does not know Hebrew.

Suppose, then, that such a Jewish individual were to ask me whether what he is doing would be acceptable from the point of view of Judaism, of the Jewish Tradition which I have presumably studied, and which I supposedly represent. Could I give him anything but an unqualified "yes"?! Would I not have to tell him that his conduct has been exemplary, not only by the canons of Reform Judaism, but that even the

Rabbinic Law allows him to pray in the vernacular?!

But the picture would change completely if this Jew were now to turn around and agitate for the abolition of Hebrew from his temple service and from the curriculum of his religious school. It would change completely because Hebrew happens to be a factor of tremendous importance when it comes to the historic consciousness of the People of Israel, if not to its very survival.

And from this perspective I am able to tolerate the man's own ignorance of Hebrew, but I cannot tolerate his imposing that ignorance on generations yet unborn. In other words, if the individual wants to be not simply a pious individual, but a pious *Jewish* individual, then—whatever his private observance or lack of observance might be—he cannot afford to work against those elements which enable Israel to stand before God as *Israel*.

Here we definitely have an area where the subjectivism engendered by the "piety of the individual" may come up against the needs of the "holy community." We have illustrated this conflict in the area of Hebrew. There are others. We could mention fixed times for community worship. We could mention the festivals. And we could mention certain basic moral and ethical commitments which the individual *qua* individual may not have felt the call to make, but which are nonetheless a *conditio sine qua non* of the holy community's approach to the problems of society and its own messianic mission.

The moment we concede that our commitment to the God of Israel also involves a commitment to the *community* of Israel (through which God's purposes are to be realized), it should not be too difficult for us—even without personal "revelations"—to recognize the divine authority behind those things which make for the historic continuity and the survival of that community.

Yes, it is a matter of *divine* authority. This means saying a great deal. But it also points up the limitations. There is no human agency in our democratic world which can impose modes of behavior on the free individual simply because a "divine authority" is claimed for them. Obviously the state cannot do it. But the synagogue cannot do it either. The synagogue today is not only a *voluntary* organization, but it is a voluntary *organization*—partaking of all the blessings and all the all-too-human curses attendant upon the machinery of modern organization. This goes as much for the so-called rabbinical bodies as it does for the lay organizations.

Happily, authority imposed from the outside, or from above, is not the only kind of authority. In our long history we have also known that other kind, which might best be described as a "self-imposed" authority.

The covenant and the oath of the returning exiles, to which reference has been made earlier, is an outstanding example of this. In the account of that covenant, as we find it in chapters 8 through 10 of the Book of Nehemiah, there are three Hebrew words in particular which can be helpful to us in our present predicament. They are: *vehe'emadnu 'alenu mitzvot*, "We also lay upon ourselves *mitzvot*."[14] These *mitzvot*, these obligations, are spelled out in some detail. They all have to do with the self-preservation of the small group of the returning exiles through the maintenance of the sanctuary and its cult, the observance of the Sabbath, and the rejection of intermarriage.

The precise details do not matter so much in our particular context. What does matter is the fact of the voluntary acceptance of Jewish obligations on the part of the people, the "self-imposed" authority. This could well serve as a precedent for our own acceptance of certain obligations, of certain *mitzvot* which are ours to perform, not so much because they represent God's Word to us individually, but because they represent the "constitution" of the "holy community."

As a matter of fact, Dr. Mordecai Kaplan has frequently made the suggestion, indeed the earnest plea, that the Jewish People today, in some formal way, reconstitute itself by a renewal of the Covenant. The suggestion is appealing. Its execution, however, is unrealistic.

The modern "Israel after the flesh," to borrow a Paulinian concept, is no longer co-extensive with the "Israel of God." Secularism has made its inroads. The personal God is no longer universally taken for granted. The divine "election" of Israel is rejected by Dr. Kaplan himself! Any "covenant" affirmed by Israel today would, therefore, have to be some compromise statement, vague enough to be acceptable to religionist and secularist alike. From a religious point of view, this would be self-defeating.

And what applies to the totality of twentieth-century Jewry applies no less to the smaller organizations. Here we should mention the futility of addressing requests for *Halakhah* to the Central Conference of American Rabbis. The seven hundred rabbis thus addressed have really only one thing in common: the fact that they are *not* "orthodox." Other than that, it will be very hard, if not impossible, to pin them down to anything. The Central Conference, for example, in spite of repeated attempts made to obtain a commitment on that score, has so far failed to achieve even that degree of self-imposed authority over its own members which would prevent the latter from officiating at weddings where a non-Jewish partner is involved. And when it comes to theological views, to such matters as the personal God, the value of prayer, the very concept of *mitzvah*, the views represented are so diverse that any "official" statement emanating from that source will have to be so vague as to be practically without meaning.

But if the precedent set by the previous commitments of the people as a whole, or of representative sections of it, can no longer be imitated by us in a slavish manner, there yet remains one other kind of precedent in our history which has a very direct relevance to our latter-day problem. I am referring to the *habhurot*, the Pharisaic "brotherhoods," organized in the days of the Second Temple. These "brotherhoods" represented those Jews who made the ritual laws more stringent for themselves, and who became more particular and meticulous in the observance of the laws governing diet and levitical purity than was the current Jewish practice of their time. These "brotherhoods," as voluntary organizations, maintained their own superior standards, and they had their rigorous "entrance requirements."

The "exclusivism" of the Pharisaic Separatists, their "setting themselves apart" from the rest of the people, may indicate a tendency at variance with the pull of "other-directed" conformity which we identify with the essence of our democratic way of life. But it remains to be pointed out that, ultimately, the Separatists won over the people as a whole. Their particular interpretation of the Law gained virtually universal acceptance, and the very stringency of ritual observance which they adopted as a "badge" of their exclusivism became, in the course of time, the *norm* of Jewish piety for everyone alike.[15]

We are not suggesting that the Pharisees be imitated in their rigorous observance of the laws of tithing and levitical purity. But we *are* suggesting that the concept of the *habhurah*, of the "brotherhood" with its *self-imposed* obligations, is one deserving of greater study by those who today are concerned about the "constitution" of the "holy community," and its seat of authority. We *are* suggesting that the basic problem, which permits of no solution on either the international or the "coast-to-coast" level, can be solved, and must be solved, on the *local* level. This is the Pharisaic way of dealing with the problem!

Unlike the old-established Jewish communities of Europe, the Jewish congregations in the United States are voluntary associations, established, at least in principle, by like-minded individuals. That is why we have such things as synagogues and temples established with the avowed purpose of maintaining the Orthodox, or the Conservative, or the Reform expressions of Judaism. Now, there would be nothing to stop the founding members of a new congregation (except, perhaps, the temptation to fall for the idolatry of mere numbers) from saying: *vehe'emadnu 'alenu mitzvot*, "We who are establishing this congregation, bind ourselves to maintain such-and-such observances and such-and-such standards which are meant to constitute our congregation as a 'holy community,' and as an integral part of that 'holy community' which is the historic People of Israel. Whoever wants to join us as a regular member will likewise take upon himself the above-mentioned obligations—over and above such other obligations as he may already have taken upon himself, or as he will yet take upon himself, in an individual capacity."

In the case of congregations already established—and that, at present, is undoubtedly the majority—it will not be feasible to introduce such a self-imposed authority retroactively. But what will be possible in the case of already established congregations is the formation of *habhurot* within such congregations. In itself this is nothing startlingly new. The traditional synagogue has always known its *hevrah shass*, its *hevrah tehillim*, its *hevrah kadishah*, and its various other societies devoted to such intellectual and philanthropic pursuits as elicited the particular devotion of the members who constituted them.

The modern *habhurah* may, in its beginning, be nothing more and nothing less than a group of people within the congregation who are particularly devoted to the *mitzvah* of *talmud torah*, and who meet regularly to fulfill it. But, as part of their "constitution," they will bind themselves to the maintenance of certain *mitzvot*—not because anybody is demanding it of them, but because they want to do so.

In this manner the solution of the problem of freedom and authority may be approached in our day. The individual's commitment to his "Jewishness" will lead him to accept voluntarily the self-imposed obligations of the group of like-minded individuals. Thus shall we be able to relive and reenact the covenant made in the days of Ezra, the covenant of *vehe'emadnu 'alenu mitzvot*. And behind that covenant at the beginning of the Second Commonwealth, as behind the self-imposed obligations of the Pharisaic *habhurot*, there is the distinct reminiscence of that other covenant, the Covenant at Sinai, where Israel responded with the words *na'aseh venishma'*, "We shall do and we shall harken," to the divine mandate that they constitute themselves as "a kingdom of priests and a holy nation."

With this memory revived, it may not be a vain hope that the modern Jew will again be able to recite—and to *mean*—the words of the ancient liturgy: "Thou hast chosen us, . . . Thou hast loved us, . . . and Thou hast sanctified us by Thy commandments."

NOTES

[1] Cf. his latest statement to this effect in *CCAR Journal*, January, 1960, pp. 11-17.

[2] *Yad, Hilkhot Teshubhah* 3: 11.

[3] Cf. Jacob Z. Lauterbach, *Rabbinic Essays*. Cincinnati, HUC Press, 1951, pp. 27ff.

[4] H.J. Schoeps, in *The Church and the Jewish People*, ed. G. Hedenquist. Edinburgh, 1954, p. 64f.

[5] Cf. *Mishnah Kiddushin* 1: 9; and *Sifre, Re-eh, pisqa* 59 (ed. Friedmann, p. 87a).

[6] Cf. b. *Gittin* 10b, parallels.

[7] Cf. Jakob J. Petuchowski: "The *Mumar*—"A Study in Rabbinic Psychology," in HUCA Vol. XXX (1959), pp. 179-190.

[8] *Mishnah Pesahim* 10: 5.

[9] Cf., for example, *Sifre, Wa-ethannan, pisqa* 33 (ed. Friedmann, p. 74a).

[10] Cf. *Mishnah Berakhoth* 2: 2, and *Mekilta Bahodesh*, ch. VI (ed. Lauterbach, Vol. II, p. 238).

[11] Cf. *Mishnah Abhot* 2: 17.

[12] Cf. the protracted discussion on this in MGWJ 1926-27.

[13] Cf. Franz Rosenzweig, *Briefe*, Berlin, Schocken, 1935, p. 426f.

[14] *Nehemiah* 10: 33.

[15] Cf. Jakob J. Petuchowski: "The Pharisaic Tradition Today," in *Commentary*, February, 1956, pp. 112-117, reprinted in *Heirs of the Pharisees* (N.Y., 1970: Basic Books), pp. 8-19.

IV

JEWISH FELLOWSHIP TODAY

Jacob Neusner

Jewish communities are mostly no longer communities at all, but rather conglomerate social groups composed of isolated individuals. Thus, in a given city, the Jews may share certain common purposes. To the world at large indeed, the Jews might seem to be clannish, for often one finds neighborhoods which are mainly Jewish, and notes that large numbers of Jews prefer the company of other Jews (no matter how desiccated their Jewishness may be). Yet when one examines the typical Jewish community carefully, one finds that the areas of common purpose and unique social experience are limited. What in fact manifests the element of "communion" among Jewish individuals in a given place, to demonstrate that there truly is community among them? One would note the common efforts in foreign and domestic philanthropy, public relations ("defense"), social service through hospitals and homes for the aged, and even common institutions for social life ("community centers") and education. Perhaps the structure of the Jewish community is impressive by contrast to that of other groups in American society; perhaps Jews are even over-organized.

The Jews are not, however, a community in the ways that once characterized the Kennesset Yisrael, the Jewish People living in a given town or village. What were these ways? One learns from any of a dozen first-class social studies of Jewish life in the past what the Jewish People once enjoyed as a community. The elaborate communal structure in the U.S.A. provides a pale contrast. The Jew in a medieval town in

51

Europe or the Moslem world (and this town would likely have survived to the early 19th century in Western Europe, and to 1940 in the East, and, perhaps, even to 1948-9 in the Arab part of the Moslem world) may have been alien to the land of his birth, but he was very much at home among the people of his faith. He enjoyed, therefore, a social security one can today hardly envision, much less appreciate. He was known to all men, and knew all men; he had his place and his hour, and if neither was particularly exalted, both assured him against the present sense of anomie and personal alienation. He belonged.

In his place, however humble, he had a living or protection, at least, against starvation; he had friendship; he had the security of a rich and complex web of human relationships, which placed him into relationship with everyone he might meet, even the stranger, even the enemy. His neighbor was his companion; he prayed with him, studied with him; shared with him the crises of life; buried him; wept for him. Community meant, therefore, one's own address in life and beyond death; it meant continuity, and it meant love, if by love one understands the effort to reach out from one self to another. The Jewish community was a representation of Kennesset Yisrael here and now, and manifested the social reality to which the Torah was given, at which the Prophets raged, and for which the Sages devised their moral and legal constitution based on revelation and prophecy. In this community, each man had his particular role to play, a role which, under the circumstances of Judaism, had significance in the historical and metaphysical drama of creation, revelation, and redemption.

The Jewish community was not alone in its debacle. All "traditional" society underwent similar strain, as Oscar Handlin describes the pattern in *The Uprooted*; and the advent of modernism—industrialization, urbanization, over-population, and perhaps bourgeoisification as well—represented the end of community for many men in many places. If one may characterize several centuries of social history in the West, and, apparently, the present social tendency in the East as well, one would conclude that most men outside primitive societies are facing the crisis of community and the advent, for good or not, of the radically isolated individual as the basic unit of society. Individuals together, however, do not create a community; they create a mass. Indeed, the very concept of the individual apparently is based on the antithetical concept of the mass, as the concept of community (or tribe, or village) is apparently antithetical to any smaller, or larger, social unit (except possibly the family).

Contrasting American Jewish communities with those that existed in other places, therefore, yields a pattern with only slight variations (mainly temporal) from those of other people on the continent of North America and, now, throughout the others as well. Western society moved from its focus on the community to that on the individual over a period of many centuries. In the hardly precise, but still useful categories of Western history, one can trace a gradually evolving pattern of individuation in the West from the time of the rise of the nation-state, through the Renaissance and Reformation, and into the eras of industrial revolution, secularism, liberalism, and only lately, totalitarianism. Today man stands alone against the state. For the Jew, on the other hand, the same pattern emerged in relatively few years, at the most (to date) three generations for the larger part of the American Jewish community, perhaps five for Western European Jewry (what remains of it), and two or even one for much of Israeli Jewry, as well as that in Eastern Europe and Soviet Russia. The Jews seem to have experienced their renaissance and reformation and nationalization and secularization and bourgeoisification and, for some "totalitarianization" in about a century; not gradually but suddenly, even brutally; and, for one-third of them, tragically.

It is no wonder, then, that the Jewish community seems desiccated and colorless by contrast to that of earlier centuries. It is no wonder, either, that most Jews do not even enjoy a community at all, most of the time and for most of their lives. Many, at least, have a rather limited experience of Jewish community: in part, ritual (and that part diminishes in importance for many), in part, ethnic. To return then to the

so-called Jewish community of a given city today, one asks
whether it is a true community, and concludes that, by
comparison with what men once experienced as "community," it is not. In most places, it is rather a collection of
communities, mostly very very small, of cliques and clans
and minuscule sibs; it is "country clubs" for some, and
community centers for some, and particular shops and
synagogues and summer resorts for some. For none is the
Jewish community co-extensive with all the Jews in a given
place (as it was in New York City as late as 1800, and in
Charleston, South Carolina, for still another quarter-century);
for few is it a community at all. One would have to look very
hard to find Kennesset Yisrael in a given place or time. The
fundamental category of Jewish peoplehood has lost its
referent in historical reality, and while it remains essential
theology, it is poor sociology indeed. If one regards the past
situation of Judaism as relevant and even authentic, however,
one will recognize that the socially meaningful entity that
was Kennesset Yisrael, that is, the Jewish people in a given
place and time, needs in some measure to be restored and
reconstituted. The relevance and authenticity of that earlier
experience are these: to a particular people, revelation was
handed down; to a particular society, the prophets gave their
teachings; the artifacts of a particular social culture were the
raw materials of the Rabbis. Judaism thus addressed itself to a
community, not merely to "individuals who share a common
destiny"; that community represented the focus and embodiment of the Jewish faith. What we have today is, alas, all that
remains of it.

One turns to analogues available in Jewish social history of
an earlier day, to find a suggestion at least as to how men met
such a crisis of community. Professor Morton Smith[1]
demonstrated how the crisis of community was met by an
earlier age. He shows that the twentieth century has no
monopoly on "modernism"; on the contrary, during the
centuries after the conquest of Alexander (ca. 330 B.C.), the
ancient Near East experienced a remarkable expansion of
trade, population, industry. New governments, ruling new

empires, effected the rationalization of commerce and the nurture of state capitalism; new men, not only adventurers from Hellas but Semites as well, brought new vigor and genius to the dormant economy and culture of the East. One consequence was the precipitous growth of great cities, and, more commonly, the founding of new cities on the foundations of ancient villages. Another was the acquisition of new values, which approved individual endeavor and ascribed positive merit to the achievements of this world. Still a third was the questioning of ancient beliefs and doctrines in the light of the new and successful ideas flowing in from Hellas; the old religions had to address themselves to a broader audience of believers and non-believers alike, in the speculative, abstract, and sophisticated language of Hellenic thought, instead of the mythic and primarily concrete discourse of earlier centuries. The crisis of community apparently was manifest, therefore, in the crisis of ancient culture, in the appearance of many men unbound by ancient bonds and ethics, and most important, in the creation of uprooted masses in cities. The primary social unit became the individual, in place of settled men in towns and villages where the primary social unit had been mainly the family and village or town itself, and in whose structure of relationships each man had found his place.

In the cities and among the masses of men, one discerns a very articulate response, through emergent, assertive individualism, to the new situation. In many places, some men separated themselves from the "masses," and in one way or another, formed social entities that provided community, a place and a definition for the individual. We have examined in some detail such "communities," formed by close adherence to laws of tithing and ritual purity. If the *havurah* was fundamentally a society for strict observance of laws of ritual cleanliness and holy offerings, it may represent a social entity which has particular relevance to men who are not wholly satisfied with the community provided by social experience among undifferentiated masses and alienated, lonely individuals. To uncover points of relevance, one may usefully articulate the social policy apparently espoused by the fellowship. First, the fellowship represented a decision to find elements of community within the common society, rather than to create a community outside of it. Second, it took a critical view of society as it was, choosing to separate its members from it by keeping strictly to its primary ideal, and at the same time attempting to educate the common society in what it considered the right way. Third, the specific method of the fellowship was, first, to define its fundamental concerns, to determine on precisely what issues there would be absolutely no compromise; second, to provide an orderly way by which an individual from any part of society might come to hear and carry out these concerns, and to elaborate the rules which would guide the fellow in every possible situation he might meet, thus defining his relationship with outsiders and his specific obligations as a part of the fellowship. Finally, the purpose of the fellowship was extremely limited; it was in no sense a revolutionary sect, but rather a finite and tentative effort to achieve particular religious and social ends. The consequences may be discerned in the endurance of the ideal of the fellowship after the social disasters of 70 and 135 C.E., when the Pharisees successfully transformed the defeated nation into a national fellowship scattered throughout many lands and conditions.

If the crisis of community has its historical analogue, so too the ancient responses find modern parallel. Thus one may regard the revolutionary utopianism of the kibbutz movement as a modern form of Essenism, in which men separated themselves from the common society to build a new and better community. The kibbutz was meant, as Martin Buber described it in *Paths to Utopia,* to make possible the creation of a real community, in which each individual had his home, and "all other inhabitants with whom he lives and works are all acknowledging and confirming his individual existence." The kibbutz definition of a community was "one in which every point of its being possesses potentially at least the whole character of community, a place in which man might feel his own home"; it represented the effort to re-acquire "in new tectonic forms, internal social relationships." As a response to the crisis of community, the kibbutz was extraordinarily successful for some men, and quite irrelevant to most.

A second modern effort to transform the situation of the French communitarian movement, is described by Erich Kahler in *The Tower and the Abyss.* Bringing together many different kinds of individuals, the communitarians created a rule, a community, neighbor groups, and a social entity (the community) which held in common the means of production, not as an effort to retire from the world but to remain in but not of it. Kahler holds that the communitarian groups, founded in 1940 in Valence, differ from other urban cooperatives in the focus of the communal effort: not primarily financial gain but rather the effort to restore the dignity of the individual in relationship to other individuals. The purpose of the communitarians was social, not economic gain. In striking ways, therefore, the communitarian movement apparently manifests similarity to the *huvurah.*

When one considers the social life of American Jewry (and perhaps other diaspora Jewish communities as well), he notes certain areas in which the idea of the fellowship may be relevant. The smallest coherent social unit of the present Jewish community is the synagogue (and its parallel, sometimes competing equivalents in organizational life, such as the lodge or chapter of one Jewish institution or another). If the synagogue was once co-extensive with the Jewish community, today it is not co-extensive even with the social life of its members. The synagogue in many places does not represent the embodiment in an institution of a community at all; it is neither the consequence nor the cause of community. It is rarely founded by men and women who themselves feel the need to give form to a pre-existent social experience; and it very often does not produce a coherent social experience for its members. It is many things to many men, but to few indeed does it represent the focus of a religious communal life.

What place, in truth, does the synagogue have in the social

life of its members? For some few, it is the place where they
sometimes go to pray; for some others, it is the instrument for
the transmission of the rudiments of Judaism to the young
(and that not very effectively); for others, it may provide the
framework for certain recreational activities. In synagogues of
more than a few dozen families, it is even possible for all
members not to know one another, and in larger places, it is
possible for the rabbi not to know each member of his "flock."
Whatever the synagogue ought to be, it is very rarely a
community or a religious fellowship. The various lodges and
chapters and posts (their name is legion) usually consist of a
small number of activists, and a long mailing list. They bring
together a very few people, for a random moment in the
month, and provide limited social experience (often recreative), but very little fellowship. Even in the more modest
forms of synagogue and institutional life, such as the
"brotherhood" or "sisterhood" or the youth group, one finds
strangers meeting strangers, remaining strangers.

If one would want Jews to cluster about their synagogues, in
small congeries of families, a solution might be possible for
some. The synagogue might indeed constitute the focus for
the social life of a given group, and, with its religious
emphasis, might indeed represent the effort to constitute
Kennesset Yisrael. One might even witness the formation of
Essenic neighborhoods in American cities, inhabited by
families whose lives are turned inward on the life of their
synagogue. They might, as men once did, live together, pray
together, study together, and know one another in the subtle
intimacies of daily life. In truth, such synagogues do exist in
America, as some villages in Israel and elsewhere remain true
representations of the ancient community.

For the most part, however, Jewish neighborhoods develop
not around synagogues, but vice versa. People who prefer to
live "with their own kind" are not motivated, for the most
part, by a desire to maintain a common school and place of
worship within an easy walk from home, or to have a
common *sukkah* at *Sukkot* and a common *mikveh* and a
common *minyan*. I am not sure what they seek among "their

own kind," but I suspect that it is a social benefit denied them elsewhere: the right to be received not as a type ("the Jew") but as an individual. Among one's own kind, the Jew is not, in fact, a member of a minority any longer, or possibly of any socially differentiable group, but he achieves the radical individuation denied him by extenuating circumstances elsewhere. The neighborhood ghetto would seem to have become, therefore, the instrument of achieving its very opposite: a place in the undifferentiated mass.

Perhaps a way of achieving community is indicated by the ancient fellowship. If men remain in the life of the city, they may still have some of the benefits achieved by those who abandon it, by delineating particular areas of meaningful observance, or ritual, or intellectual concern, the participation in which will designate a man part of an otherwise unarticulated group. The fellow did so, as we have seen, by choosing certain ritual laws which he believed to be fundamental, and by observing them under all circumstances; the result was that some men in the larger society recognized one another as a part of the same polity, and were able, for example, to eat with one another, secure in the knowledge that their meal was ritually undefiled and properly prepared according to the rules of agricultural tithes and heave-offerings. The fellowship was not made up of men who lived in the same neighborhood or had frequent social relationships with one another; and yet it sustained itself, and apparently provided a useful social relationship for its members.

One might well ask how a contemporary fellowship would differ from other such social instruments to create community, such as fraternities or Masonic groups or luncheon "service" societies. Formally it does not differ at all. Like the Mason, the fellow may live anywhere in a given town, undifferentiated from others; like him, his fellowship may be unobtrusive. The way of the ancient fellowship is, therefore, not unexplored by others. What will render it useful and unique to Jews is how they choose to articulate it. Several principles may guide thought on contemporary efforts to recover the experience of fellowship.

First, a meaningful social group among Jews ought to take its particular character and definition from the Jewish faith and tradition. It ought to be defined and formulated in terms consequential to the religion of Israel, representing the sociological effect of the religious phenomenon itself. A Jewish social group or fellowship ought to bear witness to an intrinsic sociological idea within Judaism. Is there such an idea? Professor Petuchowski's[2] proposes that there is; the idea is that the constitution of a people of Israel, in a given place and time, finds significance in the history and destiny of the Jewish people, its definitions in the faith and *mitzvot maasiot* of the Jewish people, its programme in the Torah of the Jewish people, in the fulfilment of the ethical and moral principles of the Jewish people, and in the dedication of the private person to the communal enterprise of the Jewish people. If the Jewish people came into being at Sinai, then the constitution must be the Torah, the laws, those of the Torah; indeed, the very possibility of receiving the Torah was and is predicated upon the creation of such a sacred community, worthy of bearing witness to its precepts and of realizing them in its community life. So Professor Petuchowski states:

> The Jew in the past approached his God as a member of the chosen people. He performed his Jewish obligations because they added the dimension of sanctity, which is the "constitution" of this chosen people. . . . When the Jew in the past submitted to the regimen of Torah-law, it was not so much a case of his being personally committed to this or that aspect of it, but simply of his being a member of a people which had committed itself to the Torah as its constitution.

The *havurah* represents the effort to achieve much more than friendship or companionship, the effort to overcome personal loneliness. Rather, its purpose is fellowship, a very different experience. What distinction stands between fellowship and friendship? Friendship involves two people—fellowship, two people and one ideal held in common. Friendship is the consequence of primarily interpersonal and reciprocal benefit, sometimes intellectual, sometimes emotional, sometimes psychological. Friends need each other, otherwise they cannot remain friends. It is a static relationship. Friendship rests on abiding affection, it is entirely a cathectic relationship of two people, totally focused on those two people. Fellowship, on the other hand, may very well be achieved without friendship at all, for it is predicated on a common goal or ideal shared among two or more people, drawing them together despite, not because of, their particularities and uniquenesses.

In this sense, friendship is irrelevant to fellowship. One cannot doubt that out of genuine fellowship, friendship arises, but that is a happy by-product of a quite different experience. Fellowship engages isolated individuals in a common enterprise, thereby creating between them common bonds, providing for them common experience, uniting them for reasons quite external to the structure of their own personalities. This distinction is recognized in *Avot*:

> Whenever love depends upon some thing, with the passing away of that thing, the love too passes away; but if it be not dependent upon such a thing, it will not pass away forever.

Fellowship, in an affirmative sense, depends upon a quality external to the relationships of those who are fellows of one another; it is that which unites two men who walk together down a path. When they reach their goal, they go their separate ways. To the extent that the fellowship imposes a common bond of purpose and direction upon men, it will differ from all activities intended to "bring people together" or to facilitate personal needs of its communicants, to that extent it will not be another clique or club or clan. The ideal of fellowship thus exhibits a certain austerity uncommon in the effusive personal relationships we know and expect, for it is an ideal of men's coming together for utterly impersonal—in this sense, social—purposes. Friendships never transcend individual friends; fellowship must begin with such transcendence.

Third, the fellowship is to be created by the very personal involvement of each man in the ultimate purpose of the fellowship itself, in activities directly and immediately relevant to its final goal. Most organizational life professes an impressive galaxy of purposes; if only partly successful, any single American Jewish society would already have "saved" the Jews, if not the world. The role of individuals in such organizations has very little to do with those ultimate purposes, however.

What, indeed, does the private person do in any society, including the synagogue? Mainly, the private person seems to give money and drink tea. For example, the great Jewish organizations in this country carry out enormously important tasks in philanthropic and Zionist activity, or in defence, or in education. But what do the members do? They pay dues, contribute to special "drives" or "campaigns," receive "bulletins" or communiques, and very occasionally attend a meeting? (The very military character of organizational metaphors is appropriate indeed to the status of the private in the ranks, contented to do his duty, and sometimes, to get a medal—or a plaque.) What happens at a meeting? Generally, the members hear a speaker, perhaps ask a question, but mainly look forward to the coffee hour afterwards. This is quite legitimate, it seems to me, for the coffee hour is the one moment in which each private person actually does something creative and personal. The purposes of the organization are generally carried out by professionals. No matter the "cause," most men and women who support it have very little to do themselves towards achieving it.

For "fellowship," it ought to be contrary. The individual member ought to participate at every recreative moment in contributing not to the means of the group, but to its ends. He ought to contribute himself to reach such ends, and I mean himself, and not his money. If the fellowship begins with a budget it will end with a bank account. Its goals must be so chosen that they may immediately engage each member. If each man knows and accepts the goal of the fellowship, and knows how he himself is achieving that goal personally, in his own being, then he will be more than a Lion or an Elk or a Benevolent Moose: he will be a Jew and a man.

Every activity in Jewish life, even the synagogue, permits its participants to fulfil their obligations by a money payment, a kind of ransom for the absent soul. The cash nexus, however, represents the reduction of men to things. Money is easier to collect than minds. Intellect and commitment are more precious because they are rarer. In planning the *havurot*, one may profitably eliminate, so far as possible, the things of this world in pursuit of the blessings of the next.

Finally, one ought to recognize, as did the ancient *haver* and *Talmid Hakham*, the very temporal character of fellowship or "community" itself. Fellowship has no substance. It is not a social continuum. It manifests no existence independent from that of its communicants. Fellowship is a dimension of time: one cannot say fellowship is, but rather, fellowship happens. It is created and re-created from moment to moment when certain elements, namely, radically isolated individuals, coalesce to create it. The catalyst of fellowship needs to be discovered and defined. The components of fellowship are individuals coming together out of radical self-involvement and isolation from one another, to pursue a purpose that transcends their own individual lives.

There is, moreover, an element of recurrence in fellowship, an element of temporal return: day by day and moment by moment, fellowship is re-created. In this sense, there is a mythic quality to the ideal of fellowship. Myth attempts to represent underlying, recurring realities, that may be "essences" of being, but are realized here and now only in their particularities. In this sense, again, there is a mystery to the realization of fellowship, and its very intangibility hints at this. Fellowship is the miracle that occurs when men and women transcend themselves, their personal wants, and subjective needs, in pursuit of an end, however petty, that lies beyond the horizons of their private place in life.

The fellowship in ancient times rested on the ideal of commonwealth, the sense that some men actually had common concerns and commitments which might be articulated through that particular institution. If there is in the end no underlying community in which men actually participate and for which they care, the fellowship is a useless device. From this viewpoint, however, one finds some slender hope: the Jews do seem to choose to remain a group, as the existence of Jewish neighborhoods, hotels, fraternities, and the synagogues themselves testify. If this choice is a negative one, its consequences do not have to be negative. One can attempt to transform a group which finds its definition by contrast to the "outside world" into a group which is constituted on affirmative inward social experience. Even today the Jews continue to manifest certain qualities of a fellowship; if not in a given synagogue, then in a given town, they do acknowledge their fellowship in some ways. One might well criticize the expressions of that fellowship, but one cannot ignore its presence in American cities. Attenuated ties bind Jews into an attenuated community. On this basis one may hope to recover the reality of fellowship and community.

Fellowship will not save the world, nor probably even make much of a difference to the Jewish community. It may matter, however, to the mundane life of the private person who controls very little more than how he spends his own time. I believe it may provide some men and women with a worthier "cause" than that which now informs their lives. It is an interim program, intended to meet very humble problems of social and personal conduct by directing the attention of perplexed men to higher purposes that they may achieve together. If it has any value at all the fellowship must be regarded as a tentative and austere step towards meaningful and creative use of that interim between birth and death that each man knows as life.

NOTES

[1] Morton Smith, *Palestinian Parties and Politics that Shaped the Old*

Testament (N.Y.: 1971, Columbia University Press), pp. 126–192.
    [2] Above, pp. 33 ff.

V

DEFINING THE HAVURAH

Jacob Neusner

Fellowship may be defined as a relationship among individuals characterized by both reciprocity of profound concern for one another and dedication to a goal held in common. In such a relationship, individuals respect one another's integrity, individuality, and uniqueness, thus remaining autonomous. But at the same time they submit to a purpose or a self-imposed, socially relevant discipline, which thus adds a heteronomous dimension to their relationship. In a true fellowship, individuals submit their persons to a group, which itself ought to make manifest the emergent individual. In the simplest terms, therefore, a fellowship involves the individual immediately and directly in the purposes of the group. Yet the individual may find in such a fellowship a means of achieving greater individuality by *his own* efforts to serve a common goal. Mutual respect and even affection may develop out of such shared concerns, but a fellowship, unlike a clique, does not depend on congeniality, nor does it regard love as sufficient.

Jewish fellowship rests upon the Jewish belief that where ten Jews assemble for sacred purposes, the presence of God is among them. Jewish fellowship represents the effort to constitute a group worthy of the presence of God. It is created by a small number of people who come together regularly for specific, Jewish purposes. The primary relationships of such a group are defined by the Jewish religion, and concern people (not "members" or "contacts") and God. It is an effort among individuals to create a community of people who share with one another the most precious possession, namely life, and choose to seek the fraternity of others among whom life may be sanctified. It is, quite specifically, not merely an effort to serve some cause, though good causes may be well served indeed, but a commitment of one soul to another, and of all to God. It is therefore not a purely social group, but a *way* some men may take together, united for strength upon the road.

That road leads to, and not away from, the sacred congregation, the synagogue. Jewish fellowship may in truth begin outside the synagogue. It may begin within the walls of a synagogue itself, but only as a way of overcoming the synagogue's own inability, by reason of size or some other failing, to constitute in itself a fellowship.

In the end, the *havurah* must, however, constitute a new form for Jewish religious and social existence, to replace the form currently called "the synagogue." *Synagogue* is a term applied with little discrimination to a multitude of Jewish groups over the past twenty centuries. These groups have exhibited few common characteristics, just as today there are many kinds of "synagogues," with little in common. The middle-class synagogue, serving not as a community but rather as a service station for the needs of various isolated individuals, has little reason to survive. It is too expensive, too impersonal, and quite irrelevant. That is why people make use of it, but give it no profound personal commitment, except for reasons—election to office, personal gratifica- tion—irrelevant to its stated purposes. The rabbinate of the synagogue bears little in common with the classical rabbi- nate, yet has not evolved into an attractive form of Jewish service, merely into an attenuated, unintegrated form of the old one. The ideals of fellowship therefore stand in judgment of those of the synagogue, its social and religious forms, its personnel. These ideals have nothing in common with those of ordinary folk who make use of the synagogue for their own convenience, with no deep concern or commitment, with slight learning and much stupidity. The *havurah* is not only a very old form for Jewish social and religious organization, but also a very new one. In time to come, *havurot* are likely to attract those serious and thoughtful Jews who in former times either submitted to the imperfections of the synagogue or abandoned Judaism as a social experience. Synagogues will survive, even thrive; but *havurot* will constitute a viable alternative to synagogue life, one, I am confident, which will win the loyalty of the best young Jews in the West.

The fellowship may stand as a measuring rod, against which various present societies and organizations of all kinds may be set. The great purposes of our institutions, however, may well be served through funds and not through fraternity. One must hesitate to criticize organizations for not achieving their unperceived potentialities. Great purposes never create or sustain life, but great meaning in the situation of the private person does.

Jewish fellowship, secondly, rests upon the Jewish belief that religion is social, and not merely personal, in focus. Judaism has held that one cannot be a Jew outside he community of Israel, and this contention is based both upon theology and upon practicality. Theologically, one must recognize that Revelation came not to individuals but to a group, a community, at Sinai. The purpose of that group was to constitute a "sacred nation" which might realize in its affairs the will of the divinity. The actions of the individual are deeply relevant to the destiny of the group and hence worthy objects of its concern. Practically, moreover, the community was always indispensable to the observance of every aspect of the faith. More significantly, the individual was assisted in fulfilling his religious duties by the presence of other individuals who themselves shared these obligations. Thus the capacity of a group greatly to influence the conduct of its individual members appeared as a powerful force in realizing the Torah. Discipline is less onerous if others share it, and becomes a part of social reality if it is accepted as the way life ought to be conducted.

Today, Jewish fellowship may begin, thirdly, in the evident need of many individual Jews for a richer and more complex social experience as individuals and as Jews than is presently available. Individual Jews who choose, for example, to observe the Sabbath (and no movement in modern Judaism has thought of abrogating the Sabbath) find it more meaningful to do so in the company of other observers than outside of it. Certainly the vitality of the Young Israel movement and the Conservative Leaders' Training Fellowship in the U.S.A. comes in part from the personally rewarding social experiences provided, perhaps merely as by-products, by group observance of the Sabbath and study of the Torah. This is particularly true in smaller or less contiguous Jewish settlements. The experience of the *haver* in the Talmudic period suggests, moreover, that inchoate social groups may emerge on the basis of common commitment to specific religious practices. The deep problem of Jewish community is, however, not exhausted by the shallow problems of ritual or even intellectual life in isolation. It is, in the end, part of the larger modern crisis faced by individuals who confront life radically isolated from one another and alienated from any meaningful social experience.

The manner in which such fellowship may be developed will surely be defined on the basis of wider experience and deeper insight than I possess. I would suggest a number of principles that might guide efforts to achieve fellowship. First, fellowships ought not to result from pressure from the outside upon individuals to "join" them, but rather on the inner needs of individuals to create them. Second, they ought at the outset to exclude "birds of passage," but to entail commitment on the part of the fellows to carry out the discipline imposed by the group upon itself. Third, they might well begin with a defined period of duration, so that they do not peter out and hence add to the social failures each individual experiences. Fourth, the purpose for which the fellowship exists ought to be immediately and self-evidently achievable in the lives of the individual fellows, to that the discipline is personal and not impersonal, demanding private and individual performance.

The activities of such fellowship may, again, be most varied. I would suggest only a few kinds of actions of personal and social involvement that may be relevant to Jewish fellowship. First, a Jewish fellowship ought to be a group of praying Jews. The art of prayer is difficult, and developed only through discipline. It ought to be cultivated by Jewish fellowship. I think it unlikely that a fellowship among Jews can achieve genuine religious significance without the effort to pray. Such prayers may well include, if appropriate, the relevant Jewish services; but they most certainly ought to include individual efforts to express the devotion of the fellowship to the divinity.

Second, a Jewish fellowship ought to be a group of *studying* Jews. Some Jewish text ought to provide the center of the group's concern, although it may function only as a point of departure. Jewish study is most creative when it is a study of, *and digression from,* a text. It then has a beginning and a continuity, and becomes a means of giving new life to the text itself. Two approaches may be considered: first, open and free discussion of books read by all in advance; second, group study led by individuals, but, I think, only by individual members of the group itself. The dangers of this approach are self-evident, but the potential results, measured in significant and disciplined learning, may be formidable.

Third, a Jewish fellowship ought to be a group of Jews who perform acts of compassion *(gemilut hasadim),* and perhaps specifically those acts of compassion which no others do nowadays. For example, except for the efforts of rabbis, Jewish inmates of prisons are ignored by individuals in the Jewish community, and , perhaps worse, their families are frequently isolated from other Jews. If the Jewish community is not presently able to serve these men except through the efforts of the rabbinate, perhaps individual groups might consider how they could assist in the rehabilitation of those who have left the right path. Certainly such groups could do much to relieve the loneliness and anxiety of prisoners, both for their own future and for their families' welfare. Another example of an area of real service *(avodah)* may be found in hospitals for the aged, chronically ill, and mentally ill. Here again, except for the efforts of the rabbinate, old people, bedridden people, and mental patients are not the concern of many individuals in the Jewish community. Yet they would be greatly comforted to receive the concern of their fellow Jews. The aged may be given a renewed share in the affairs of the active community; the chronically ill may be given a bright moment in the somber day; and the mentally ill may be given new sense that others care about and share their troubles. These are, moreover, areas of service which require the individual to give his own time and effort, not merely his funds, and which are hence particularly appropriate for Jewish fellowships.

Fourth, a Jewish fellowship ought to be a group of Jews whose lives are illumined by the sacred calendar. Hence these Jews might find ways of celebrating together the Sabbaths and the festivals of the Jewish year, presumably within some one synagogue but perhaps after individual fellows' participation in the prayers of several synagogues. Such celebrations are, of course, the heritage of all Jews; but the fellows might make certain that the Sabbath is a day of delight, and the festivals, of rejoicing, and they might find ways of keeping the Sabbath which are appropriate to their religious viewpoint. (I have in mind, in particular, liberal Jews who reject the traditional viewpoint on the Sabbath. If at the outset they affirm the Sabbath as a day of rest and not of commerce, and if they find together means of observing the Sabbath according to their convictions, the result must surely be the sanctification of the Sabbath among them.) Moreover, a Jewish fellowship might very well consider aspects of the Jewish way of marking the passage of time which are currently ignored. For example, the month of Elul was traditionally, and of course remains for traditional Jews, a time of penitence and supplication, Av of mourning, and Adar of merrymaking. Perhaps a fellowship might develop specifically for the purpose of observing Elul, or Av, or Adar; or Pesach, Sukkot, or Shavuot. Perhaps a fellowship might begin with a simple task of building and living in a Sukkah once a year; or of conducting brief *selihot* (penitential) prayers during Elul.

Fifth, a Jewish fellowship might keep in mind the practice of preserving the record of its experience as a group. It might, for example, keep the writings that may mark its life, such as prayers or even individual comments worth preserving. Such records ought to enter into the living literature of the "people of the book," and in time constitute a kind of scripture.

Whatever its program, the fellowship must realize the teaching, "Not by might nor by power but by my word says the Lord of hosts." It must not abandon its spiritual concern for the concerns of the world, though its spiritual life ought well to involve it deeply in the affairs of the world. Its single goal must be to create a place where the Presence of God may dwell among men. Whatever the means and however virtuous the results, without dedication to that goal, the fellowship must in the end produce another, perhaps especially effective, organization, and acquire for itself institutional patriotism rather than piety for God.

Perhaps in another place and age, the idea of Jewish fellowship may have been commonplace. Indeed, today in some places, the Jewish community is in many ways a Jewish fellowship, and that is how it ought to be. But the failure of the "Jewish community" to realize a true sense of community, of commonality and common concern for spiritual affairs, makes it important to reconsider other ways to the same end. Among them the way of fellowship has been walked before, and perhaps again it may lead to a corner of God's kingdom on earth.

VI

TOWARD AN ORDER OF 'B'NAI OR':

A PROGRAM FOR A JEWISH LITURGICAL BROTHERHOOD

Zalman M. Schachter

There are ample precedents in Jewish history for liturgical brotherhoods—*havurot*. Josephus and Philo have apprised us of the work and lives of the Essenes; and the Dead Sea Scrolls, of course, have yielded a *Manual of Discipline,* increasing our knowledge of the constitutional and functional aspects of liturgical group life. Even within normative Judaism there are many examples of such societies. The following pages are the result of the discussions of concerned individuals who see it as their vocation to establish such a community—an "Order of B'nai Or" (Sons of Light)—and to live its life, in our own time.

We take it for granted that the present "business-as-usual" *status quo* does not express the highest and most desirable dimension of Judaism and that this condition does not necessarily meet with divine approbation. On the contrary, it must act as a stimulus challenging us to overcome it. To be motivated by a wish to "save Judaism," "to make for a more meaningful Jewish survival"—or whatever the current formulation of the *shelo lishma* is—may have salutary effects; but we want it clearly understood that we are interested in *shlemut ha'avoda,* the perfection of our service to God, so that He, be He blessed, may derive *nahat* (pleasure) from us. Or, to put it differently: we are concerned to realize God in this lifetime; to achieve a higher level of spiritual consciousness; to liberate such hidden forces within us as would

Dr. Schachter is Professor of Judaic Studies at University of Manitoba.

energize us to achieve our highest humanity within Judaism. Regardless of the particular formulation of the meaning of *shlemut ha'avodah*, we regard ourselves as not only working out our own concern, but in our concern we also see God's blessed Providence in action, calling us to the life of the *hevrah* as well as His abiding involvement in it. Responding, we see ourselves as yea-saying partners with Him.

The most serious reason urging against the establishment of such a brotherhood is that this constitutes a forsaking of the larger community. But this is not our intent. In a later section, describing community services, we will deal with this in detail. For the moment, suffice it to say that the means of earning a livelihood for the total community and its individual members would be found largely from serving in areas of urban Jewish *zorkhey zibbur*—community needs. . . .

Groups like ours are usually bound by the three vows of *poverty, chastity* and *obedience.* To us *poverty* means no private individual ownership of resources. These will be pooled in a common treasury (and shall be guaranteed in the event of leaving). That which is owned by the group is considered to be *hekdesh,* dedicated to God. A waste of these resources amounts to desecration.

Chastity, to us, means no mitigation of the full implication of this word. The eyes, the mind, language and the senses have to be guarded, so that they remain in the condition of chastity. Such sexual activity to which the Torah obligates us must be engaged in with chastity. Thus we interpret chastity not to mean total sexual abstinence, but that the fulfillment of such *mitzvoth* as are tied to sex are to be engaged in a manner befitting God's continual, even more intense Presence as it obtains between husband and wife in the joyous fulfillment of the *mitzvah.*

Obedience, to us, takes on a Halachic character. Any Jewish society receives sanction for its *takanot,* constitution and statues by virtue of the principle *shavia al nafshey hatikha d'issura,* in that whatever the statutes forbid takes on the forbidden aspect of *t'refah.* Positive levels of obedience take

on a character of positive commands. As God's delegate—
more rabbakh k'more shamayim—the ultimate arbiter of the
takanot will be the overseer chosen by secret ballot by full
members of the community. Any immediate superior
delegated by him will also be accorded the same obedience.
The overseer's rule will, God helping, not be a capricious use
of power. In this sense the overseer is accountable to God and
the community.

As various income functions become more clearly defined
and take on dynamics of their own, it may very well be that
other *B'nai Or* groups will have to split off from the original
group. As it is, we have quite a bit of work to do, which may
turn out to be more than we can well handle. We expect that
functions will be split off according to the planning of the
group and the promptings that come through the individual
member's heart from Him Who ultimately is the holder of our
destinies. . . .

Time and time again we must consciously and deliberately
center down to our main calling which is the service of God in
prayer. There are Torah *Kolelim* who organically represent
the head—the "apostolic" shock troops, representing the
mouth and language—but we must be the heart. It is for this
reason that our excursions into such income-bringing
functions as will be mentioned later are at best economic
means. True, we will want to choose such means as will be
closest to our central vocation, but *it* must remain central and
be pursued in sober seriousness.

We are basically dissatisfied with "the world." Our
dissatisfaction stems mainly from the fact that as well-adjust-
ed members of it we would have to live as ardent consumers
of goods which we do not really need but which in fact inhibit
our best possible functioning in terms of *shlemuth ha'avoda*.
We have to isolate ourselves from a contaminated environment. Only then can we make sure that the laboratory
conditions will be met which will permit us to proceed in our
chosen direction.

We believe that the experience of the cosmic and the divine
is potentially given to all men and that, depending on one's

style of life, one can become a receptacle for the Grace of God. We believe that there is enough psychic and pneumatic know-how available to us within the Jewish framework. To serve God better, we will not even hesitate to borrow extensively from the know-how of others. We feel that the seriousness of the vocation to serve God has largely become lost in the exoteric assertion of the reception of the unique gift of grace which is the revelation possessed by a group. To put it differently, if I am sure that I possess the clear statement of what God demands of men, this possession ought only humble me and challenge me to fulfill the demands of that revelation. Yet some "guardians of the revelation" see themselves as exempt from the humbling challenge to live up to it, as if their chosenness implied that they need not struggle with their own recalcitrant wills, slothful habits, etc. For us, the need to establish a liturgical community actually means that we have become aware of what William Law calls "the serious call to a holy and devout life"—issuing daily in the *bat kol* from Sinai.

Not only are we dissatisfied with the secular world, we are also dissatisfied with the "religious" world at large. That world lives under the same consumer compulsion as the secular world. Under this consumer compulsion (and kosher goods and their producers are as relentless in driving us to consume them as are others) one is far too busy to obtain the means for consuming and then far too busy to consume all the means. One consumes without having any time left for *avodath hashem*. One may become a kosher sensate reprobate. Economically, four hours of work per day, five days a week yield enough of the necessities of life for people whose only "Joneses" are those who live as frugally as they. With twenty hours of work per week one should have enough for one's self and one's family to give one all such necessities as will prompt one to be in the best shape for *avodath hashem*. We will work forty hours. It is our hope that in the absence of all sumptuousness there will be no need for ascetic self-denial in the vulgar sense.

Another reason why we are dissatisfied with the religious

world is that it lives the religious life of hardly more than verbal assertion, at best a feeble vote *for* the good, *for* God and *against* sin. We are not interested in formulating a new religion; what we seek is to live the esoteric implications that inhere in our religion as it is. The esoteric side of any religion not only tells about the core-experiences behind the exoteric facade but also how one is to achieve such experience. It may not be "democratic" to hold that the esoteric experience is not given to the masses, but masses are not given to the highest functional striving in the religion to which they give assent. Their assent is static. The static view does not recognize that as a person progresses and grows, new emphases are necessary. Mass people are frightened by the seeming inconsistency in balancing emphases that strike them as contradictions. No static philosophy can express all the levels of the dynamic range of the process of inner growth. This is another reason why we cannot anchor ourselves in any specific philosophy and why our psychological ceiling must remain open.

The exoterically minded will accuse us of antinomianism. We are as antinomian as Yom Kippur and Pesach. If they were to fall on one and the same day, it would be quite impossible to fast and eat *matzot* at the same time. But there is half a year in between.

To gauge the level of postulant will be the responsibility of his spiritual director; he will give him a temporary theological-conceptual framework. There are some souls who may ultimately not fit the contemplative life but who nevertheless will need to be set into growth by being associated with us for some time. We pledge ourselves not to be possessive about them but to allow them free egress whenever they feel that the time has come. Thus, besides being theologically and psychologically open, we must be socially open. It is also conceivable that non-Jews will wish to spend some time with us. They may run into some functional difficulty on their part, but we have no intention to demand from them that they give up their present faith (or lack of faith) before they join us.

We are not pledged to any particular philosophy. However, in order to communicate with one another and with the Jewish past we need a comprehensive, subtle and precise language. We are aware that the terminology of Habad Hasidism embraces both rationalistic and mystical ends of the continuum of Jewish thought. It is best suited for our purpose. To become proficient in the use of this terminology will be important to those who join us. We hope that a postulant will outlive a dozen philosophies in his progress from level to level.

All this may give the impression that only persons of high I.Q. are suitable for the work of the *hevrah*. This is not so. Spiritual generosity is a far greater prerequisite for the communal contemplative life. Simpler souls often have as God's gift to them a better intuitive grasp of unseen realities than intellectually complex ones.

If our community were to be "busy" and wanted to heal all the ills of the world, it would not have time for the very time-consuming exercises with which our purpose burdens us. We must not be "busy." We hope to divide our day into eight hours of livelihood-work (which we will describe later), eight hours for bodily needs, sleep and food, and eight hours of intensive and serious spiritual work. We are not worried about recreation in the vulgar sense. We feel that living the cycle of the liturgy, we will experience joys such as are not given to the pleasure chaser, and that the Sabbath and holy days will suffice to recreate us in a far more natural and soul-satisfying way.

We are sure that no one will survive for long in the community if he were not to be engaged in a noticeable process of sober growth. There must be no emergencies occasioned by the other day segments (except, of course, when a problem of the actual preservation of life arises) which would cut into the eight hours of *avodath hashem*. This is the sole purpose of our community, and nothing must interfere with it. This aim, then, would be pursued as relentlessly as we have been pursued by the "Hound of Heaven." There has been far too much romanticism in religion in connection with spiritual advancement. We intend to proceed with this work to achieve a level of craftsmanship that will equal other precise professional skills. Yet we are aware that despite their apparent vagueness such inner promptings as are authentically experienced by certain souls, are often far more valuable than any book knowledge. These promptings will have to be clarified by spiritual direction, but the work proceeding from these promptings will have to be pursued soberly and consistently.

We are also convinced that life makes for adaptability and the readiness of organisms to accept education. To have been given the privilege of the use of the bodily senses means to us that these, too, must be educated to enhance the spiritual life. We will, with God's help, want to find the sensory triggers which are capable of opening us to a wider consciousness. We hope with His blessed help to learn in the spiritual laboratory what physiological fulcra to utilize that will be of help in our work. Any kosher means that our community will decide as proper and helpful we will want to study in their application and usefulness and learn to control. Depth psychology has given us many insights and placed good tools at our disposal, and we hope to use them.

We dare not give Him worse service than that which is expected on other levels of life and vocation. We hope to winnow out of our own Jewish and general religious literature such *etzot* (counsels, hints, bits of empirical advice) as are to be found in them, to classify them and to apply them where conditions indicate their use. We hope, God willing, to use every phase of life for the bettering of our service for Him—food, sex activity and rest, breathing and body posture, dance and song, sight-light and dark-color schemes, olfactory stimuli, etc.

As a result of spiritual direction we hope to chart our own mind-body-spirit phases and to apply such positive or negative feedback as seems indicated. We hope in this manner to be able to rediscover some of the pneumatic clues which are to be found in the observance of *mitzvoth ma'asiot-*

—which transform them into *hovoth hal'vavot* and thus to relearn the art of achieving *Yichud*, the God-one-ing function, which will enable us to be more intensively, more frequently, and over a greater range, in *d'vekut*-absorptive union with our God. All this, then, is based on the assumption that it is still feasible in our day and age to fulfill the commandment of *k'doshim tihyu*—"Holy shall you be."

We need to maintain contact with the Jewish world at large and to offer a service that many do not find in their synagogue. Furthermore, there are a great number of unaffiliated people who may be able to overcome their reluctance to seek information and guidance if they were offered such outside the regular synagogue setting. In short, a reading room in a downtown area may supply this need.

People are reluctant to sit down in the sanctuary of a synagogue simply to relax for a while from their pressing cares and burdens. A chapel in conjunction with a reading room would make this possible for them (and ultimately serve as a model for synagogues). The chapel would also serve as a laboratory for classes to be conducted in the reading room.

An experienced counsellor may lend a sympathetic ear to allow a heavy-laden soul to unburden itself. It is conceivable that some psychotherapist will at some juncture wish to refer people with value-problems to a counsellor affiliated with the reading room. This counsellor will, besides possessing clinical training and native ability, need to be an integrated person with a rich inner life. He will be on good terms with people who are situated in the world and will have to avoid being a soul-trapper for the *hevrah*. He will, we hope, as a result of his contemplative training, be able to look at his counselee as he stands in God's primeval thought and lead him to realize that potential in himself.

Such souls as will be moved to enter the community will be tested through a probationary period to see if they are motivated by a divine stirring in them or by a need to escape some unwholesome immediacies. In case the two coincide, it would be our principle to have the person resolve first the problems that immediately face him and only then enter the community.

For many Jews it is an unknown fact that Jewish answers in depth are available to them. Non-Jewish esoteric and pneumatic societies that promulgate one or two esoteric insights are full of Jews. We acknowledge that we are pained by this, for we think that the majority of Jews who frequent these societies do so not because they are pneumatically fulfilled by them but due to lack of available Jewish facilities. It is hoped that at least some of them will find their way to the reading room and chapel.

We need, too, atzarot—weekend retreats—for our men and women. The object of these atzarot would be to become re-acquainted with their inner selves, and with their early struggles to live a God-directed life. Here they could become acquainted with an enlarged repertoire of Jewish experience and striving. Here they could relearn how to daven with kavanah, and how to learn Torah. Here they could sharpen their spiritual sensitivities. Until such time as we have ample facilities for retreat guests, we may have to conduct our atzarot at some kosher hotel during the off-season.

An atzeret program might begin with a briefing, a spiritual house-cleaning to be followed by an earnest Minhah. A half-hour of representative study could be followed by a joyous Kabbalat Shabbat. After Ma'ariv all the participants would then gather at a tish; with the exception of conversation pertaining to Torah or prayer, silence would be desirable. Now zemirot could be introduced. The tish would take up the entire evening. Instruction as well as questions and answers could take place right there. After the bentshen the group would retire right on the premises. In the morning there would be a shiur, a time for meditation before the davening; the service would be with all the group, followed by Kiddush with another tish. After the second meal a silent rest period with books would be desirable; another shiur, and the third meal with Ma'ariv, and Havdalah. A Melaveh Malkah would provide an outlet for discussion and evaluation.

Perhaps the retreat ought to extend through Sunday in order to present an extension into the week of the renewal of the spirit. A group might perhaps wish to experiment with other modes of inner expression, thus bringing to light some of the gems contained in our spiritual storehouse.

Perhaps, and this is not such a remote possibility, we could again infuse the observance of Yom Kippur Katan with contemporary relevance. A Yom Kippur Katan retreat would serve as a periodic stock-taking experience. Most of our self-employed professionals and businessmen can and do, when they so desire, take a day off for whatever purpose they choose. They could convene at the retreat house in the evening, eat in silence, in fact impose silence for the entire stay, while someone reads to them a passage of, let us say, the Mesillat Yesharim. After a period of Torah study, they could, as a minyan, and taking their time, retire with K'riat Sh'ma Shel Hamittah, awake at about 5:00 A.M. and, perhaps for the first time in their lives, recite the Tikun Hatzot (for most of us the Tikun Hatzot has the emotional connotations of a romantic legend). Then, after reciting T'hillim, they could study some more, daven without hurry, and return to study. They could fast during that day, spend some time on heshbon hanefesh, meditation, proceed with the Yom Kippur Katan liturgy at Minchah time. Ma'ariv and supper could be followed by a discussion, after which they would return home.

The idea behind the atzarot is not only to give a one-time experience but to demonstrate the practicality of transferring and incorporating in one's own home and synagogue observance some of the dimensions experienced during a retreat.

We are disturbed to note the gradual decline of the comprehensive liturgical repertoire once alive in the synagogue. We feel that we must prevent its complete loss. Who knows whether a generation which is yet to come would not have to resurrect for use, or at least find roots in, a non-European synagogue tradition? Idelson and others had the holy restlessness that moved them to collect and record for posterity such things as *Die Synagogengesänge der orientalischen Juden.* We think it imperative to acquire and perpetuate the skills of praising God in the *nussah* of Italy, Cochin, Baghdad, Yemen and Rhenish Ashkenaz style, etc.

We are also painfully aware of the lack of *piyyutic* material created in the last 250 years. People engaged in praising God with a vital and joyous desire are always on the lookout for new modes of expression of love and longing. How incongruous is it that in the last thirty years mostly people who lived in a secular world have found it necessary to find poetic expression for spiritual and liturgical feelings that welled up in their hearts. We hope to make these two problems our own.

We think the solution lies in alternating the different *nusha'ot* liturgically, musically, and rhythmically six out of seven years. The seventh, the Sabbatical year, would be devoted only to a skeletal framework of Talmudic liturgical institutions, which would then be enhanced and clothed with the sinew, flesh and skin of contemporaneous liturgical expressions from the realms of poetry, prose, music, chant and rhythm—on days when instrumental music is Halachically permissible to the accompaniment of "harp and the timbrel" (even to the inclusion of such experiments as *musique concrète).* We hope that the people who will be exposed to retreats from time to time will take their impressions with them and bring about the adoption of such liturgical modes as fill the contemporaneous needs of Jewry at large.

Currently the ideal artist is the one who expresses himself . . . It is quite obvious that only the individuated person has a unique self to express. For us an individuated self that is not also sanctified has no warrant to clamor for expression. Besides the contribution that sanctified art can make to religious art in general and to Jewish religious art in particular in stimulating other art aspects, there are particular liturgical values that can be realized through rededicated sacramental artistic expression that springs from real spiritual sophistication.

Hasidic masters have already shown the way of what can be

done in the field of musical creation. Taking ethnic tunes they found appealing, they transformed them into profound religious paeans of praise. But these creations have largely been of an ecstatic nature. They may not lend themselves to a more "Appollonian" mode of worship. On the other hand, their uncomplicated rhythms are also not quite contemporaneous; even on the ecstatic musical side, the lively syncopation of jazz has for the most part introduced vulgarities to the Jewish scene. The field still awaits its artist. . . . The imagination contains the only barrier to the kind of musical creativity that awaits us as a result of the activity of *B'nai Or* . . .

From a Halachic point of view, abstract painting is to be favored. After some of our people will have become adepts, we hope that they will see fit to arrest and project that which happens in their interior contemplative eidetic field through their skills in painting. The *Zohar* and the entire Kabbalah with their visual (as differing from the Talmudic aural) emphasis offer countless themes for the artist who prefers abstract forms.

Nowadays, there are far more and more pliable media available than ever before. It will be our task to utilize them. Much philosophy and science has been redeemed and made serviceable to God in our faith. The "muses" are still awaiting redemption.

Many synagogue appointments, such as arks, *parokhot* and Torah *mantelach,* are now mass-produced. Though from time to time Jewish artists are employed to design new patterns for them, these do not always correspond to the spiritual business of the *shul.* To design and produce them is a work of love and ardor that stems from the awareness that these things will be utilized in a palpable way for the greater glory of God. This is motivation enough for some of us to pursue this work as a means of livelihood. It is quite conceivable that one of the people who will join us will be an architect or an interior designer or will have leanings towards that field plus innate talent. He would be sponsored by the community to study this field and pursue it. Perhaps much of the bizarre would be obviated and objects more simple and spiritual take their place. It stands to reason that people who work at prayer would be able to distinguish between that which enhances worship and that which distracts the mind. At the same time a person who is engaged in sinking his roots in the classical experience of the past will be able to make use of such traditional forms as are available in our heritage without necessarily copying them.

For whatever work we do inside our own home we would design such khaki or denim work-clothes as would permit us to attach *tzitzit* to them. For occasions of spiritual work a *tallit*-like coat will be worn. For studying and spiritual work during weekdays we want to reintroduce the practice of wearing the *t'fillin* all day (even after prayer). Wherever possible, we would like to fulfill the dictum of our Sages: "'This is my God, and I will beautify Him.' Beautify *Him*? Beautify Him in *mitzvoth!*"—a beautiful *tallit* and a well-wrought pair of *t'fillin*, the *tallit*-stripes in many colors.

Some people at present involved in the teaching of Hebrew do this for extrinsic reasons. It is as good as any other job and better than some. The hours may be convenient and the surroundings congenial—all in all, a good way to get through college or seminary.

Every sermon on education points out that we stand in need of dedicated educators capable of empathy with their students, transferring to them information and, what is more, the proper attitude to utilize this information. Teaching is a holy act, a *mitzvah* in itself. Members of our community will be particularly well-suited for the profession of teaching, if this coincides with their talents and inclinations. Knowing that they are engaged in a *mitzvah* they will know how to resist the temptation to kill time. And besides making sure that the information transfer involves authentic Judaism, i.e. Torah, the skill drills will be in their direction of *t'fillah be'zibur* and *limud hatorah*. They will foster the stance of piety of body, mind and soul. . . .

One or two of us in a Hebrew school or a day school may be capable of involving the entire staff of that institution in a wholesome change. We pray and are hopeful that some day there will also be teaching orders. To us, however, the income derived from teaching will afford an opportunity to engage in a contemplative life: and the contemplative life will influence our teaching. . . .

The masculine liturgy is not designed to raise women to spiritual heights. They are bereft of the sacramentals which men experience in such *mitzvoth* as *tallith* and *t'fillin*, and they have, therefore, been liturgically dependent on the men's synagogue.

The solution for the problem of women lies in a full separation of their entire spiritual work from that of men. Halachically, our women are largely free to experiment with the liturgy and to fit it to their own physiological curves. Chances are that women with different monthly cycles could not act in concert with a *minyan*. Thus, they will largely have to chart their calendars and do their interior spiritual work according to it. In the absence of masculine sacramentals, they would have to invent for their own *minhag* such sacramentals as would be prompted by the stimulus of tradition and reinforced by their own personal insight, aesthetic feelings, and experiences. (We do not refer to such functions as remain *en famille*, but to such functions as are performed at public worship.)

While, in the beginning, women might have to be under the direction of a male spiritual director, it is hoped that very soon spiritual direction of women for women may be achieved.

We expect a larger turnover in the women's novitiate for such who, after a period of initiation into the spiritual life, would wish to return to the world. Furthermore, we do not expect to accept as permanent members women of marriage-able age, and those female adepts who are single would remain as postulant novices of a higher degree than recent arrivals until they marry and remain in the community, when they would be accepted as permanent members. Chances are that fate and exigencies will demand a special classification of non-participant dwellers in the community. Thus, for instance, the spouse of a member who happens not to be inclined towards this work will have to be integrated on the sidelines of our community.

What we have presented above is a tentative program for our projected "Order of *B'nai Or.*" It is not yet a rule of our Order. That will have to be fashioned as a result of actual communal living; at the present we have not yet begun as a group in any permanent sense. You who read this are asked to help us by letting us know your reactions. And if you are sympathetic toward our hope but feel yourselves not called to join us, we will request your prayers for our sake and reciprocate with ours for you.

PART THREE

FELLOWSHIP
AND
ETHICS

VII

JEWISH FELLOWSHIP AND JEWISH ETHICS

Jacob Neusner

In the classical Jewish tradition, one cannot distinguish between narrowly defined moral and other religious actions. That tradition, which takes shape in the Babylonian Talmud and cognate literature, recognises a myriad of commandments, some ethical, some ritual, and differentiates as little as possible among them. All are means of serving the will of the Creator of the world, and all provide an opportunity to sanctify this life. This does not make our task appreciably simpler. The questions we raise are these: What were the "norms" of Jewish tradition? Are there now any legitimate ways of speaking normatively?

1. The Classical Situation

One norm, and one alone, exists within classical Judaism, and that is the law (Halakhah), believed to be derived from the Torah, or Revelation, given to Moses at Mount Sinai in both written and unwritten form, transmitted by him to Joshua, then to the prophets, scribes, sages and rabbis, down to the present day. Ethical and moral questions, like any others, should in theory find their answers within the literature of Jewish law when properly investigated by men who themselves exemplify the ideals of that law and tradition. The norms of the tradition are, therefore, to be discovered in this fashion. Surveys of the legal periodical literature reveal a very lively continuous inquiry in this field. To cite at random issues under recent discussion: Is artificial insemination an

93

act of adultery?[1] Do workers have a right to strike?[2] Is it permitted to settle in the State of Israel against one's parents' wishes? Hence, does the duty to honor parents override other religious obligations? May Jewish women use oral contraceptives?[3]

Consideration of matters which others might regard as of other than ethical consequence come to the fore. For instance, how are spacemen in orbit to fulfil religious observances which depend on the count of the days and nights? May ritual circumcision be performed by a non-observant circumciser? The responsa of Rabbi Moshe Feinstein, a leading Orthodox legal authority, include attention to whether co-education is permissible, how women whose husbands disappeared in concentration camps may be permitted to remarry, as well as the religious requirement of honesty in the telephone booth or at the subway-station turnstile.[4]

This is not the place to spell out in great detail the theological convictions which underlie such a view of ethics. It is generally known that classical Judaism sees the Jewish segment of mankind as a covenanted community, which exhibits the marks of the Covenant in the flesh and in the spirit, in the private world and in the life of the streets. The terms of the Covenant apply to all of this age and to all circumstances within it, binding Israel together as a singular community in the service of one God. The Jew under the Covenant is the freest of all men, and the slave of all men—freest in that the terms of the Covenant at Sinai impose upon him commandments entailing a new moral freedom, and slave to all men in the duties of compassion and responsibility so imposed. He is second to none, there being no priest to mediate, nor official to determine the relationship between the community of which he is a part and the Maker of the Covenant. He is a part of a kingdom whose constitution was made at Sinai, whose citizenship imposes numerous moral and spiritual obligations, whose worldly artefacts are the collective religious life of Israel, and whose requirements are to do justice, love mercy, and walk humbly with God. That kingdom aspires to no worldly dominion, but rather to a time in which all men will proclaim the praises of their Creator.

Nor is it necessary once again to lay the ghost of late nineteenth-century misconstruction of rabbinic Judaism. The externality, the "automaton" of the law, the self-satisfaction and self-gratulation of the law-abiding Jew, not to mention the hypocrisy, the arrogance, and the mean-spiritedness of his observance—these spiritual libels have long since passed from serious men's minds, living on only in uninformed or reactionary scholarship.

The more serious issue is the relationship between the individual and what is expected of him as part of the community of the faithful. As Eugene Borowitz says:

> . . . how to reconcile these two seemingly irreconcilable factors, law and self. In the 19th century, the science of ethics might perform that function, for the self was essentially ethical, even as was the Halachah. Such a self-evident, self-justifying ethics no longer exists. Indeed, as against the Kantian turn, we need Faith to ground ethics, theology to validate. And the same is true of man. Jewish belief is needed to affirm what much of modern society does not in practice believe, that man is full of worth and dignity, that every self is truly precious. Judaism validates and motivates both the deed and the individual, but because Judaism has historic scope and concern it sees them both within a larger context and structure, the Halachah. What then might it mean to create a Halachah which is fully modern in its concern with persons as it is yet true to Israel's Messianic continuity? That is the contemporary statement of what once went under the name of Jewish ethics. While we are no nearer to its meaning than were the men of another generation who sought to define the distinctive characteristics of Jewish ethics, still we may have begun to ask the right question for our day and thus have made it possible for us better to face up to our real responsibilities.[5]

Borowitz alludes indirectly to the now classic essay by Emil Fackenheim, "The Revealed Morality of Judaism and Modern

Thought, A Confrontation with Kant."⁶ The Kantian challenge, Fackenheim says, is this:

> If in order to be moral a law must be self-imposed, not imposed
> from without, then how can a law given or imposed by God
> have genuine moral qualities? Thus the religious man must
> either concede that the will can and must impose the
> God-given law upon itself, but then its God-giveness becomes
> irrelevant in the process of self-imposition and appropriation;
> or else he insists that the God-givenness of the law does not
> and cannot at any point become irrelevant, but then the will
> cannot impose the law on itself, it can only submit to it for
> such non-moral reasons as trust in Divine promise or fear of
> Divine threats.⁷

Fackenheim holds, however, that the revealed morality of
Judaism cannot be classified as "either autonomous or
heteronomous in the Kantian sense." He criticises the
Orthodox Jewish response, that the morality of Judaism is
revealed but heteronomous, and the liberal one, that it was
autonomous but not revealed. The real issue is, "How can
man appropriate a God-given law or commandment, accepting and performing it as though it were his own, while yet
remaining, in the very act of appropriation, essentially and
receptively related to its Divine Giver?" Fackenheim's
response is to stress that, in the moment of commandment,
the finite content of commandment is not communicated,
but rather, the fact that one is commanded:

> . . . The Divine manifests Itself as commanding, and in order
> to do so it requires real human freedom. And since the Divine
> is Presence as well as commanding, the required human
> freedom cannot be merely condition; it must be unconditional
> and absolute. . . . The freedom required in the pristine
> moment of the Divine commanding Presence . . . is nothing
> less than the freedom to accept or reject the Divine
> commanding Presence as a whole and for its own sake—that is,
> for no other reason than that it is that Presence.

But this freedom of choice is not autonomous, for the Other makes possible the power of choice, and, Fackenheim adds, "If and when a man chooses to accept the Divine commanding Presence, he does nothing less than accept the Divine Will as his own." But, he notes, the Presence does not become irrelevant once revealed moral law has appeared: "The Torah is given whenever men are ready to receive it, and the act of receiving Torah culminates in the confrontation with its Giver." The moral law is not a bar, but a bridge. In the revealed morality of Judaism there is a three-term relationship between man, his neighbor, and God, for whose sake, and for whose Name, men act justly and mercifully toward their neighbors. Fackenheim explains:

> Moral commandments, to be moral, must be performed for *their* sake. For unless so performed, they do not realize a three-term relationship which takes the human neighbor in his own right seriously: they function merely within an attempted two-term relation between man and God. . . . And yet the commandment remains fragmentary if performed for its own sake *alone*. For if such performance discloses the human neighbor, and ourselves, too, as beings of intrinsic value, it is ultimately because the Divine commanding Presence so discloses them. . . . He discloses Himself through all intrinsic value as its ultimate source.

These extensive citations from Borowitz and Fackenheim are meant to indicate, apart from their intrinsic interest and importance, that the rather wooden description offered earlier of the classical scheme of Jewish ethics conveys little of the vitality, the worldliness, the conceptual vigor of Jewish ethical ideas. That the law is revealed and exposited raises more issues than it settles. That various men of wisdom remain to be consulted does not mean that their task is an easy one, nor that the consultation is even easily formulable.

The content and method of Jewish ethics, though not its theological foundations, are discussed in Max Kadushin's

Worship and Ethics, A Study in Rabbinic Judaism.[8] Kadushin stresses the theme that "worship and ethics are cultural phenomena [in rabbinic Judaism]. Each individual has his own personal experiences in both spheres, but what makes the experiences possible are the values of society." It is the law that, "working with the value concepts of the folk as a whole enables the individual to achieve religious experience." These value concepts include Torah, commandment, charity, holiness, repentance; and these in turn endow situations with significance. Just as, in Judaism, ethics is both personal and yet governed by revealed law, so, too, is worship meant to be both communal and personal. The worship service, which is so deeply theological and personal, is meant to conform to numerous legal requirements, such requirements bringing the individual together with the fellowship of the faith through the ages. What is important for our purposes in Kadushin's study is his stress upon the sociological and historical foundation of Jewish ethics. He states:

> Rabbinic ethics is not the product of philosophical reflection
> but of a historically evolved tradition. It has to do with the
> moral life of a people to whom that tradition has given
> character and continuity over many centuries. It is concerned
> with day-to-day issues, takes account of social, economic, and
> political factors, and affects the relations of individual to
> individual. . . .[9]

The breadth of rabbinic morality is very wide, for it includes, Kadushin points out, matters of behavior such as dress, food, and etiquette, which are not usually thought of as located within a moral system. Since the people and the rabbis were so closely related, one might suppose that rabbinic morality is merely a folk product; but this Kadushin rejects: "It is the product of the interaction between a society and its best minds, the product of the continuous interaction between the folk and the rabbis."[10]

To return to our opening question: One can indeed speak normatively within the Jewish tradition, by basing oneself upon the revealed Scriptures, the oral traditions handed down concerning their interpretation and application, and upon the guiding teachings of the rabbis themselves. This "normative" system continues to operate to the present day more or less as it always has. Yet one cannot escape Kadushin's warning that the formulations of Jewish ethics and morality depend upon "the interaction between the folk and the rabbis." Therefore, when one asks what is normative in contemporary Jewish ethics, one cannot merely open books or consult those who understand them.

If the sources for norms in Judaism include the values of the people, who after all constitute a fellowship of faith and live by a sacred constitution as citizens of God's kingdom, then one must seriously doubt the possibility of discovering *today's* norms. The very character of rabbinic ethics was presumably shaped by the moral life of the people to whom the Torah has been entrusted. The issues of ethics were allegedly defined *by* the day-to-day life of that people, and they were resolved for a community responsive to the tradition and loyal to its expositors and exemplars. For two centuries, however, it has been quite clear to all that there is no longer a fellowship of faith uniting all or even most who regard themselves, and are regarded by others, as Jews, and hence one must doubt that the classical ethical enterprise as Kadushin sees it continues to operate in the old ways. One need not doubt that for numerous religious Jews, whether of traditional or liberal orientation (for both Fackenhiem and Borowitz, exceptional expositors of the tradition, are Reform rabbis), the classical literature and its values retain broad relevance and considerable influence. But this cannot obscure the fact that what being a Jew means, or does not mean, is by no means as clear as it once was. Jewry has entered a lingering, at times irritating crisis of identity, which does not, to be sure, demand immediate solution.

That crisis does, nonetheless, pose substantial barriers to the discovery of what is, and what is not, Jewish ethics under the old system in new circumstances. *If* the classical ethical system depended upon the interaction of religious virtuosi with the ordinary community of faithful, then how does one uncover its contemporary structure when large parts of the community no longer regard themselves as faithful in the old or any other sense? Part of Jewry continues to stress the law and to live by it, though in different ways according to the Reform, Orthodox and Conservative formulations. But even that segment of Jewry can hardly be thought to constitute a "community of the faithful" but is rather a conglomeration of sects within a broader ethnic-cultural continuum. The Orthodox lawyers do not legislate for other than Orthodox Jews, and the divisions even within Orthodoxy are no less substantial than those that separate it from the modernists.

Even if one wished to postulate the existence of a "believing community," broadly defined, to provide the referent for an examination of norms in Jewish ethics, one wonders how precise and specific such an examination might become. The Jew today is many things, plays many roles; most of these he does not play as a Jew at all, as he once did. There was a time, not long ago, when the legal system which best embodied Jewish ethical values actually governed the lives of Jewish communities; when the rabbis were lawyers and judges, rather than pastors and preachers; when the community subjected itself to its own, rather than to the common, secular law of nations; when the spiritual and worldly sovereignties were more or less one. Today, paradoxically, while a part of Jewry has recovered a "Jewish sovereignty,"[11] that sovereignty is not intended to be Judaistic so much as Israeli. Whether or not an effort should be made to base Israeli law upon classical Jewish legislation is not at issue here. The fact is that where there is "Jewish sovereignty" it does not, as it once did, coincide with spiritual convictions about living by God's word and by His laws upon earth, and probably does not intend to. Thus whether in the State of Israel or in the Diaspora communities, one cannot any longer find the "folk" to which Kadushin's references apply, nor is the nexus between rabbi and people quite the same. The State is a new nationality; the Diaspora is a function of urban, middle-class society. Ethics comes from other places.

It is quite obvious that the "values" of the Jews no longer conform to those of the tradition, so that creative efforts might result from the tensions between the given of the world and the revelation of the past. Should one seek the "values" of the people, he will probably discover that those of the greater part of the community differ from the values of the outside in rather inconsequential ways. It is true that the traditional modes of living and the inherited value-structure retain a certain inertial force, so that, for example, Jews long divorced from a tradition that lays great stress upon study of the Torah nonetheless produce brighter-than-normal children, or, more realistically, would like to. But one can hardly decide upon such a basis that intellectualism is a "norm" within contemporary Judaism, and begin to build a system of normative ethics upon the values of the mind.

The obvious conclusion is that one cannot locate a "norm" within Judaism as we now have it. We may at best discover "Jewish sectarian norms," applicable to those who coalesce in segments of Jewry responsive to the tradition, or not responsive to it at all and yet still in some measure shaped by it. Or we may restudy the tradition itself, at the outset admitting that we are going to locate the norms of the past, again to be advocated in the present. Obviously, those who retain the classical faith have no difficulty whatever, for the norms, their basis, their ramifications—all these *are* now what they always were, and for precisely the same reasons: the revealed morality of Sinai, the values of the community shaped by Revelation. For the philosopher, these represent the three obvious alternatives, by no means excluding one another.

As a historian of a segment of the history of Judaism, however, I do not find myself quite so limited, because I do not believe the history of Judaism itself to be so impoverished of alternatives, so unilinear in development, or so rigidly one-dimensional in its growth. We have so far remained very narrowly within the limits of the perspectives on the history of Judaism and the formulation of Jewish tradition inherited from rabbinic Judaism. That formulation was given above.

But if one looks at things as an historian, one may come to a very different understanding of how norms took shape, an understanding which will reopen the *theological* inquiry that seems to have been closed to "normative Jews" for two centuries.

The central issue is: What *was* normative, and what ought to be normative? If one can redefine the first question, he may reopen discussions of the second. And the first is a strctly *historical*, not a theological issue. To face it squarely: in the period about which Kadushin writes, one cannot accurately say that the rabbi played the role Kadushin assigns to him, nor that he did so for the reasons and in the ways Kadushin thinks. It is quite correct that in rabbinic Judaism, worship and ethics were very much a part of a culture, but that culture did not so much emerge from the masses as it was the creation and unique possession of the rabbinical academies, their masters and disciples, and those who could be influenced by them. These were *by no means* all or most of the Jews of the time.

Its norms were not ever popular to begin with. The masses of the Jews in Palestine and Babylonia, where the two Talmuds were produced which supposedly embody the folk-culture of the Jews as of their religious leaders, did not conform to the rabbinic value system at all, if only because, for the most part, they were hardly exposed to it. They did not have so intimate a relationship with the rabbis. The rabbis were mainly teachers and judges of the law. They were also believed by many, including themselves, to possess extraordinary theurgical powers. They were thought to be men who could do miracles, cast an evil eye, or whose merit, through their knowledge of Torah or through their "pure" genealogy, was sufficient to bring rain, or protect a city better than walls. Their direct influence over the people was, however, peripheral in many areas of life and important in only a few. Their direct influence, as one would expect, derived from their administration of the law. Yet in third-century Babylonia, their courts were able to deal effectively only with those parts of the law which involved civil litigation, exchanges of property of all kinds, and matters of personal status in which property exchange took place. These were affairs of life which *had* to come before them and in which they were, therefore, able to impose their ideals without difficulty or significant opposition.

In religious matters, narrowly construed, things were very different. The "blessing after meals," a compendium of rabbinic values, is discussed at great length in the Babylonian Talmud, and yet the laws pertaining to it, supposedly conveying or embodying its values, applied, according to the evidence available to us, only in the academies, among the masters and their disciples. Synagogue worship, upon which the people naturally laid great stress, was not half so important to the rabbis, who believed that study—that is to say, *their* study—was far more important than synagogue prayer, and said so. Indeed, the synagogues excavated in both Babylonia (Dura-Europos) and Palestine, and the literary evidence about the synagogues, reveal that the rabbinical laws concerning ornament, so deeply anti-representational in spirit, were simply not observed among the people who built them. This does not mean that those people were "not nomative" or were outside rabbinical control, but rather that the life of the *synagogue* itself was not then within rabbinical control.

So when one speaks, as does Kadushin, of how the rabbis gave form to the value concepts of a folk, he refers perhaps to later periods, but not to the period in which rabbinic Judaism itself took shape and with which Kadushin is specifically concerned. It is true that rabbinic ethics is the product of an "historically evolved tradition," but that evolution (and I think there was very little actual evolution) took place in the rabbinical academies, which, like the Christian monasteries in Syria and Mesopotamia, were in many ways deeply influential in in the life of the faithful community, but in many significant ones quite separate and different from it. The academy, like the monastery, was not merely a place where the ideals of the common faith were realised in an intensified form, but where some quite different ideals were cultivated and exemplified from those of the towns and villages. It is true, similarly, that rabbinical ethics was concerned with day-to-day issues, which the rabbis observed, and in time was eminently practical *both* in formulation *and* in execution, but in the seed-time of rabbinic Judaism it was, I think, only or mostly in *formulation*.

Both the late Professor Louis Ginzberg and Professor Saul Lieberman have referred to these facts. Ginzberg stated: "The Talmudic scholar is the normal type of Jew by which rabbinic Judaism is to be judged, though it is true, the normal Jew must not be confounded with the average one. The average Jew was not a Talmudic scholar, but the normal one was. The development, however, of the average to the normal is one of the most interesting features of the history of the Jews. By the seventeenth century the average Jew, at least in Eastern Europe, was a Talmudic scholar."[12] More explicitly, Saul Lieberman states: "It is hardly possible that the great masses of the Jewish people in the big towns conducted themselves in conformity with the idealistic views of the rabbis. . . . The mirror of rabbinic literature reflects a continuous war between the rabbis and the masses. . . ."[13] Ginzberg's statement, that the "Talmudic scholar is the normal type of Jew," is in fact to be assessed theologically, not historically. Lieberman's is quite another matter, for he makes it abundantly clear that the masses of the people were not "lesser Talmudic scholars," whose values and ideals were shaped by the influences of rabbinic thought, but were quite different in spirit and values. The issue is not whether some Jews broke the law. It is: What was *normative?* Whose values were expressed by the Talmudic rabbis? Lieberman leaves no doubt whatever that one cannot think of the rabbis as "embodying the values of the folk." Rather, they sought every means to shape the lives and values of the people, and in time they succeeded—but *not* in the period in which *they* were shaping Judaism. What became the theological norm was not the folk norm when it was in formation. It did not embody popular but rather academic values. It did not express the aspirations of the people, who had to be cajoled, intimidated, and, when possible, forced to conform to what the rabbis desired. This is true of law *and* of ethics in Jewish society in Talmudic times.

The relevance of these facts to our inquiry is obvious. If one seeks a "norm" in Jewish thought and ethics, he should not begin with the the sociological question at all. The impasse reached above represents the end of a blind alley. The "norm" is not the way ordinary people lived, nor does it embody their values. It is invariably, I believe, and in the case of rabbinic Judaism most assuredly, shaped by the ideals and values of a class of religious virtuosi, who, certain of themselves and believing in heavenly approval for their values, turned to influence where possible, to impose where necessary, these values upon the lives of the people. And the shaping of the norms of the virtuosi depends not upon the folk, but upon academic theological inquiry and investigation. In a word, ethics is not a matter of sociological inquiry, *nor* a function of culture. It is not formed in the streets, but in the school house. The "normal Jew," in Ginzberg's felicitous phrase, is not the ordinary one, unless (or until) the masses conform to the ideals of the theologians, as happened in time in the history of Judaism.

2. The Centrality of Persons

We, therefore, revert to our questions: What are the "norms" of "Jewish ethics," and *are* there legitimate ways of speaking normatively?

It is clear to me that no serious person within the Jewish tradition will at first find comfortable a situation of subjectivity. Jews have disavowed being prophets; in the words of a fourth-century rabbi defending his legal decision, "I am no sage or visionary, nor am I unique, but I am a teacher and a systematiser of traditions, and they rule thus in the academy, just as I do."[14] It is quite clear that any ethical teaching within Judaism must satisfy the condition that it have "authority" or represent a consensus of some kind, shaped in communication with the realities of the Jewish

world and able to speak to and influence that world. On the
other hand, I think it is equally clear that the recovery of an
"objective" ethical system, based upon the realities both of
the rabbinic tradition, which alone of the historical variations
of Judaism remains alive today, and of the condition of the
Jews—the best testimony to their conviction of the world's
unredemption—is not a simple task.

Modern Jewish thought has not moved very far beyond the
limits imposed by the rabbinic tradition, and it is here that
one may locate the most difficult obstacle in the way of a
renovation of Jewish ethics as well. As Nathan Rotenstreich
points out,[15] "Jewish thought has been preoccupied almost
exclusively with systems of ideas. Hardly any note was taken
of living patterns of culture, living problems, concrete
circumstances. The image of the modern world, however, is
shaped by ideas incarnated in living patterns of culture; by
ideas in action, by ideas which play a regulative role in
everyday life. This aspect of the modern world has yet to be
confronted by modern Jewish thought." Rotenstreich explains
the isolation of Jewish thought by reference to two facts, first
of all the prestige of the law itself "as the crystallized
expression of Judaism and as a code of law." My opening
statement is a valid illustration of this fact. Yet Rotenstreich
points out:

> As a code of law, the Halachah crystallizes prevailing
> conventions and concepts. No innovation can be introduced
> into the Halachah except by the authority of the Halachah. Yet
> only a view which transcended the Halachah can constitute a
> foundation for suggested innovation. . . . Today Jewish
> thought seems to be paralyzed by the long time-span between
> current questions and past solutions resulting from the
> occasional meeting, in individual Jewish thinkers, of philoso-
> phy and the Halachah. . . . If, accordingly, the Halachah is the
> realm in which Jewish thought is confined, how can the
> Halachah itself make available to its inhabitants the means of
> breaking through its walls?

Secondly, Rotenstreich notes that religious Judaism is invariably identified in Israel with Orthodox Judaism, which has yet to face the problem posed by non-Orthodox piety, nor has any other form of religious Judaism faced the problem posed by non-religious Jews who wish to create a secular Jewish culture.[16] Further, Rotenstreich says:

> Not even the objectivistic interpretation of Judaism is entitled to ignore the nature of man. It, too, must take into consideration the fact that man is a creature endowed with consciousness and self-consciousness. For even the Jew who is, presumably, inextricably entangled in an objective network does not for that reason cease to be a self-conscious subject. Hence it is incumbent upon Orthodox Jewry to recognize the individual consciousness of the concrete Jewish individual, without assuming *a priori* the existence of a pre-established harmony between his individual consciousness and the objective meaning which the Halachah assigns to the fact that he is a Jew. . . . The problems posed by modern Jewish reality cannot even be clarified, let alone solved, in terms of the assumption that if a man's will does not coincide with the objective fact that he is a Jew, then the will and the consciousness of that man do not count.[17]

Rotenstreich and Borowitz here came together, for what the former demands, the latter regards as the task of the hour, "to create a Halachah which is fully modern in its concern with persons as it is yet true to Israel's Messianic continuity."

I think the way ahead is illuminated by Rotenstreich, who says:

> In Judaism, the encounter between divinity and humanity is not relegated to any institution whatever. In so far as an encounter of this kind is represented as occurring, it appears in the words and actions of pious persons, such as the prophet, the scholar, the holy man; and in the conduct of the chosen people. In Judaism, then, the meeting between divinity and humanity is personal and dynamic, not depersonalized and static, as it

inevitably becomes when solidified in institutions.[18]

The evidence of Talmudic times supports Rotenstreich's contention, for it was as much the *person* of the rabbi as the alleged authority of his tradition which shaped the values of Talmudic Judaism. How one is supposed to act in order to be deemed a disciple of the sages was so carefully, thoughtfully defined that none can doubt the importance of personal *exemplification*, in the academy and also in the streets, of the values of rabbinic Judaism. Indeed, I think it was the effective charisma of the rabbi, preserved in the accounts of his capacity to do unusual deeds, in the stories of just how he behaved in such-and-such a circumstance (with the implication that so must all pious men act), in the lore of his conversations with heavenly beings and of his extraordinary knowledge of the world—that charisma constituted the real source of his *influence*.

Judaism took shape around the grand and striking personalities of one age after another, or, even more, around memories of those personalities whom later generations chose to regard as "authoritative" or "normative." The prophet, sage, rabbi, *zaddik*, or holy man—these were the figures who shaped the ideals and the conduct of the "chosen people," not because of their power in the courts, but because of their piety and sanctity outside them. Naturally, the normal variations of personalities characteristic of any community permitted, indeed required, the recognition of numerous variations in emphasis in ethical and moral ideals. It is quite obvious that the revealed Scriptures placed limitations on the range of such variations. But the emphasis of one differed from that of another, and he who had the capacity to learn could find a learned man to emulate, as he whose spiritual capacities were promising could find a saint to help him cultivate them. Rotenstreich states:

> Israel has made it possible for Jews to create thematic, ideological, institutional, and social forms of collective Jewish life which they can choose voluntarily. The desire to take

advantage of this possibility represents a new, subjective trend in Judaism, a trend which makes subjectivity the source of its own objective expressions. Whether the subjective trend will triumph, or whether it will produce a new objective form of Judaism, or whether it will culminate in indifference to Jewish questions—all these are possibilities which cannot be determined in advance. It is even possible that the subjective trend will ultimately admit defeat, admit the impossibility of a subjective form of Judaism, and retreat to the position of the objectivistic trend embodied in the Halachah. . . .[19]

The conditions to which Rotenstreich refers are by no means alien to the Diaspora. Western Jews have turned out to be just as subjective, just as selective, as those in the State of Israel, as the varieties of Diaspora Judaism, including its Orthodox segment, make abundantly clear. The opportunities of freedom abound everywhere. Jewish men, in the past supposedly expected to conform to a single, mostly objective scheme of what is right and what is wrong, now find themselves free to choose without thereby necessarily selecting heresy. The possibility now exists "to create a Halachah" which concerns itself with persons, both humble and extraordinary.

3. An Ethics of Jewish Fellowship

One must stress *a* Halachah, for none can hope that changes outside the classical framework of decision-making will find recognition as *the* Halachah. (Yet, except for those among the Orthodox groups, it hardly matters.) As all thinkers about modern Judaism have stressed, there can be no Judaism without a system of law, though the authority for, and the content of, that law may differ radically from the classical beliefs. The first, most obvious difference must be the concern for persons. The classical law seems[20] to have a single set of expectations with numerous variations for particular cases, but none for particular individuals. Indeed, the central focus of a renewed system of law must lie with the private person, his best interests, his needs, his particularities. It should be able to make provision for the time of life in which he finds himself, for we have again learned from psychology what artists have always known, that each stage of life imposes its own set of problems and expectations, from the ascetic idealism of the early and middle twenties to the mellowing preparation for the "long pull" of the middle thirties.[21] Even prayer may play a more important role in the life of the late adolescent or the elderly person than it does in that of the young parent, whose responsibilities require that his children become his prayers. One law for young and old, perhaps, but a law with different requirements as life unfolds is the only law that can conform to the realities of the individual.

Yet it is clear that stress upon the individual alone is not sufficient, for law relating to the private person can emerge as little different from personal idiosyncrasy. But what social referent can one locate except the already available, but for many unacceptable, segment of conforming Orthodox, or Conservative, or Reform Jews? It seems to me that the search for law must first entail a search for community, out of whose collective life a law can emerge. Community is not to be found, however, in the massive Jewries of Western cities, any more than one can uncover it in Haifa or Jerusalem. These have in common the anonymity and anomie of modern life, the fragmenting of large numbers into numerous segments and sub-groups. No one seriously hopes, or even wants, to return to the fabled life of the village, with its routine sacralities and ordered social patterns. It is rather to be looked for among men who can accept a common discipline, who can form a community because it already exists among them and needs only to be perceived by them.

Within Judaism, the example of the ancient fellowship, or *havurah*, comes most readily to mind. The fellowship, which was constituted as a society for the meticulous observance of parts of the law which common people mostly neglected, formed an inchoate society of people who kept the law among those who did not, and who recognized in one another fellows with whom, for technical, legal reasons, they might enjoy a common meal. The circle of the master and disciple, also deriving from ancient times but with numerous examples through the centuries, provides a second and more accessible form of fellowship. Just as some came together for ritual reasons, so did others for intellectual ones. In Hasidism, similarly, communities took shape around the charismatic masters, whose deeds and piety won the awe of common people, and who could therefore form the circle of a new society. Such is one possible social form for collective Jewish life, in which random individuals might come together to find what collectivity exists among them, and to explore it. Out of such relationships can emerge a pattern of expectations and requirements, of service to others, of cultural and religious actions, of prayer, of ethical concern, which one could understand as Halakhah in an austere and unexpected form.

The experience of fellowship seems at first glance too narrow, however, to make much impact upon the formation of ethical laws, and it is these which lie at the heart of our investigation. The occasional formation of group life, on specific ways and for specific purposes, represents too narrow a segment of life, too specialized a concern, to produce a broad pattern of ethics. What can emerge is only an ethics of the fellowship itself, that part of law which is emergent in the experience of small-group life. And yet, one may suppose that out of such a limited context may emerge experiences and insights applicable to a broader spectrum of experience. Should the fellowship sufficiently engage its communicants, it will create among them an open, supportive society for some moments in their life, corresponding to the therapeutic situation, in which they can find out truths about relationships among human beings, work out such truths in the objective reality of "the world," yet a world in which all come together to express, and to help others to express, the individualities which they find they have in common. The hours of fellowship are different from those of anomic life, but they can create a kind of laboratory for the larger world, a

pattern of right actions which the fellows find not only
relevant to, but necessary for, life among ordinary people. As a
fellowship deepens and the communicants broaden their
range of ethical self-consciousness in a narrow circumstance,
lessons are likely to emerge for application in the commonplace situations of life. Such lessons would represent
norms—norms of a Jewish *fellowship* to begin with, but to be
exemplified and worked out elsewhere as well.

The sources for such an ethics must, I believe, be twofold.
First, it would be an act of spiritual vandalism to ignore the
ethical and moral resources already available to Jews in their
classical legal tradition. That tradition is mostly centered
upon the proper relationships between human beings, upon
the proper conduct of social, commercial and personal life. It
is the specificities which have come to seem to many Jews to
be irrelevant, and the means of applying the law to be either
remote or repulsive. But the ideals remain a rich source of
ethical insight, and studied from such a perspective, may
produce ethics deeply consonant with historical expectations
(or, as Borowitz says, Messianic ones). Second, the insights
and ideals of individual Jews, derived from the experiences of
family and home, of common schooling and the common life,
cannot be set aside as irrelevant or inconsequential—or
inauthentic. Psychological realities prevent it. It is to
overcome the impersonality of the classical tradition that a
modern fellowship is envisaged, and stress upon personality
and the private person's insights is the only means of serving
his individuality.

We seem, therefore, to have returned to the classical
situation, in which the objective law stands in tension with
the subjective needs of the individual. But this is the
difference: while in former circumstances it was the law
which predominated, in the circumstances of fellowship it is
the individuals forming the collectivity of the fellowship,
whose lives must shape the ethical dimension. The tradition
provides insight, but it is the individuals who form the
fellowship, whose insight determines the usefulness and the
truth of that tradition. The traditional law requires study, but

it is the individual who determines the worldly consequence of that study. And the final authority can only be the living person, he who may decide to give life or deny it to the otherwise dead words of the past. I believe this to be a fact whether one likes it, being of Rotenstreich's mind, or not, adhering to the classical viewpoint. The difference between the two is this—and I do not intend an invidious comparison: while the classicist accepts the issues set for debate by the classical tradition and determines only whether to accept or to decline (being Orthodox or Reform) the expectations of the tradition as he understands them, the participant in a fellowship enters into the issues of the fellowship, and these are set by the lives of the individuals, deriving both from their individuality and from their collective experience.

In my view, the "norms" of Jewish ethics are to be derived, therefore, from the life of the individual Jewish human being living in community with other Jewish human beings, and engaged by concern for the varieties of Jewish traditions—not only that formed by rabbinic literature through the ages—in an eclectic search for values congruent to present but unarticulated values of his own and for insights and guidance appropriate to, making sense out of, the current circumstance. I naturally stress the this-worldly and the human, but not by any means with the intention of excluding revelation. Rather, I call for reopening the question of revelation in a modern mode: What is it that Jews can understand by revelation? How do they make sense of the concept and of the content of Torah as revelation? What is the contemporary capacity to receive, or be illumined by, revelation? These are issues which underlie any ethical inquiry within the Jewish tradition. Yet without a social referent the results of the inquiry mean little and matter less.

Thus, it is most important, first of all, to recover a sense of community and Covenant, and from there to proceed to explore the meaning of that Covenant and the nature of that community, questions that lead directly to the fundamental issues of Jewish existence in any age, including this one, and center upon revelation. But what is normative cannot in the end be found in books, but among faithful people, and what is revelation can only be decided by living people who give an assent not only to what has gone before but also to what takes place here and now. The norm must lie in the context of the lives of living men and women, must be uncovered where men are. If one believes, as I do, that Providence shapes the realities each of us knows as life, then it cannot be otherwise: those who live here and now must uncover in the artifacts of their lives, illumined, to be sure, by the discoveries of other lives about the working of Providence in other times and places, the "contextual norm."

It cannot be supposed that such a norm will not be "Jewish," or that it will be uniquely so. So far as Jews have been shaped by their parents, and their parents by theirs, for many past generations, thus far do they bear the psychic and cultural consequences of the Covenant. So far as they continue to search their traditions for insight and revelation, so far will their consciousness take shape in the light of the Covenant. And yet Jews are human beings, and their crises are normal human ones; they bleed and die, and can be made into soap, like anybody else. So it would be hard to find a Jewish truth that is not a human one as well, or a Jewish ethical insight that would not, properly construed, bear application to the common circumstances of men. And yet some of the insights of Jewish ethical fellowship are likely to be shaped by peculiar, classical Jewish concerns, experiences, and emphases, and others by commonplace human ones. Some will be congruent to the existential issues confronting other men, and some will not. Some will apply, but in the very touch will shape experience into a covenanted moment, and form out of a common hour a segment of eternity, as only a Jew, whose imagination is shaped by memories of many centuries of devotion to God and yearning for His kingdom, can perceive it.

My effort here has been to isolate historical and sociological from theological issues, and to open the way to competent theologians to discuss the questions of norms in Judaism without the intrusion of historical data. And yet, I cannot claim much success, for I do not know what is to prevent the insights of a fellowship from becoming not only contextual but quite subjective, not only merely descriptive but wholly cultural, hence relative. The only answer to the question must derive from theology, for it will in the end depend upon how we reach valid, *non-subjective*, knowledge of God, the source of norms and the foundation of any ethical imperative. An ethical inquiry, shaped by sociological interest and historical imagination, therefore leads directly forward to the issues of revelation and theological inquiry. In Jewish terms, quite clearly, the meaning of the adjective "Jewish" requires thought. I have suggested that the "norms" of *Jewish* ethics derive from the life of the individual *Jewish* human being, living in *Jewish* community with other such people, and engaged by concern for the varieties of *Jewish* traditions. I believe this to be a valid approach. Yet who is to say what is *Jewish* about ethics, or about human beings, or about traditions? Enmeshed in a massive, gnawing, two-hundred-year crisis of identity, the historian and sociologist and ideologist had best recognise the limitations of the present "state of the art." These disciplinary approaches cannot even say who is *not* a Jew. Once again, the hour has come for the theologian to occupy the podium. But, with Rotenstreich, I do hope he will not repeat what we have already heard—and found wanting.

In my view, the first question for the theologian must be the metaphysical one: what is the reality alluded to by the religious language? If one speaks of creation and a willful Creator, then what does one understand to be the act, moment, or process of creation? If he turns to "revelation" then one asks, what does one mean by it? How does what we know of creation permit us to assign purpose, meaning, or order, to talk of a "Law-giver"? One cannot merely say, "I believe," and retire from the field, as if belief were possible without understanding and intelligence. The most difficult questions were closed a long time ago: What is before, above, beneath, beyond? These are precisely the questions that now emerge as decisive. The theologian cannot come to faithful

Jews with the sentimental appeal of empty rhetoric or mere emotional bathos. He claims that "God" is "real" and purposive, and it is his task to explain the intent of his claim but, more important, its implications about reality. Even if one supposes that *Torah min hashamayim* is a true and valid concept, he still needs to explain what he means by Torah—and by heaven. The "Jewish problem" is, therefore, what it always was: not a matter of politics or economics, nor an anguish assuaged by flags, philanthropy, or even by mere repetition of the formulations of others' faiths. The Jewish problem is: What does it mean to be "Israel," a singular people covenanted to the service of one God?

NOTES

[1] These questions are all drawn from the surveys of recent legal literature by Immanuel Jakobovits in *Tradition, A Journal of Orthodox Thought*, as follows: 8, 2, 1966, pp. 81-2, on artificial insemination.

[2] *Ibid.*, 7, 4, 1965 (8, 1, 1966), pp. 98-9.

[3] *Ibid.*, 7, 2, 1965, pp. 121-26.

[4] Aaron Kirschenbaum, "Rabbi Moshe Feinstein's Responsa," *Judaism*, Summer 1966, pp. 364-72.

[5] "On the New Morality," *Judaism*, Summer 1966, pp. 329-36. Quotation on p. 336.

[6] In Arnold J. Wolf, ed., *Rediscovering Judaism: Reflections on a New Theology* (Chicago, 1965), pp. 51-76.

[7] *Ibid.*, p. 61.

[8] Evanston, 1963.

[9] *Ibid.*, p. 20.

[10] *Ibid.*, p. 62.

[11] For an analysis of this concept, see Ben Halpern, *The Idea of the Jewish State* (Cambridge, 1961).

[12] *Students, Scholars, and Saints* (Philadelphia, 1928), pp. vii-viii.

[13] *Greek in Jewish Palestine* (N.Y., 1942), pp. 14 ff.

[14] R. Nahman b. Isaac, Babylonian Talmud, *Pesahim* 105b.

[15] "Secularism and Religion in Israel," *Judaism*, Summer 1966, pp. 259-83.

[16] *Ibid.*, p. 275.

[17] *Ibid.*, p. 276.

[18] *Ibid.*, p. 279.

[19] *Ibid.*, pp. 280-81.

[20] I stress *seems*, since I am not a scholar of the history, content, or method of Jewish law, and claim no expertise whatever in the matter.

[21] On these periods I do claim to know what I am talking about.

PART FOUR

THE *HAVURAH* AS COMMUNE

VIII

THE *HAVUROT*

Stephen C. Lerner

Two views of 1970: Somerville, Massachusetts. In a yellow frame house on College Avenue, seven young people sit around a bare table with books before them. Their clothes, the hair, are very much in the style of this college and graduate generation. But the six men wear *kipot;* the books are copies of a Hassidic text. On the wall a sign announces: *"Shavat vayinafash*—slow down and live."

Cambridge, Massachusetts. In crowded Harvard Square, a few miles away from Somerville, six girls pass, beating tambourines and chanting "hari krishna." Two young women sell incense sticks and one fellow stands with a sign: "Philosopher available."

We have come to expect the Cambridge scene. We have come to lament—and accept—that young people, a disproportionate number of them Jews, go questing after every off-beat movement. For many, however, the Somerville scene is a surprise. The modest house on College Avenue is the home of Havurat Shalom, an experiment which marks a new direction in American Jewry and which, for many in America's Jewish leadership, is as threatening as the action in Harvard Square. In much the same way that the firebrands of Orthodoxy castigate Conservative Judaism more than Reform, because Conservatism is close enough to the real thing to confuse and mislead, there are many who worry more about Havurat Shalom and its younger counterpart in New York than about

Stephen C. Lerner is Rabbi of Tifereth Israel—Town and Village Synagogue, New York City.

the more prevalent manifestations of young Jewish activity across America.

Havurat Shalom does not afford a foretaste of the messianic age, but neither does it presage the fires of Gehinnom. It is a serious attempt to provide a new alternative to the traditional modes of Jewish study carried out in seminaries, Hebrew colleges and universities. Dissatisfied with the model of Jewish *wissenschaft,* it values the religious quest above the dispassionate search for knowledge. Turned off by the formal and often cold relations between faculty and students in the established institutions, its members seek to develop an atmosphere of fellowship in which serious study is pursued without fixed lines separating teacher from pupil.

The Havurat Shalom Community Seminary opened in the autumn of 1968. After a year and a half of operation, it has its own building, approximately thirty-eight members, and an *elan* that few institutions possess. By virtually any yardstick, it has made more than modest progress toward its goals and it has stimulated the establishment of a similar, if less ambitious, group in New York as well as rudimentary organizations elsewhere. The basically anti-institutional nature of the *havurah* may endanger its long-term survival, but at this writing, it constitutes as vibrant a center of Jewish life as may be found in these United States.

The idea of a *havurah* did not begin with the Boston group. The notion had been in the air for some years among young Jewish intellectuals. More than six years ago Rabbi Jacob Neusner spoke about *havurot* or fellowships which existed in talmudic times, and commended their application to our day. The Reconstructionist movement had also talked of building *havurot.* It remained for Rabbi Arthur Green, a brilliant if erratic Seminary graduate, to give shape to the amorphous concepts. Rabbi Green traces the genesis of his active interest in the project to a discussion, while still a Seminary student, with Father Dan Berrigan, a radical priest, about the underground church and the inner-city Protestant parishes. Rabbi Green began to speculate about the establishment of an experimental synagogue where intensive study would be carried on and where a more total sense of community would prevail. He explored the subject with Alan Mintz, a Columbia student and former National President of USY, who was also deeply interested in such a venture.

Returning to graduate study at Brandeis after his Seminary ordination in 1967, Rabbi Green pursued his ideas in discussions with Rabbi Albert Axelrad, the dynamic director of the Brandeis Hillel Foundation. Green was especially troubled by the fact that many young religious seekers found nothing of value in Judaism, while Axelrad's particular concern was the alienation of politically active youth from Jewish life. They hoped a new kind of institution might meet both needs. "When we realized we weren't out of our minds," as Green phrased it, they began to look in earnest for students, teachers and an advisory committee. All three searches proved successful. The Havurat Shalom Community Seminary opened its doors in the fall of 1968, with twelve students and a faculty including Rabbi Zalman Schachter and some of the brightest recent Seminary graduates. Its impressive advisory committee included leaders from all walks of Jewish religious and intellectual life: Brandeis Professor Nahum Glatzer, *Commentary* writer Milton Himmelfarb, Hillel directors Max Ticktin and Richard Israel, and Conservative rabbis Jack Riemer and Herschel Matt. (In most cases, however, the men on the advisory committee lent nothing more than their names to the enterprise.)

The students who found their way to the *havurah* had impressive academic credentials, and most had good Jewish backgrounds. One chose the *havurah* and the Harvard Graduate School of Education over the Jewish Theological Seminary; one came after having been rejected by the Seminary; another came from Shlomo Carlebach's West Coast House of Love and Prayer after being somewhat unhappy there. Personal association with Green and Axelrad brought some members; others were recommended by sympathetic Hillel directors. Not all found the *havurah* to their liking. Three dropped out during the first year, variously finding the center too Jewish, too "straight," or too communal. Axelrad dropped out as well, citing the demands of family and Hillel. But most of the students continued and during its second year of operation the enrollment has grown significantly. In New York, meanwhile, Alan Mintz and a group of graduate students formed the New York Havurah in the fall of 1969.

Though it is at odds with the shape of America's educational institutions, the *havurah* necessarily maintains some of their trappings. It is chartered by the Commonwealth of Massachusetts as an educational, non-profit corporation. Its full-time students (those taking a four-course program) may receive 4-D draft classifications, since Havurat Shalom is recognized by the authorities as a rabbinical seminary. (Green is quick to point out that only half the students have availed themselves of the 4-D's.) It projects a four-year curriculum leading to the title of *haver* (fellow). There has been some discussion about the future ordination of rabbis. According to Green, those students desiring ordination would be given a bibliography of Hebrew texts and secondary sources which they would be required to master. Then a board of examiners, consisting of the ordained rabbis on the faculty with the possible addition of outside rabbis, would pass on the candidates' qualifications.

The absence of sophisticated administrative procedures makes it difficult to gauge enrollment accurately, but there are apparently thirty-eight members this year, of whom eighteen are full-time students, six are part-time students, seven are teachers and seven are wives who belong to the *havurah* but neither study nor teach. There are also wives who are student-members. Admission to the *havurah* is not easily gained. The members feel that the size of the group must be limited in order to maintain a communal experience. Some may be admitted next year to replace those who drop out or go to Israel. The institution, according to Rabbi Green, is interested in Jewish religious seekers rather than in those with either an "Orthodox mentality" or a Jewish secularist orientation.

All members are expected to participate in the religious and communal life of the fellowship, in addition to its study program. There are financial obligations as well. Each member, whether teacher or student, is expected to contribute $500 toward the upkeep of the house on College Avenue. A $10,000 grant from the Danforth Foundation enabled the group to make an $8,000 down payment on the building. The group employs a part-time secretary; two of the younger teachers receive small salaries; the other members of the faculty receive no pay.

Rabbi Green hopes that the *havurah* will eliminate the category of part-time student (except for wives) in the future, and permit only such outside graduate study as dovetails with the learning at the *havurah*. At the present time the group is far from this ideal; nor is it true that all members share equally in the life of the *havurah*. Rabbi Joseph Lukinsky participates at best tangentially in the group's activities, but the *havurah* appears content to retain him as a member. (Lukinsky is a rare person who manages to have entree to and to feel at home in a multitude of Jewish spheres. He is a member of the *havurah*, a faithful *davener* at Brookline's Congregation Kehillath Israel, and a faculty member of both Brandeis University and the Jewish Theological Seminary's Teachers Institute.)

While the institution has no true hierarchy, and lines of authority are fluid (all are equal members), there is nevertheless a leader—Rabbi Arthur Green. The force of Green's personality, his primary role in the founding of *havurah*, his devotion to its goals, have made him clearly a sort of *mareh d'atra*, although the term *rebbe* might more properly describe his position. Green has always been a seeker, fascinated by *agadah*, *kabbalah* and *hassidism*. He was once described by a fellow student as an *epikoros* who *davens* like a *hassid*. Green is more interested in experimenting with the full range of religious tradition than in maintaining the *halakhah*, and the *havurah* generally shares these emphases. As Havurat Shalom's most constant shaping

force, Green's charismatic personality has led the institution
along a certain line of development. Its spirit, as Green defines
it, is the "ethic of becoming a religious human being through
the sources of Judaism rather than through the ordinary
concepts of Jewish commitment." To this end, there is a great
stress on developing meaningful prayer styles, and on
openness to fellow members and to the tradition. Saturday
morning services, informal *Kabbalat Shabbat* gatherings, a
group *seudah shelishit*, communal weekly meals, and a
general willingness to work together and share chores all
contribute to the growth of a total religious and interpersonal
relationship. The spirit of Buber's writing reigns supreme.

The one *havurah* activity open to the public at large has
been the worship service on *Shabbat* mornings. Many
outsiders come to *daven* with the group regularly, and
onlookers and observers come from near and far. Services are
held in the main room of the building on College Avenue.
Many sit on cushions scattered on the floor. A different
hazzan each week has leeway in leading the service. The
traditional liturgy is followed for *Shacharit*, and when English
is used it is chanted to traditional *niggunim*. The weekly
Torah portion is not read in its entirety but is studied
intensively, utilizing various approaches. Sometimes the
atmosphere is that of a Quaker meeting; people read silently
until someone wishes to comment. At other times there is
simultaneous Hebrew and English reading (Hebrew in an
undertone and English aloud). There is no *Musaf*, but services
conclude with singing and dancing.

What the *havurah* has created, it may be said, is a
contemporary *shtiebel* where intensity of feeling and unem-
barrassed exuberance are combined with study in a modern
vein. Even those for whom prayer is not a central quest find
that participation in a service conducted in an atmosphere of
fellowship has heightened their religious perceptions.

The moderately traditional style of worship evolved by the
havurah is typical of what has transpired there in other areas
of Jewish practice. Green admits that he has been surprised by

THE HAVURAH AS COMMUNE

the marked growth or re-emergence of respect for the Jewish tradition on the part of most members. The *Shabbat* in particular is a meaningful experience. Green estimates that approximately 90 percent observe the Sabbath (not necessarily according to *halakhic* guidelines). Seventy-five percent of the members maintain kosher homes while only a third observe *kashrut* outside the home. One quarter have gone beyond traditional Jewish law and are now vegetarians. These figures indicate where the *havurah* differs from a more typical sampling of committed American Jews. Within the American community, more Jews observe *kashrut* as a symbol of family loyalty, of national identity, than observe *Shabbat* as a day of spirituality, of relationship between man and man and between man and his God. In the *havurah*, however, it is not the claim of group loyalty which draws the members' allegiance, but rather the potential for religious growth.

Study is at the center of the *havurah* program as it is at the center of the Jewish tradition. Last year, courses offered included a study of Buber's *I and Thou*; a survey of the biblical, legal and *agadic* sources relating to Sukkot; Zalman Schachter's varieties of spiritual quest which included a lab in *davening* techniques; an introduction to Talmud; an introduction to Jewish mysticism; and courses in *Siddur* and *Chumash*. In addition, students arranged individual readings with the members of the faculty. Besides Rabbis Lukinsky, Schachter and Green, last year's faculty also included Rabbis Edward Feld, David Goodblatt, Burton Jacobson and Mr. Michael Fishbane, an instructor in Bible at Brandeis University. By September 1969, Zalman Schachter had returned to his academic post in Canada, David Goodblatt had left to study with Jacob Neusner at Brown, and Edward Feld had become the Hillel Director at the University of Illinois. They were replaced by equally able and interesting figures: Rabbis Everett Gendler, Hillel Levine and Michael Swirsky, plus non-rabbinic faculty.

The current courses in large measure are following last year's pattern, although there is no apparent sequential arrangement to them. Among other offerings, Rabbi Green is teaching two courses in Hassidism, Rabbi Jacobson, a course in Amos and Rabbi Lukinsky, a course in Talmud. Rabbi Gendler offers a course in male and female symbolism in the Jewish tradition and, with Rabbi Levine, leads a seminar in Judaism and contemporary social problems.

The choice of courses seems to derive from the interests and competence of the teachers. Given the general tendency of the *havurah,* it is not surprising to note that formal courses have as yet not been offered in such a classical fields as medieval Hebrew poetry, medieval Jewish philosophy, modern Hebrew literature or Jewish history, and that, by traditional standards, a disproportionate amount of time has been devoted to mystical, mythic and *hassidic* thought.

Perhaps the most old-fashioned program of the *havurah* is the *bet midrash* organized this year. This is designed for the small number of members with weak or non-existent backgrounds in Jewish learning. These students study Hebrew, *Chumash* with Rashi, *Siddur, Pirke Avot* and other traditional texts five days a week, four hours a day.

Although it is extremely difficult to judge the academic standards of the *havurah* faculty and students on the basis of a few cursory visits, it is this writer's feeling that they are an unusually able group. Except for Albert Axelrad and Zalman Schachter, the rabbis have been graduates of the Jewish Theological Seminary, generally among the Seminary's outstanding students of recent years. Whatever their deficiencies as accomplished scholars, they are a knowledgeable, imaginative and committed group although they are not *baale halakhah* in the *yeshiva* sense.

A session with Rabbi Gendler, for example, leaves one more impressed with the moral and visionary concerns of the man than with the rigorousness of his knowledge. At a class the writer attended, Gendler read and discussed a Sephardic-Kabbalistic compilation for Tu b'Shvat, *Sefer Pri Etz Hadar.* Interspersed among his grapplings with the Hebrew names of the various fruits and his remarks about the significance of each kind, were asides about the importance of developing contemporary rituals for the holiday, and of creating a mood which would enhance appreciation of the world of nature. After class, Gendler told the writer that he wanted to reintegrate Judaism with the vegetation cycle. He sought to "provide the *Kudsha B'rich Hu* with His consort," to "lead Him out of solitude," and to develop a Jewish style in which "rabbinic asceticism and *mitnagdic* defensiveness" were not the norm.

Classes were held in an atmosphere of informality. Interchange between student and teacher was easy and pleasant and there seemed to be a genuine interest in learning. Green's intermediate-level class in *hassidic* texts, for example, was marked by interesting comments about Catholic quietism and Agnon, and references to the *Zohar*, as well as close scrutiny of the class text, *Sefer Baal Shem Tov*. Each of the seven students participated, and the discussion was intelligent if not illuminating.

To this writer, the most remarkable revelation is that the students are clearly contented. Whereas students all over the country express widespread dissatisfaction with institutions of higher learning, both Jewish and secular, the members of the *havurah* actually like their courses. According to Joseph Riemer, a graduate of Queens College and a product of New Xork *yeshivot*, the teachers are "very competent and very inspiring." He praised the atmosphere of "fellowship with people of my generation" in which study was carried on. For Riemer as well as for others, study in the *havurah's* religious environment contrasted favorably with the non-religious, depersonalized approach which they believe is common to universities and seminaries alike. For some, the *havurah* represents the essence of *Torah lishmah*. Other mystically oriented young people seek exposure to the Jewish tradition as a source of nourishment. Richard Siegel, Brandeis '69, was excited by a college course in Eastern religion; at the same time, he realized that "there were Jewish parallels to Eastern concepts." He became steadily more interested in religious attitudes and discovered that an intended career in law was not for him. Wishing to continue his religious search, he came to Havurat Shalom. He has found his choice a good one: "I'm engaging in the most serious study I've ever done in my educational life, in the most positively creative atmosphere I've ever been in." This is not the sort of comment we expect to hear from a student in an American Jewish academy.

While the mood of the *havurah* is introspective, the image of an urban commune or latter-day Essenic settlement is not entirely accurate. Most of the members are involved in outside activities. Rabbi Green had been a graduate student at Brandeis until January and currently lectures to Jewish organizations on the theme "A Critique of the Jewish Community." Rabbi Gendler is a member of Packard Manse, an ecumenical retreat in Stoughton. Rabbi Jacobson is principal of the Temple Emunah religious school in Lexington. Joseph Riemer is principal of the Kehillath Israel Hebrew high school in Brookline. Others are graduate students, Hebrew teachers or Jewish youth leaders. Furthermore, while political activism is not the major thrust of *havurah* life, members of the seminary were active in the Washington protest against the war in Viet Nam, and in the Boston campaign to pressure the Council of Jewish Federations and Welfare Funds to allocate more money for Jewish education and Jewish culture.

Though many members work in the community, a definite current of antagonism to existing Jewish institutions and a clear sense of apartness and superiority do exist. The members see themselves as non-conforming young Jews. Some do, however, wish to become new-style Jewish leaders who would attempt to revitalize the Jewish community. For this group, Jewish education, Jewish community work or Hillel positions are all viable options. The one field excluded by virtually every member is the congregational rabbinate. For other members, communal matters are of no great concern. Indeed, as Green noted, there has never been a resolution of the basic tension between those who see Havurat Shalom as a center for the creation of new types of religious leadership and those who see the fellowship only as a place in which the members may experiment with new forms of religious and community life.

While the *havurah* judges the Jewish community and finds it grossly wanting, the "establishment" is somewhat equivocal in its views of the fellowship. A leading Conservative rabbi in the Boston area welcomed the contribution of *havurah* members to Jewish education and youth work. He felt that they were fine teachers and had good rapport with adolescents. As for the *havurah* itself, "It's a kind of *shtiebel.* . . . But I don't mean that as a criticism. I was raised in a *shtiebel* and I like them." Rabbi Herbert Rosenblum of Temple Emunah (Lexington), where the school principal and members of the teaching staff are drawn from Havurat Shalom, agrees that the presence of the fellowship has enriched Jewish education in the Boston area. Nevertheless, he laments the isolationist stance of the *havurah:*

> To the extent that they may verbalize the psychotic gulf between themselves and the synagogue, they have made an absolute type statement which is just a misconception. People change and mature, synagogues change, and perhaps a meeting can take place in a more relative way, if not completely.-
> . . . These kids are still fighting to retain the umbilical cords of Camp Ramah and their college experience. They are postponing the acceptance of mature responsibility.

Professor Jacob Neusner, too, has expressed reservations about contemporary *havurot.* In a recent column in the *Boston Jewish Advocate* he wrote:

> One of their problems is the selfishness of the quest; another is the episodic quality of their fellowships, which have no place for married, mature people already embarked on the adventure of raising children and making a living.
> The *havurot* depend on a great purpose to unite the *haverim* and give their social life worthwhile tasks. Otherwise, they are destined to continue their present irrelevant and solipsistic life, to concentrate on their spiritual belly-buttons, so to speak, and to exclude from their concern the larger part of the Jewish

people.

At the Jewish Theological Seminary, the *havurah* receives both support and criticism. Stories of the real and imagined doings of *havurah* members at Camp Ramah in Palmer, Massachusetts, and vague reports of excessive permissiveness in Somerville are factors in the critical assessments. In turn, some of the *haverim* feel that Ramah leaves much to be desired religiously.

Rumors of drug-taking at the *havurah* seem greatly exaggerated. In fact, one of the few rules existing in the *havurah* is that there may be no use of drugs on communal property. (Another rule is that only kosher dairy cuisine may be served at communal meals.) Of course some *havurah* members may experiment with drugs privately. Nonetheless, Rabbi Green calls the atmosphere "post-drug"; he feels that the challenge now is not drugs. Anyone who wants to can get high, but "the question is how to integrate the highs into daily living."

The impact, actual and potential, of the *havurot* student recruitment is one that Jewish seminaries will have to treat seriously. The Jewish Theological Seminary has already lost one applicant to Havurat Shalom, as has the Jewish Institute of Religion (Reform). The challenge becomes clearer if one looks at the roster of the New York Havurah, the Boston group's younger relation. Virtually all its members have strong backgrounds in Jewish learning and Jewish leadership. Among the nineteen members, one is a Jewish Theological Seminary drop-out, two are Seminary rejects, two are current rabbinical students at the Seminary, and one is a Seminary graduate. Three are rabbinical students at the Jewish Institute of Religion, one has withdrawn and one is on leave from that school. Others at one time or another considered applying to one of the seminaries. Thus, this group may exert a strong pull on present or prospective seminaries by providing a supplement or alternative to studies in "establishment" institutions.

At present, the New York Havurah represents the same anti-institutional and communal tendencies as its New England prototype, but differs somewhat from it. Both as a group and as individuals, its members are much more involved in liberal or left-wing political and social action projects. But it is not yet an all-encompassing framework. Generally, its members see the *havurah* as a supplement to other areas of study and community activity in which they are engaged—often together. For most, it is an attempt to build a religious community of people who share similar concerns—politically, societally and religiously. As one member explained his dissatisfaction with "normal" Jewish life, "Why spend *Shabbat* with people with whom one wouldn't spend the weekdays?" Its members from the seminaries, upset with the matter-of-fact careerism and formality of their institutions, find that the *havurah* gives them a community in which they may truly participate. Ronnie Kronish, Brandeis '68, and Arthur Ruberg, Haverford '68, students at JIR and JTS respectively, hope that what is created at the *havurah* can be a paradigm for the Jewish community—more concern, more fellowship, more real religious learning. Not everyone shares these hopes. Rabbi David Sperling, JTS '67, has no illusions about American Jewry. "It's future," he quipped, "is at Kennedy Airport." But study and prayer with this fellowship have brought him renewed appreciation for religious study and for the religious life. "I got positively high on *tefillot*," he noted when speaking about a recent *Shabbat* service.

Less structured as to communal programs and less demanding in terms of study requirement, the New York Havurah has begun to build a spirit in which learning, prayer, community and social action are embraced as vital norms. Nevertheless, it lacks a dominant and guiding voice like Green's, and the requirements for participation are so minimal as to be almost non-existent. Most members feel that they should give more time to the fellowship, but since all are involved in other ventures, this is most difficult. The future of the New York Havurah is still questionable. It may develop a total community experience—or it may become an "after-hours" Jewish study group with the power to grant 4-D's.

At this junction both the *havurot* seem remarkably successful, but they could break up at any time. They have little institutional structure and no real lines of authority. There are, as noted above, tensions between the socially committed who turn outward to the community and the religious seekers who turn inward to the self. Then again, the *havurot* may currently demand too much or too little. A knowledgeable observer told me that Havurat Shalom recently has been challenged by the possible resignation of a group of members who seek an even more total communal experience—perhaps in Israel—than the group now provides. Finally, there is the potential and real conflict between the full-time and part-time members. These problems may be more real for the Massachusetts fellowship which has a fairly clear-cut idea of its aims, than for the New York group.

Whatever their success, the *havurot* face recurring knotty questions. It is difficult to see how the *havurah* pattern could be followed in America, outside of a few centers where extra-institutional scholars and rabbis are fortuitously gathered. By cutting themselves off from the existing "establishment" institutions, the *havurot* may simultaneously limit the number of knowledgeable resource personnel available for additional groups. Surely, it is totally unrealistic to expect the *havurot* in other cities will have rabbis of the caliber of Green, Levine and Swirsky available to them if they write off the synagogues and their professional leadership.

Most unsettling and most shortsighted of all is the facile way in which the *haverim* scornfully condemn the institutions of the Jewish community. Most had good Jewish backgrounds; many were active in Ramah, USY and Conservative synagogues; a much smaller number were active in the Reform movement. Yet despite their positive experiences, few entertain any real hope for the synagogue. For them, the congregation and the congregational rabbinate are not where the action is. And perhaps, in view of the existing synagogues, the *haverim* may be right. However, there is no law which says that congregations cannot change, and no unwrittten law denying the possibility of *havurot* being formed within existing congregations. Few of the *haverim* consider this to be a realistic goal, for they seem to share a certain Puritan sense of the corruption of the existing order and the concomitant requirement for a New Zion. With their generational obsessions and their biases against buildings and budgets and the bourgeois, they refuse to grant that within synagogues one may find small numbers of like-minded people, rabbinic and lay, for whom study is important, prayer a challenge, and community a desideratum. They want little part in supporting this group, in strengthening the content and quality of the synagogue program, in acting as the leaven within the larger congregation. Ultimately, they are acting out, in the Jewish sphere, the broad generational rebellion. They want to study with and learn from people of their generation or close to it (the exigencies of serious Jewish study may demand that the *havurah* members trust people until they're forty or thereabouts!), to pray with them, to live and interact with them. Clearly, they think that they can't "do their thing" meaningfully with the corrupted or deadened elders.

Havurah members are willing to work with Jewish youth whom they, like the radical movements, consider good material to mold. In this regard, it is incorrect to suggest, as Professor Neusner does, that they exist in splendid spiritual isolation. Most of the *haverim* in Somerville do sally forth regularly into the community, nourished by the *havurah* experience, to teach and to lead Jewish youth. However, they share with the Lubavitcher Hassidim an exaggerated sense of the correctness of their ways, an explicit condescension toward the institutions which engage them. Ultimately, this would seem to limit their effectiveness as builders, for to teach positively one must have some stake in the community in which one works. The *haverim* lack this, and thus it is difficult to expect that they will nurture the kind of creative rebels who will seek to improve the quality of synagogue life.

Alternatively, if they do create revolutionaries who reject the establishment, they will lose their present entree into establishment circles.

How long can one remain a member of a *havurah?* For many members of Havurat Shalom, affiliation is considered a life-long enterprise. Yet Professor Neusner is probably correct when he questions the ability of *havurot* to continue to function with their idealistic assumptions about community and study once families arrive and full-time obligations are undertaken. (Rabbi Rosenblum notes that there are perhaps sixty or seventy people in his congregation who constitute a fellowship of sorts for study and worship, but who participate within the context of family life and a complete working week.) Furthermore, given the currents of our time, one cannot be sure that a twenty-five-year-old would care to participate in a *havurah* half of whose members might be over forty. Would there have to be *havurot* for different age groups; or more intensive groups for graduate students who have free time, and less intensive fellowships for family men? How would the programs of the latter differ from the best a good synagogue has to offer?

A real *havurah* must remain small—forty to fifty members at the most—and thus its potential for influence is limited. For many *haverim* this is not a paramount consideration. Some have written off the Jewish community except for the "saving remnants." Moreover, the continued survival of Israel the people, or Israel the state, is not a subject of major concern. The *haverim* have their own souls to worry about.

It is precisely the failure to value the religious component of the survival of the Jewish people that weakens the power of Havurot Shalom, and may destine it to become no more than an interesting footnote in the history of time. This is not a necessary development. One wishes that the *havurah* would try to coordinate more of its activities with the creative elements in the "establishment." One would hope that with the holocaust a scant generation behind us, the continuing existence of the Jewish people would be a concern to which all of the *haverim* would be willing to devote themselves. (Until recently, a course on the theologies of the holocaust was given to interested members of New York Havurah by Rabbi David W. Silverman of the Jewish Theological Seminary. Although himself not a member of the group, Rabbi Silverman conveys the *havurah's* commitment to other faculty members and attempts to inhibit polarization and stereotyping judgments on the part of each group.)

The *havurah*, then, is not without glaring faults and mistaken emphases. Nevertheless, its existence and its real achievements provide a challenge to the Jewish community. It emphasizes that there is a small but growing number of young people who want to study seriously and to worship intensely. Many of them have received their initial impetus in this direction through programs run by our synagogues or by the Conservative movement. As adolescents they found no place for their commitment in the synagogues, where prayer is rote-reading, community is expressed in suburban soirees, and learning is best described as a Harry Golden lecture. Large synagogues ghettoized the youngsters in the youth service, *de facto havurot*. Rarely did the adult service attempt to integrate youthful energy and creativity into channels of worship or education. Rarely did the youngsters feel that they really shared in synagogue activity. Thus was lost the ideal of the synagogue as a center which could bridge the generation gap and bring together Jews of all ages, as it had for centuries.

If the *havurah* does nothing else, it should remind Jewish leaders that, as successful youth services have indicated for years, religious creativity, fervor, and a sense of community have not passed from this earth. Business as usual at the *shul* is no longer acceptable. Rabbis will have to surmount their own inertia, the resistance of synagogue boards and ritual committees, and get youth involved in every aspect of synagogue life. They must make sure that services provide at least some modicum of informality, youthful participation and creative study.

The challenge to the seminaries, and to the Jewish Theological Seminary in particular, is even greater. More and more students want to study in a setting in which relevance is at least as important as depth, where informality and openness are valued alongside scholarly attainments. Jewish *wissenschaft* is no longer a necessary and sufficient cause of learning. Furthermore, the schools must acknowledge that as many students are interested in courses in *agadah* and mysticism as in Talmud. While the seminaries should not alter their curriculum merely to suit a current fad, they should expand their offerings to provide adequate courses in areas of Jewish study which they have undervalued and which attract vibrant students today. With the increasing number of alternatives currently available, the seminaries cannot assume that students will automatically flock to their admissions offices. If the establishment fails to respond to the request for new styles of learning, more and more students will find supplemental sources of enlightenment or bypass the seminaries altogether.

In sum, the *havurot* offer a strong challenge to the present shape of things in American Jewry. The *havurah* as an institution will not solve the malaise in the American Jewish community; it presents problems of its own and it may not even endure. But it has indicated that a way can be found to make serious study of Jewish sources more relevant, and religious services and the religious life more meaningful. By and large, the *haverim* evince great and genuine affection for their program. Would that the same were true of the students in our seminaries and the young people in our synagogues!

IX

THE MAKING OF A
JEWISH COUNTER CULTURE

Bill Novak

As we quickly approach the end of this decade, to the profound surprise of those of us who had assumed that the world would never see 1970, certain of the social patterns in the 1960's are already becoming fairly clear. Perhaps the most striking characteristic of American life in the sixties is not so much that things are so very different than they have ever been before (although for most of us this is certainly true), but rather that the rate of acceleration of these various changes has been so exceedingly rapid. While one might have expected there to be obvious and even fundamental differences between life-styles in 1928 and in 1963, the changes that have occurred in American life since 1963 (particularly among young people) have been equally imposing. It might, then, be instructive when considering young people to look at what has changed over the last decade and a half, and to note briefly some of the developments that have taken place during that time. While this in itself has already been done (and surely by more competent thinkers), the task of looking at the past fifteen years with particular emphasis on Jewish young people still stands before us. For the data are still being produced, and the motion has not yet slowed down. But if we are sincere about understanding current trends in Jewish life, we run the risk of premature analysis before news becomes sociology,

Bill Novak is Editor of *Response*. This paper is the text of a broadcast over station WBAI-FM on November 26, 1969 in New York City.

and before sociology becomes history.

One hears a great deal these days about the importance of "image." I have found that despite its turning into a bit of a cliche, the idea of the image as a tool in social thought is an extremely useful one, for it brings to mind more subtle data than are usually discovered through more normal channels. It can be equally correct, while at the same time, less "factual" than routine analysis. Let us consider, for example, the image of the 1950's. In considering image, facts are secondary while interpretations, nuances, expressions and impressions take on a primary importance. So whatever really happened—something we may never know because most things never really happen—the image of the 1950's symbolized so very well by a paternal, kindly and dull general, was a picture of complacent serenity with a tinge of fear, gadgetry, and a hint of the plastic world that was soon to come. One tends to picture the era (at least if one is young and depends heavily on images for one's conception of things past) as a time when millions of Americans sat blankly in front of their newly purchased television sets, abandoning books in favor of building banks, making children and raising money. In much the same way that Sinclair Lewis' immortal portrayal of the life of George Babbit caught the spirit and particularly the image of an earlier era, Philip Roth's masterpiece *Goodbye Columbus* captured in print (and less successfully on the screen) our image of the 1950's. Symbols abounded in the Eisenhower years. Fraternities and football games, Elvis Presley and James Dean, Rock and Roll and motorcycles, leather jackets and crew cuts. A whole style of life lay behind those symbols.

Campus politics was another term for student councils. Liberals found themselves looked upon with suspicion (they still do, but now of course it is from at least two directions), while civil liberties was an idea discussed in law schools. If American youth was not completely happy, it was at least nominally satisfied with the way things were. Discontent was still around the corner, while actual ferment was several blocks away.

Jewish life in the 1950's was something less than glorious.

Youth activities on an organized level made today's look good by comparison. If a Hillel foundation provided its quota of Jewish boys for Jewish girls, it was doing a fine job. And Jewish education—if you can imagine this—was in worse shape than it is now. It was certainly not a hopeful picture, and, given the mood of America at that time, there was little reason to expect a significant change.

But as the new decade began, things did change, and very rapidly, as new symbols arose to replace the old. The election of John Kennedy was at the heart of this symbol switch, as new qualities and ideas were paraded before the nation. Fashion and glamor. Minorities and politics. Youth and vigor. Involvement on all levels by all people. Charm and wit and chivalry. A sense of humor and a belief in the future of mankind. A new sense of cultural excellence. The country responded to all this as young people awoke one morning in 1961 to find themselves in a new age. Michael Harrington told them about poverty, John Galbraith about corporate capitalism, Paul Goodman and Martin Luther King about youth and dignity, while Bob Dylan (and later on, of course, the Beatles) filled in the gaps by drawing a more complete picture of the world and its visions. The system itself took on a new life, and Washington again became its focal point. The Peace Corps was born, and folk music swept the country. There was a great march on Washington, and the sit-in movement began in the south.

Jewish students were very much involved in the projects associated with the Kennedy administration. To be sure, they were involved as Jewish young people rather than as young Jewish people, but we should find nothing surprising about that. They became involved in the civil rights and peace movements. Liberal rabbis pointed at them with pride, while the more conservative elements in the Jewish community were frankly embarrassed by the Jewish identity of the activists. And, unfortunately, many of the young people themselves shared in that embarrassment.

The new spirit continued to grow, until the bullet that killed the youthful President brought that short-lived era to an abrupt and violent end. Another swift change in symbol sets, as ugliness moved into the White House. Power and Prestige took over. Quantity replaced quality, authority replaced style. And finally, Vietnam.

Aside from the well-known and documented effects that the war has had on the youth culture, there were, I suggest, two key events during the Johnson administration that had a profound effect on Jewish young people and their situation. The first of these events was the gradual but obvious shift in what until that time had been called the civil-rights movement. In effect, black people told their white counterparts, and Jews in particular, that the struggle was more particular than universal. As a black movement there was really nothing that whites could do to help, except by withdrawing from the struggle. This was naturally a bitter pill to swallow for many Jewish liberals who had been honestly and significantly involved in the black struggle up to that point. When cries of antisemitism were heard, and when some of the blacks allied themselves out of ignorance with the Arab cause, many Jews gave up on the whole thing. But some of the younger Jews responded differently, and understood the message that had emerged. The lesson was, ironically, a Jewish lesson—identify with your own people. You are fortunate, said the black to the Jew, for you have a people: work with it. You are fortunate, said the black to the Jew, for your history is recorded: study it. You have your own culture so dig it. That was the message in 1966. But it was a little too subtle, and had to be repeated, in a different form, a year later.

The massive response of the world Jewish community to the 1967 war in Israel was just that—the reformation of a world Jewish community. For the most part, the response did not extend to the American campus, except in a very personal way. While the war of 1967 had an effect on all Jews, it seemed in many cases to reach young people a little later than their parents. Perhaps their parents had other spectres haunting their collective memory. Whatever the reason, the Jew on campus reacted to Israel far more in 1968 and especially in 1969 than he did immediately after the Six-Day War.

In view, then, of the black revolution and the six-day war, what has become of the Jewish activist on campus? Many of them are still in the picture, as they have always been, ready to participate in any cause but their own. But a small minority has responded to recent events by attempting to merge their political views and their Jewish tradition. The New Left, at one point the only hope for a political morality in this country, sold him out by its pointless acceptance of the "good-guy-bad-guy" dualism in the Middle East. The logical response, one might think, would be for the young people to channel their energy into concerns that are at least in some way Jewish. But it is not as easy as it seems. Above all, many of my generation have been turned off long ago by an organized Jewish Community which is neither Jewish nor Community—only organized. Consequently, many young people have the impression that America Jewish life is really Judaism, and they want no part of it. So, to their minds, Judaism is another part of the system, because their elders have allowed it to happen.

We turn now to some of the results of this ferment. The new Jewish counterculture, it must be remembered, is in its initial stages. The entire movement is dfficult to study because it is (intentionally) fragmented, decentralized, and particularistic. These anti-organizational tendencies are common to the new politics in general, as there is a built-in distrust of structured mass movements, often as the result of bitter and frustrating experience.

In an attempt to categorize the various features of the new Jewish counterculture, one turns first to the most obvious aspect—politics. The political counterculture in Jewish life is composed for the most part of people who have been involved in progressive or leftist causes of various kinds in the past few years. In many cases, they are just now realizing that there is some connection between their political radicalism and their Jewish backgrounds, however thinly they might have been exposed to Jewish values in earlier years, and however poorly they understand the link between the two. Examples of these political projects are the Jewish Liberation Project in New York, *Na-aseh* in Philadelphia, the New Jewish Committee in Minnesota, and Jews for Urban Justice in Washington. The Philadelphia group, for instance, has been active in calling for draft counseling in local synagogues. Groups in New York and Boston have been more concerned with how money is spent in the Jewish community. Just this past week a group of three hundred Jewish students picketed the national convention of Jewish philanthropic organizations, demanding that higher priorities be given to Jewish education, culture, and social action. In the recent peace march in Washington, hundreds of Jewish students met together under the banner of the National Jewish Organizing Project in an attempt to determine how they might best combine their politics and their heritage within the peace movement. And in Montreal, Madison and Toronto, new progressive Zionist groups have sprung up out of thin air at the local universities. In Long Island, the well-publicized Ruskay case attracted national attention when a Jewish student presented evidence to prove that it was impossible for him to be granted the status of C.O. by his local draft board, because his religion was not recognized as being traditionally pacifist.

But it would be a misreading of the situation to see the counterculture strictly in terms of politics. In Toronto, for instance, a group of young college people, faced with the dreary prospect of attending High Holy Day services at the local temple, as they had been doing for years, decided not to go, and instead formed their own underground congregation, and held their own services in the basement of one of the member's homes. In various other communities, young people are forming their own religious services, often radically different from the traditional Jewish liturgy. The *Havurat Shalom* in Cambridge and the House of Love and Prayer in San Francisco are but two of the more known communal places where a new form of experimental service is being developed, and where younger Jews can come to find appropriate modes of expression for their own religious quests.

Jewish culture and education have not remained unaffected by the increased activity in the youth community. In certain afternoon Hebrew schools, committed college students have taken over whole departments and are experimenting with new types of Jewish education. The 1960's have also seen the growth of more exciting projects within the establishment, such as the Ramah camps, and better youth programs. But these institutions are inadequate in themselves, and the impetus has finally come from the young people themselves. Performing groups in Hebrew music and dance have sprung up in the nineteen sixties, particularly in the New York area. In addition, Jewish kids are now reading Jewish books. Not only Philip Roth, who has been scapegoated by parts of the Jewish establishment for being, in a word, too good a writer, but also authors such as Agnon, Nellie Sachs, and Elie Wiesel, along with Americans such as Singer and Malamud are part of the new reading list. And, at long last, there is finally some agitation at various colleges for the establishment of departments of Judaica. At the State University in Albany, students have taken matters into their own hands by creating a free Jewish University.

One could go in listing projects, but there are two in which I have been involved which I would like to describe. Last year there were a number of conferences and meetings as it became clear that developments all over the country were leading in similar directions vis à vis radical Judaism. There were a number of individuals who felt that the movement in its totality was greater than the sum of its parts, i.e. that a merely political affiliation was in itself inadequate. What emerged was the Havurah in New York City. Havurah is the Hebrew word for fellowship or community, and its is within that framework that courses have established to study Judaica on the graduate level. The Havurah is dedicated to a free personal type of learning, and with a total membership of twenty-five and no administration at all, it is able to achieve this desired goal. Anyone interested in starting a course has an opportunity to do so, and the students decide whether they need a teacher, and, if so, they seek one out. Havurah members have a communal meal once a week, and spend shabbat together at least once a month. The group decided that the November retreat should take place at the March on Washington, and we participated in that event as a group. There is also a Havurah (group) in Boston, as well as New Brunswick. New groups will probably emerge in other cities as local people are ready to create them. The Havurah provides human contacts in a way that the university can not, and as a system of learning it may well become very popular in the near future among religious and even secular students. It should be added that most members of the Havurah continue their graduate programs at other colleges at the same time.

If the Havurah is sort of a culmination and summary of the recent developments, then *Response* is surely at the other end of the spectrum. When *Response* was started three years ago by a few dissatisfied undergraduates, there was no hint of a counterculture in Jewish life. The editors of the magazine wanted a forum to discuss the problems in American Jewish life, and suggest new models and ideas that might be useful, especially to other students. The first issue appeared in 1967, with five hundred copies. Two years later, *Response* is now a quarterly with over five thousand readers. The magazine has become somewhat of an unofficial intellectual organ for the new Jewish counterculture, for it is in the pages of *Response* that new theoretical models are discussed, while current structures and concepts are analyzed.

The counterculture I have spoken of is a new and growing organism. It is very small in actual numbers, but involved in it are some of the brightest and most creative young people in Jewish life today. The overall movement is intentionally vague, ad hoc, and decentralized, for its members have learned to fear structures more than anything else. The Jewish establishment might do well to take note of the new counterculture, which seeks not so much to destroy what already exists as to bypass it. Rather than concentrate on attacking and destroying what is irrelevant, the movement has chosen instead to create new models and experiment with their uses.

As Jacob Neusner has pointed out, fellowship in Judaism is not exactly new. In fact, it is evident that most of the elements in the counter-culture are very old ideas. Young people are going back to traditional models and it is in this sense that they are most truly radical.

1. In Boston

X

HAVURAT SHALOM:

A PROPOSAL

Arthur Green

Havurat Shalom is a group of men and women involved in an ongoing religious quest, largely nurtured by our contact with the insights and traditional forms of Judaism. The search each of us has thus far undergone in seeking his own path in the celebration of life's divinity and in seeking out his own role in the realization of the Kingdom of God in human affairs, has brought us to the need for *Havurah*, for religious fellowship, and to the establishment of *Havurat Shalom*.

Each of us strives to make the above statement true concerning his role in *Havurat Shalom*. We all know that each of us is here for all kinds of other reasons as well: emotional, intellectual, sentimental, academic, etc. Many needs are fulfilled by an undertaking which occupies so much of one's emotional energy. Yet we seek to subordinate these to the needs of the Spirit as the most essential meaning of *Havurat Shalom* and of our being here. That all decisions we make are in the context of the *Havurah* should be borne in mind.

If the human spirit is to survive in our age, there will need to be many attempts at its intentional cultivation. We see ourselves as part of a great effort in this latter part of the

Rabbi Green comments: "This is the most complete essay I have written on my ideal of *havurah*. It was a proposal submitted as part of a reorganization effort in January, 1970. It was never accepted in full and should not be taken as a description of the present *Havurat Shalom*".

149

twentieth century to preserve human values and religious truths which are elsewhere being swept aside. A small but terribly significant spiritual subculture is being created in the West; we seek to identify with the highest elements in that cross-cultural and cross-religious effort.

We further stand in the context of a particular religious tradition and a particular people in the world's history. Our living commitment to Jewish tradition is one of study and experimentation; we have a particular commitment to the spiritual renewal and meaningful religious survival of the Jewish people.

The particular path of this *Havurah* is one that recognizes the legitimacy of religious personalism. We know that each of us must find his own spiritual path, and we would seek in the *Havurah* the context, knowledge, and atmosphere that would enrich this search for each of us. It is hoped that we will grow in the ability to share elements of this search with one another, and that we will all be concerned with one another's spiritual and personal growth.

The range of particular religious paths is and may healthily be a broad one. It would appear, however, that on either far end of the spectrum there are those who could not be comfortable in this *Havurah*. Those whose Orthodoxy in attitude does not allow them to accept the legitimacy of alternative paths for other Jews, and those who find no validity in the entire enterprise of personal religious search, are probably beyond our scope.

When we enter into the *Havurah*, we accept certain obligations upon ourselves. Without obligations the *Havurah* could not exist. We affirm that the *Havurah* has a right to make serious claims upon our time and energies. Each of us is in the *Havurah* because it is of great importance to us; it is an expression of those matters which are (or which we hope to make) central to our lives. While nearly all of us need to work outside the *Havurah* to earn our material sustenance, and outside personal involvements are of course not discouraged, we agree to take most seriously the *Havurah's* claims upon such as meals, worship, retreats, etc., and such menial but nonetheless crucial obligations as household chores and financial contribution.

Each of us takes upon himself the obligation to participate in all activities of the *Havurah*, unless there is some substantial physical or spiritual reason why he cannot do so. Each individual will remain his own arbiter as to the validity of such reasons, but we are asked to take the question of group obligation quite seriously, much more so than we have done in the past.

Study of Judaism is a central defining task of membership in the *Havurah*. While hopefully not an end in itself, but rather an expression of the more basic attitudes outlined above, study of Torah occupies an essential place in our group value system and a major portion of our time. We seek to develop new models of religious study, to make study itself once again a form of worship. We also recognize, however, that constant learning is needed as a source of access to our tradition, and that we cannot tolerate Jewish ignorance in ourselves. Inability to become involved with a serious program in the study of Judaism may well be sufficient reason to leave this particular *Havurah*, to which study is so central.

A specific study requirement is the acquisition of skill in Hebrew language to the point of ability to read classic unpointed texts in the original with some minimal fluency. It is to be understood that no one who enters the *Havurah* without this ability will be allowed to remain a *Haver* for more than one year without embarking on a serious effort to master the Hebrew language. (If such a person chooses not to do so through the regular course offering in Hebrew, *Havurah* will ask its regular teacher of elementary Hebrew to evaluate for it the seriousness of such efforts.)

One of the purposes of study in the *Havurah*, in addition to personal spiritual development, is the cultivation of well-taught and personally sensitive leaders for the Jewish community. To this end certain *Haverim* will require carefully planned courses of study, in some cases leading to the granting of titles which may help them to serve in leadership roles. Such programs will be described in detail elsewhere, but the *Havurah* as a group here undertakes a responsibility to those *Haverim* to see to it that such serious study is possible in our context. This is a commitment of both teachers and fellow students.

The attitude of the *Havurah* toward traditional patterns of Jewish ritual observance and liturgical worship is one of open-ended experimentalism of great seriousness. While no particular observance pattern is insisted upon, concern for and willingness to attempt the ritual life patterns remains essential to our vision of Judaism as the sacralization of the everyday. Those for whom the possibility of living their lives in deep accord with the Jewish ritual rhythm of Shabbat and holidays does not exist, those who see no chance for the meaningfulness of the prayer experience in any form, and those for whom being an heir and transmitter of the symbol-system of Jewish piety is not significant, should not be a part of this *Havurah*. On the other hand, we hope for the emergence of new ritual and liturgical forms of the *Havurah*, and frankly deplore our own lack of such creativity thus far.

Participation in communal worship experiences is an important part of our participation in the *Havurah*. It is hoped that the frequency and variety of such experiences will increase, and that absence from them will not be taken lightly by *Haverim*. Of course the *Havurah* will always respectfully appreciate the fact that participation in a religious service is not done casually by most of us, and there may often be good spiritual reason why certain *Haverim* do not feel it right for them to take part in certain forms of religious worship.

We recognize that the present *Havurah* is a large and highly diverse group in terms of personalities and life-styles. None of us will have relationships of equal intimacy with all of his *Haverim*, nor can real personal closeness be legislated. Nevertheless, we have chosen to join the *Havurah* out of a need for religious fellowship, and none of us would deny the relatedness of the personal and religious dimensions in human relationships. Some attempt at the religious appreciation of one's *Haverim* as fellowmen and companions must be part of the *Havurah*. Such appreciation, which involves being open to viewing the other in the light of one's own religious ideals, will mean a certain degree of seeing through defences and letting down one's own masks. For all of us, the very recognition of one another's defences as such may be a terribly significant step in this direction.

It must be emphasized that the way to such a style of the interpersonal has to be trod with great delicacy, respect, and patience. Openness does not happen automatically when we join the *Havurah*, and is not something that can be delivered on demand. The goals are long-range, and pressure is not the way. On the other hand, the attempt on the part of all of us is essential. It would be hoped that there is no one who is not seriously working on himself in these areas, and that none of us have closed off the possibility of seeing all of our *Haverim* in the light of the Divine Image.

Married persons are generally accepted into the *Havurah* as couples, unless otherwise stipulated. While it is understood that it will often be one member of the couple who is engaged in full-time pursuit of Jewish study, it is expected that all members of the *Havurah*, both male and female, will be involved in study at least on a one-course equivalency basis, and will make equal commitments to all other *Havurah* responsibilities. Spouses of *Haverim* who do not feel they can fulfill the requirements of *Havurah* membership, or who are not comfortable in the spiritual climate of the group, are, of course, welcome to attend all functions of the group, but are asked not to participate in *Havurah* meetings.

Many of us are not comfortable with the idea of formal legislation in the *Havurah*; we might be still less comfortable with a *Havurah* judiciary. There are times, however, when we feel we have legitimate complaints against one another with regard to the shirking of communal responsibilities. It would be hoped that we will first attempt to clear up such matters by personal contacts. If such informed approaches fail, the matter should be brought to the attention of the coordinator. He may then decide, after consultation with the individuals involved, to bring the matter up for discussion at a meeting of the *Havurah.* The coordinator is trusted to be aware of the injunction forbidding the public disgracing of one's fellow-man.

In the case of extremely serious or continued neglect of responsibility to the *Havurah* as outlined above, the group in meeting may issue an ultimatum to be backed up to the point of terminating that individual's membership in the *Havurah.* It is of course hoped that such decisions would be mutual.

While it is agreed that the *Havurah* does not exist primarily for the purpose of group therapy, as that term is generally used, it is also recognized that there arise in our group tensions and hostilities that take us away from our goals. It is recommended that the *Havurah* create a ritual, based on the tradition of *Yom Kippur Katan* on the eve of the new moon. It is recommended that on that evening each month the *entire Havurah* come together for a half-hour silent meditation service, to be followed by a communal meal, real or symbolic. During the course of the half-hour silence we shall try to regain perspective on one another. Anything that need be said, addressed to the group or addressed aloud to any other individual, for the sake of reconciliation, may be said in the course of the meditation service.

XI

SOME LITURGICAL NOTES FROM HAVURAT SHALOM

Arthur Green

The liturgical life of an evolving community, insofar as liturgy is allowed flexibility, is a great indicator of the directions of that community's movement and growth. Such is the case on a large scale with the history of Jewish liturgy in America; on a very small scale the same seems to be true in examining the liturgical history of the *Havurat Shalom* community, now in its fourth year. The purpose of this report is to share with some friends news of the religious direction we have been taking, and also to suggest some general and specific approaches to Jewish worship which might be instructive elsewhere.

When *Havurat Shalom* began having regular Shabbat morning services four years ago (Shabbat morning was then and still is our central service), we were very much committed to the idea of "creative worship." That meant, among other things, that each service required careful planning (by a committee of *Haverim*), that specific themes should be explicitly emphasized each week, and that there should be sufficient variety in the service so that we were not oppressed by the repetitious quality of the basic liturgy.

"Creativity" sometimes meant original work on the part of *Haverim*: composition of new prayers, etc. More often, however, it meant a kind of patchwork creativity: finding sources, both Jewish and non-Jewish, which could be added to the liturgy to provoke thought and inspiration. The poetry of Rilke, Eliot, Cummings, and others combined with passages from Agadah and Hasidut; musical selections (a phonograph was permitted) from as far afield as Beethoven, Stravinsky, and the Incredible String Band became parts of Shabbos.

I do not mean to put this down, though, as will be seen, we have moved in other directions. There were times of positive exhilaration in weaving together elements of our general and Jewish cultures. The String Band's "You Get Brighter Every Day" really *did* make a beautiful *Yotser Or*. Stravinsky did feel right after reading the flood story from the Torah scroll.

The decline of this approach to liturgy in the *Havurah* began toward the latter part of our second year, and is now almost complete. The change came about for both practical and spiritual reasons. First, the practical: It became extremely difficult to produce anything really creative on a week-to-week basis. Even the creativity of choosing readings became a burden. Friday afternoons would be the time of frantic phone calls among the committee members: "Can you think of anything good for this week?" It was found too that governance by committee was not feasible, especially when there was to be one *Shaliah Tsibur* for the Hebrew portions of the service. He would take the group in one particular mood direction; readings by committee members would often be at variance with his liturgical mood. It was then decided that the planning of the entire service (aside from the Torah portion) would be in the hands of the *Shaliah Tsibur*, and that he would be responsible for additional readings and interpretations as well as the *davening* itself.

From a spiritual point of view, I think we reached the point where we realized that we were burdened by a combination of modes of expression that simply did not sit well with one another: a good poetry reading, a good concert, and a good *davnen* just cannot be mingled to produce anything other than a staccato hodgepodge. The choice was for *davening*: poetry was largely eliminated and music became group singing, with and without words. Outside readings are today sometimes used as an introduction to the service or as part of a comment on the Torah reading, but the main body of *Shaharit* employs the Siddur alone.

Much of this semi-conscious process became clear to us in an important conversation we had last year with Alan Grossman, of the English Department at Brandeis, who spoke to the *Havurah* on "Poetry and Prayer." We came to realize there that poetic experience and liturgical experience differ deeply from one another; the former is deeply personal and private, the latter communal and public. Poetry can celebrate a moment in itself; the task of liturgy is, by evoking its myth-structure, to bind that moment to eternity. We have come to realize that ridiculously poor poetry (*eyn kelohenu, adirey ayumah,* etc.) can be great liturgy *davke* because of its repetitive quality and its power to evoke group response, while a magnificent poem can simply fall flat as liturgy.

Now let me turn to a brief description of our current liturgical patterns. Our current weekly liturgy revolves around three events: *Kabbalat Shabbat, Shaharit* on Shabbat morning, and *Seudah Shlishit.* The public is invited only to the Shabbat morning service, though of course anyone who attends the other two events is welcome. But in tone *Kabbalat Shabbat* and *Seudah Shlishit* are more intimate moments for the *Havurah* "family"; on Shabbat morning we *Haverim* are in a minority.

Kabbalat Shabbat (before dinner), said by candlelight, begins with a few moments of meditation and *nigun* singing (often *Yedid Nefesh*) and then proceeds into the regular Hebrew liturgy. The Psalms are usually chanted *shtibl*-fashion in a rather loud cacophony; there is a real build-up of intensity climaxing at *Lekhah Dodi.* That is the focal point of the service, sung to various tunes but always with great intense involvement. *Ma'ariv* is quiet, rising to outcry only for *Shma Yisrael,* and concludes with a *nigun* after the *Amidah.* The *nigun* there is important; it allows for a release and downward flow after the service; it takes us from *Amidah* to *"Gut Shabbos"* without abruptness. The passages after the *Amidah,* on the other hand, are seldom recited—they seem to make the service too long, or rather to draw it out beyond its moments of greatest power, where we feel it should be left.

Shabbat morning worship begins at 10:30 (a reasonable hour

for a *shul* of young people—but a bit late for this early riser's personal taste), and lasts about two hours. I should say that throughout our liturgy there is no emphasis on "getting through" quantity of material. We much prefer an abbreviated service to a rushed one; if the *nigun* around *El Adon* goes on for ten minutes, that can be a highlight of the service.

The service begins with a preparation period: that can be a *d'var Torah*, a reading a *nigun*, some selections from the Psalms in the *Siddur*, or some combination of the above. It is assumed that the *shatz* has thought this out, and really is leading the group into the particular mode of that week's *davening* as he sees it. *Shaharit* itself begins with *Nishmat* and goes through the *Amidah*. The leader may choose to *daven* for a while from the English rather than the Hebrew page, he may (and usually will) intersperse the *tefillah* with wordless *nigunim*, he may offer some interpretation of a particular passage, he may tell a relevant story at some point. All this is highly informal; obviously the *Haverim* place great trust in the *Haver* who has volunteered to lead them that week.

A few words about our Shabbat-morning congregation: we generally have seventy-five to a hundred people, mostly of college age. More than half are familiar enough with Hebrew liturgy to follow, if not to understand. Perhaps a third of the *kahal* understands the Hebrew text without translation. The others are encouraged to sing along with the *nigunim*, to *daven* aloud in English, or to use the chant as a background for meditation. Some obviously have felt left out by the Hebrew in the service, but we try to make up for that by general informality, friendliness, and encouragement. It is clear that we live with two often competing claims: a liturgy that is authentic to us as a *Havurah* versus a liturgy planned for the outside people who come. We try to do it somewhere in between, sacrificing neither personal integrity nor friendliness; it's sometimes a tough balance.

We do not repeat the *Amidah*, but rather allow the *Kedushah* (often the climax of the service) to proceed aloud from the silence of the *Amidah*. Repetitions generally don't seem to make sense to us, and the passivity of the *Kahal* during the repetition would be a burden on the totally participatory flavor of our service.

The Torah is taken out, carried through the *Kahal*, and a part of the *Parashah* is read. We have only one *Aliyah* (Women or couples together are welcome; we have occasionally had female *shelihot tsibur* as well, with great success). The *Aliyah* is read from the scroll in a sort of undertone, and a modern English translation is read simultaneously. The *Oleh* concludes the *Berakhah*, after which the reader will either give a *D'var Torah*, or, more commonly, say just a few words to open discussion on the *Parashah*. Informal discussion often goes quite well, and can last as long as half an hour. It has to be well fielded by the reader (who sits in the middle of the *kahal*), but people often feel free to say both intellectually exciting and rather personal things.

After the return of the Torah there is a bit of singing—from the *Siddur* or wordless *nigunim*, and the service is concluded. We have not felt that *Musaf* works for us—not for any ideological reasons, but rather structurally. Once the *davnen* mood has moved into discussion mood it seems a mighty effort to go back—and hasn't yet really made sense to us. *Kiddush* after the service is a time for communal announcements, general socializing, and meeting some of the new people.

Seudah Shlishit is more of a free-form liturgical moment for us. We have neither *Minhah* nor *Ma'ariv* together; those who want to say them do so privately; for most of us that would be too much. The meal itself is largely symbolic: *hallah*, wine, and *nasherei*. We do it around a long table, in the relative darkness. *Motzi* will be followed by *nigunim*, which can go quite some time. There may be informal *Divre Torah*, continuation of the morning's *Parashah* discussion or, occasionally, a prepared talk by one of the *Haverim*. By tacit agreement the meal is mostly silent; private conversations in corners of the table are seen as a disturbance and generally don't happen. *Birkat ha-Mazon* is followed directly by *Havdalah*, still around the table.

We have become quite traditional in our forms, though not bound by Halakhic requirements. The *Havurah* today is perhaps best described as a non-Orthodox *shtibl*. It should be noted that most of our *Haverim* come from backgrounds where these forms were not unfamiliar: most of us are post-Ramah, USY, day school education, visit to Israel, or some deeply formative Jewish experiences. Those who do come to us with little previous Jewish background at this point seem to fit well into our rather traditional liturgical pattern.

The ongoing struggle for appropriate liturgical forms within the Havurah has at times been a painful one. Surely each of the Haverim, at one time or another, has been deeply uncomfortable with a given service. But that very uncomfortableness is a moment of growth, and the struggle that emerges from it, in this area as in so many others, is what makes Havurat Shalom so exciting for us.

2. In New York City

XII

THE HAVURAH IN NEW YORK CITY: SOME NOTES ON THE FIRST YEAR

Bill Novak

In *Response* No. 5 (Fall 1969) there was a brief report on a new project called the Havurah in New York. Written several months before the Havurah actually began to function, the article proved to be a bit unrealistic. On the other hand, it was Stephen Lerner's impression early in 1970 that "the future of New York Havurah is still questionable. It may develop a total community experience—or it may become an 'after-hours' Jewish study group with the power to grant 4-D's." As the Havurah begins its second year, it seems apparent that neither option has taken place. What has occurred, rather, is a modest but growing step toward an active community group.

The idea for the New York Havurah developed in the spring of 1969. When it became fairly clear that something new was happening in the young Jewish community—particularly in political terms—there were several hastily convened meetings and conferences in the New York area. Probably the most important of these was the Brewster Conference, which was sponsored by the World Union of Jewish Students, with the purpose of establishing whether or not there was a radical Jewish community in the making. Brewster was a key event in that groups, projects, publications and individuals from all over North America met together and discussed what they had been doing in their own communities and colleges. Among the participants were *Na'Aseh* from Philadelphia,

161

Jews for Urban Justice from Washington, radical Zionists from Montreal, the House of Love and Prayer from San Francisco, and *Response* . equally important was the the presence of a good many interested individuals who for various reasons were not formally affiliated with any of the new groups. On the surface, the conference was only moderately productive. The only formal result was the establishment of an office to supply information to all the various projects. Although NETWORK has been somewhat active, the job is apparently more difficult and complex than anybody had realized.

But another result of the Brewster conference was that a group of people began to meet in New York to discuss a possible community-living project for the following year. The meetings lasted only a few weeks, and the participants went their separate ways once again. But the idea continued to exist as a realistic alternative to the organized Jewish community. At this time the only active model for such a group was the Havurat Shalom in Boston, which was in the midst of its first year. What was needed was a crystallizing event that would provide the impetus for people to get themselves together to seriously plan such a project.

That event appeared in the person of Burton Weiss, a draft resister who sought sanctuary in the chapel of Manhattan's Jewish Theological Seminary. Although in the end, as expected, Weiss was taken to jail by federal authorities, the day had been spent in meditation, study, song and fellowship by several hundred young Jews. Many of the participants felt a bond of common purpose and community spirituality, and some were anxious to pursue the idea further. Shortly afterwards, in Rabbi Eugene Weiner's apartment overlooking Central Park, the Havurah in New York City was born. In the time between the formal establishment of the group and the search for potential members, the seven founders were more than a little reluctant to set too many guidelines or make plans for the Havurah. They did, however, agree on several basic assumptions. First of all, and most important, the Havurah was to become a center of study. For some, it would be an alternative to rabbinical school, to others, a supplement. This did not mean that the element of study would be the same as that of any university or seminary. On the contrary. The Havurah was to be at the same time less and more than that. It would be less in the sense that there would be no prescribed course of study, and almost no minimum number of courses. In addition, decisions as to the direction of each course and its teacher (and not every class needed a teacher) were to be made by the students who were interested in that course. It would be more, on the other hand, in the sense that the study would take place in a well-rounded context that would include other activities with the group.

When the group met together for the first time in September 1969, one of the first actions was the setting up of a study program. I clearly remember sitting in a big circle in Nyack, New York, waiting until each member declared exactly what sorts of things he wanted to study in the Havurah. Whenever three or more interests would overlap, the *haverim* involved would meet together to decide on the details of schedule, direction, teacher, and so forth. To be sure, not all of the classes decided upon in September were still meeting in May. Indeed, several never even got off the ground. But at the same time, new courses were constantly starting. Those courses that were unsuccessful during the season had no problem—they naturally came to an end. In other words, to a certain extent only successful classes could be in operation as long as there was no administration to satisfy. Some of the more successful classes included The Psalms, the Minds and Lives of the Prophets, Non-Violence in the Talmud, Jewish Social Movements in Europe, the Theology of the Siddur, and Theological Responses to the Holocaust.

Thursday night was set aside for the communal meal. Originally, it was hoped that the Havurah would develop into a sort of semi-commune. In New York, however, it proved difficult to meet together even for weekly meals. These were originally held in the homes of the members, and were later moved to the more centrally located headquarters on the upper west side. After the dinner, the business of the community would be taken care of. New projects might be considered, and old ones reevaluated. In addition to the monthly retreats, during which the group would spend a weekend together in the country, *Shabbat* services were held every week. As one of the few Havurah activites that was open to non-members, the services varied greatly depending upon who attended and which *haver* was leading the service. Most often, the service would consist of a modified *shacharit*, with good deal of singing and recorded or live music, a small reading from the Torah, and a lesson on the portion of the week. There was generally no *Musaf*.

If one had to point to a single outstanding failure in the Havurah, it would probably have to be the inability of the group to unite for any form of joint political action. To be sure, the Havurah did participate in the November moratorium in Washington, and the group stayed together and shared the traditional Friday-night meal before taking to the streets in the massive March Against Death. But from November until May, when Kent State and Cambodia revitalized the anti-war movement (and when the Havurah was active in organizing in the Jewish community) there was no concerted action on the part of the group. *Haverim* as individuals did take part in various secular and Jewish concerns, such as the Peace Movement, the confrontation with the Federations in Boston and particularly in New York, and various projects on behalf of Soviet Jewry and Israel. For the most part, those members who were politically oriented continued their work through the channels and organizations with which they were already familiar. It is probably also true that the Havurah in its first year was simply not a strong enough body to support political action. This will very likely change as the second year begins, with a very different membership.

Admission to the New York Havurah involves a series of meetings in which the new applicant meets with as many *haverim* as possible. An applicant is accepted if he has a Jewish background appropriate to the level of the group, if he is willing and anxious to extend and explore that background, and, most important, if there are warm feelings between

THE HAVURAH AS COMMUNE

himself and other members of the group. In the beginning, there were suggestions that a project of this type ought to be open to the entire Jewish community, but due to the unique kind of commitment expected of each member, and the importance of the bonds operating within the group, this idea was wisely disregarded.

One of the most frequent complaints voiced both by critics and friends of the Havurah concerns its alleged isolation. Critics contend that the Havurah serves only to fragment an already disunited Jewish community. Friends, on the other hand, often suggest that if the Havurah is indeed such a good idea, its members should be actively crusading across the country to "save " other Jewish youth. Unfortunately, both comments tend to miss the point. The Havurah and other similar groups are not fragmenting the Jewish Community any more than that community is already split in various directions. On the contrary, the new movements in Jewish life are actually bringing together various alienated segments of American Jewish life. The Havurot are saying, in effect, that between the way things are now being done and the alternative of not doing them at all there is another distinct alternative: doing the same things differently. As for the crusading for new members, the New York Havurah was set up by and for its twenty-five members. It may, in the end, prove not to have been the wisest possible action; it is too early to tell. But it would be entirely inappropriate for the members of such a group to tell other young people how to run their lives! Interested parties may visit the Havurah at appointed times, and members are constantly being asked to meet with interested groups and individuals.

By the time this article is published, the Havurat Shalom will have started its third year. The New York Havurah and the Havurah at Rutgers University will have started their second years. Havurah groups or similar projects will have started in Philadelphia, Chicago, Seattle and Toronto. What the groups have in common is a realization that the essence of Judaism and the way that it is frequently studied and transmitted and observed may have little to do with each other. To be perfectly fair, a good many people have felt this way for a rather long time. They haven't all joined Havurot; they will not; perhaps they should not. There is a bit of a tendency in some circles to glorify the Havurah movement as the only bright light in a sea of decadence. That, of course, is nonsense. But seen in proper context and perspective, the choice by some Jewish young people to take these types of matters into their own hands is a significant one. The search for small, more personal group experiences goes on as we begin to learn and seek, together, to rediscover a heritage which, for so many, for so long, has been more apparent than real.

XIII

ALONG THE PATH
TO RELIGIOUS COMMUNITY

Alan Mintz

The editors of *The New Jews* state:

The term *Havurah* means religious fellowship, and is classically used to describe groups of pietists and mystics which emerged in the first century A.D. and in the Middle Ages. The term now applies to several experimental religious communities, most notably in Boston and New York City. The *Havurot* are comprised of young Jews, usually of graduate school age, both single and married. The first group was founded in September 1968, in Boston; the second in New York approximately a year later. Although they do not necessarily live together, members of the *Havurot* join one another often for religious study, experimental worship, experiencing of the Sabbath, communal meals and retreats, and political action. The attempt is to create a small authentic Jewish community, the most important bases of which are interpersonal understanding and serious commitment to the confrontation of religious and moral issues and experiences. The *Havurot*, by their very existence, constitute an indictment of and a turning away from the traditional American Jewish community.

Small communities are often hesitant to describe themselves; their self-conscious identities are always in flux. But in the piece that follows, Alan Mintz discusses the forces and feelings that led up to the establishment of the *Havurot*, and

Alan Mintz is a doctoral candidate in English at Columbia University.

suggests, at least in part, what they hope to achieve. His approach is personal and describes his own experiences in the secular culture, experiences which led him to participation in the *havurah*. He also sketches his personal understanding of the nature of Judaism, and tells why he feels this experimental Jewish community to be so important.

I

I am a religious communitarian. I am interested in small fellowships of Jews who study, worship, and act together in a setting of interpersonal understanding. I am a member of the *Havurah* in New York City.

Such is my identity in programmatic terms. The subject here, however, is not program but rather the roots of the commitment—that is, how, in a very subjective fashion, I arrived at this identity. . . .

The Fragmentation of Community. For any Jew today, including the Israeli, who decides to live in some open relation to the world, the tension of living in two civilizations is alternatingly enriching and lacerating but always interminable and inescapable. Such is one's condition, the given of existence, the nature of things. The ambiguous insights of the secular present and the demands of the Jewish past are thesis and antithesis which will not be dissolved in a comfortable synthesis. The selfhood of the young Jew today must, consequently, be so defined; he cannot expect to exist in a milieu in which his full person can be actualized and exposed, but must accept the realities of fragmentation and compartmentalization. He chooses one group for his political involvement, another for his intellectual growth, another for his religious practice, still another for spiritual search, and so on. . . . To each group he presents an encapsulated aspect of himself to be shared; nowhere must he expect fully to reveal himself.

The emerging concept of decentralized fellowship seeks not

to avoid the tensions of living in secular society but rather to create a milieu in which Jews can grapple together with a shared appreciation of struggle, a base from which to look outward on the world. That is, a setting where personal relations can be formed, based on the knowledge of the full person, where being rather than performance is encouraged. Here, hopefully, the sparks of self-integration and group trust might begin to be regathered.

The Middle-Class Ethos. It is, of course, indisputable that well-off Jewish middle-class society has bequeathed valuable norms to its children: strong family bonds, generous financial giving, concern for education, steadfastness in accomplishing communal goals, etc. The evils of this society are made all the more dangerous and insinuating because they are the perversions and excesses of these same virtues; positive traits become ugly and defensive in reaction to the general American society.

OBSESSION WITH PERFORMANCE. The genuine concern for learning and culture which existed has been transmuted into an obsession with performance in school and before other audiences. Achievement and intellect exist only as commodities defined by the school, artistic sensitivity only as its display confirms the parents' success as parents. "Let my son play something for you" belies something more insidious than motherly pride. Moreover, education can only be measured by achievement in school, not by the presence of intellectual curiosity, critical instinct, creativity, or any characteristic through which the development of the child might be unfolded. This would not be so bad if Jewish middle-class society did not hold performance as nearly the only standard of judging the child's worth. Who doesn't know many smart people who, as children, because they could not be *brilliant* in school, deliberately began to fail, then to lie in order to avoid the anxiety of being discovered, and so on? Who doesn't know men who carry throughout their adulthood a suspicion of their own worth on this account; women who could only see themselves marrying "professional types";

people whose ability to enjoy themselves is mitigated by vestiges of the "only-if-it-doesn't-interfere-with-your-school-work" ethos?

OVERPROTECTIVENESS.   One of the major tragedies of Jewish child-rearing is the isolation of adolescents one from another at a period when the family ceases to affect their values and to be able to hold them by power alone. At this time, contact with other kids is of inestimable importance, as is exposure to alternative adult models, ones more idealistic than the parents. Many adults, stunted in their development and afraid in their personal relations, could have worked out their problems in adolescence if familial protection had been relaxed enough to allow them to spend more time in a supervised setting with other teenagers. If more daughters had been freed for such exposure there would not be so many women who consider themselves primarily princesses.

SUPPRESSION OF THE EMOTIONS.   Jewish middle-class life possesses no language of the emotions, no words to express subtleties of feeling, no freedom from self-consciousness. Where there are no exterior symbols to express interior states, the latter disappear also. If this is the classic plight of Western bourgeoisie, the Jews have done little that is exemplary to make things better. We have nowhere to look for release from the oppressive dullness and standardization of feeling, no chance for breakthrough into occasional joy and reverie. Even the natural expression of anger has been contained in my generation in favor of artificial politeness and even-temperedness. One can only wonder, when such an elemental emotion has been driven underground to brood in black interiors, in what perverted forms it will reappear.

The Desanctification of Experience.   Life events devoid of spirituality, the slithering by of time unpunctuated by holy moments, process without periodic disengagement for overview and resentment, physical acts which fail to point beyond themselves, and the delusion of genuine love in diffuse lovingness—such is the fluid in which we seem inescapably immersed. Even the few extant illuminati think they constitute a new phenomenon and avoid encountering models of past religiosity through which they might enrich and refine themselves. Generally, the reductivist thrust of positivism and scientism annihilates the possibility of symbolic ambiguity; the mass media make all language suspect. Those moments of special meaning that we indeed experience are isolated and accidental occurrences in an otherwise meaningless style of life, nor are we able to create a ground for their more frequent occurring. Even the culture in which many of us exist, academia and the intellectual world, drowns out the spiritual with its self-confident humanism. We have nowhere to look for models, for *rebbes* who are involved in the world but not imprisoned by it, and who seriously seek religious knowledge but are not enslaved by scholasticism and legalism. . . .

II

Although I have never been distant from Judaism in my activity and personal observance, my involvement has recently been illuminated by a series of new realizations which make me very happy about possibilities of the future. Although I shall speak of "discoveries," these matters have been implicit all along. It seems, however, that American Jewish culture, having absorbed the worst of Americanism and the most insipid of Judaism, has conspired to keep these realizations from me in my upbringing and Jewish education, which textually was among the better to be had. A shift in consciousness in the past few years has fortunately allowed many young Jews to participate in a sense of a renewed possibility of personal ties with Judaism. What has amounted to a transvaluation has enabled many to conceive of Judaism once more in images of vitality and richness. My own realizations about Judaism run along the following lines.

Root Identity.   When I came to school, I was impatient with my limited exposure to the world and was eager for radically new experiences. I wanted my life decisions and identity formation to be undertaken out of choice and knowledge rather than ignorance and desperation. It was very important for me then to discover that Jewishness was an irrevocable element in the defining of my being, that my differentness and particularity were part of my condition, givens in my existence. The awareness was different from ethnic pride or the newly fashionable particularism; rather, it constituted the degree zero, the point of departure for the consideration of entry into religious style, communal association, and historical process.

Why? Perhaps the way I was raised, perhaps my Jewish education, perhaps the polarized world of "them" and "us" into which I was socialized very early. But certainly as of late the consciousness of the holocaust has been decisive; the almost metaphysical necessity of my particularity, the indelible nature of my uniqueness have jolted me, and I have come to aver that my lot is with the Jews. What happens to them, happens to me.

But please note that for many this realization is identical with survivalism: the commandment that after Auschwitz a Jew remain a Jew, and the Jews remain a people. If the discussion remains on this level, there is nothing here for me more than regressive minimalism, an increasingly defensive posture which seeks to preserve Judaism as she is and Jewish institutions as they are. That is not my fight. The phrase "what happens to the Jews" does not mean to me "what the world does to the Jews and how they react" but rather "what kind of community the Jews build for themselves, what quality of existence they will choose." The imperative is not to survive in the aftermath of destruction but to create a vital and just future out of the extraordinary materials offered us.

If this is the case, we must turn inward toward Judaism and the Jewish community as the stage on which to play out our social and religious aspirations. One does not like the Jewish community, but one feels responsible for what it becomes. Three areas of action become apparent: sensitizing the community to the social dilemmas of our time and helping to formulate a religiously based response; criticizing and attacking institutions and demanding they conform more closely to Jewish values; and most importantly, constituting as many uncompromised counter or parallel institutions as possible. We seek not defense of the community but participation in its becoming.

A Fuller Past. A most startling discovery has been that Judaism does not have to be identical to the scheme of middle-class values. Even though the two are taken as the same entity today, the equation is not determined and necessary. A new consciousness of the past has brought us to believe that a more fundamental and nourishing Judaism existed, was discussed, and did not need a middle-class life-style and its constellation of values.

The United States has up to now read its past as a series of consecrated values current at the time and, by so doing, has been blind to entire sections of its history. Similarly, the Jewish community has persuaded us to believe that certain periods and tendencies in our history constitute the sources of what is "normatively" and "legitimately" Jewish. Our discovery has been that the Jewish past is pluralistic and multi-traditional, and that no degree of institutional power can label one period or one tradition as *the* source of legitimate Judaism. We now begin the scrutiny of that which was either kept from us or despised as deviant: mysticism, sectarianism, Hasidism, liturgy, religious poetry, the traditions of non-violence and sensuality, the *gemeindschaft* of *shtetl* (small community) life, the Holocaust, and many other areas.

Why have Torah and Halacha (Jewish law) been excluded from the list? Because here our discovery has not been of their existence but of their contemporary meaning. Torah and *mitzvot* (biblical commandments) constitute in our lives the demanding Other, the qualifying presence which commands us to transcend in deeds what is natural and gratifying for us. Torah is the crucial component of the religious scheme which respects but does not indulge the subject.

Politics and Shabbat. I locate myself in Judaism because I find it is fertile to both social striving and spiritual growth; because I find both possibilities symbiotically contained in the performance of the *mitzvot*; because as we recover lost segments of our past and refurbish old models I can feel sincerely grounded in Judaism; because I need a past with which to interrogate and be interrogated; because I want to demonstrate politically and experience *Shabbat* with the same people; and because my *neshama*, my soul, cannot be refined and do right without the community.

III

I have discussed the roots of my commitment, I have talked of needs, pressures, and discoveries rather than programs, projects, and projections. I wish to add a note about these latter categories. I mean by the term religious communitarianism a tissue of independent communities which might be described in this manner: small groups of persons involved in the creating and determining of their communal becoming, who do not necessarily live together but interrelate as whole persons, who aid each other in the growth and actualization of each, who study the Jewish past and draw from its riches in creating their own individual and communal religious patterns, who turn to the world and act on its stage for the realization of Torah, who celebrate together individual and historical moments of joy and sorrow, who are not afraid to expose their children to other adults as non-parental examples, who *daven* together and seek new songs to sing to God, who seek to reestablish ties with the natural world, and who, in the future, will be able to say, "May we be proud of the work of our hands."

3. In Washington

XIV

PROPOSAL FOR FABRANGEN

Paul Ruttkay and Robert Agus

I

The determination to work for the development of a new community has grown out of a reaction to the series of problems facing us as individuals and as members of the American Society. The force generated by the reaction is both directed and reinforced by our vision of a better, more human existence. The manner in which we proceed to make the dream realisable must depend on the relationship between the vision, the generating forces and the facts of external reality. What follows are some initial thoughts about these three subjects.

Fragmentation, disunity, alienation—these are some of the words that describe the most strongly felt problems oppressing us. Our lives are cut up into arbitrary, unnatural units such as work, play, love, religion, secular, routine, exceptional, etc. The present system operates along the "division of labor" notion of efficiency: the product is a squared off blob of feelings and experiences called modern life. We feel no natural relationship between what we are feeling and what we are doing, between the one-third of our time spent "on the job" and the other two-thirds spent living, and between our perception of ourselves and our predetermined roles in society. Above all, we feel that our lives lack the sense of wholeness that grows out of being in an organic harmony

175

with ourselves, with our friends, and with nature.

A second aspect of this fact of non-integration is suggested by the disunity with people or the lack of positive communal relations. Just as the present system fragments the individual, it divides and separates each of us from each other. A system that promotes or values the characteristics of competition, exploitation, and aggression is one that works against the communal values of cooperation, sharing, and love. Just as America has succeeded in amassing vast material wealth, so has it succeeded in tearing people apart and reducing us to a mass of paranoids fighting for a more comfortable survival rather than a more fulfilling living experience.

In addition to being fragmented, alone individuals, we feel alienated from aspects of our personality, our life, and the lives of others within society. The type of alienation we feel is characterized by an inability to incorporate all the aspects of our lives into a total personality. The deeply felt sense that "things" are not real develops out of the inability to relate meaningfully to many experiences we have during any one day. An example of the phenomenon of alienation is found in the nation's love of "antiques" and the use of the word "comfortable" to describe older items. At the same time we are also attracted to new products not because of their improved quality but almost solely because of their advertised newness. One of the very real tragedies of the modern age is that when we have the greatest mental and physical ability to create new things that will serve men in ways better than ever before, all we are producing is more packaged junk. Aside from the fact of poor quality, the significant fact is that we do not feel close to these "things" or, in another manner of speaking, we are not able to incorporate them into our lives.

While it is possible the feelings just described are reflective only of psychological problems besetting a few immature radicals, we think they describe a mind-set common to many in America today (and a partial explanation for the frustration and tensions that every so often burst into acts of violence and destruction). They have developed out of the conflict between the human needs for love, security, and integrated wholeness and the American cultural values of competition, exploitation, and aggression. . . . These values lead people to view themselves atomistically as units working for the accumulation of power and wealth; of course, this is to be accomplished within the framework of a society dedicated to peace, freedom and justice for all regardless of race, religion or country of national origin. The values justify, in the name of individualism, a system where people have no control over major aspects of their lives, where they are unable to relate wholly to their friends and where the items and experiences that surround them are merely "things." Everybody and everything is viewed in the context of how it advances the power or status of the individual and not in the context of how it relates one aspect of life to another.

In an organic culture all aspects of life are related to each other and to the expanding consciousness of the individuals. A plastic culture, on the other hand, produces no natural flows and relationships and no ability to incorporate one aspect of life into another—just as plastic is not biodegradable in the ecological sense. Rather than producing an expanded consciousness or broader understanding of the nature of reality and one's evolving relationship to it, such a culture closes the mind and heart to thoughts and feelings. It produces individuals who are able to achieve self-development in only the most fragmented, skewed manner rather than wholistically as truly human creatures. These paragraphs are meant to suggest, if not explain, why we feel new cultural directions are needed.

As Jews we feel an extra sense of the conflict between the plastic culture's values and the vision of a Jewish communal existence. As an organic evolving religious, wholistic civilization, Judaism is in direct contrast with the fragmented and alienated existence produced by the inhuman values of competition, exploitation and aggression. Through its unique symbiosis between visions of the Ideal and facts of reality (both those internal and external to human beings), the Halacha, Judaism attempted to project the values of wholeness, group loyalty, social justice and individual development.

The notion of individualism was that of each person striving to achieve self-realization by attempting to manifest that aspect of the Divine Presence found within him. Hence each individual's development related to each other's and to the whole of nature through the shared relationship to the Divine or to the Wholeness of Life. This religious or organic concept of individualism lent itself naturally to values of cooperation, sharing and love because the individual views himself as part of a community of living creatures all of whom must be free to develop if the Divine Purpose is to be realized.

In America this type of culture runs counter to the basic forces of society; just as plastic is not incorporable into nature, so the American culture and the Jewish culture (as we have portrayed it) are not moldable. Therefore, the pressures have produced a washed-out assimilated version of the Jewish culture (and for that matter, all other organic, living cultures) that bases cultural pluralism on the types of foods we eat, the days we call holidays and the language of public prayer. The organic sense of community that made Judaism a dynamic force for change and development of both individuals and societies has been destroyed in the "land of freedom" in the name of brotherhood. Rather than promoting cultural pluralism or integration, the American system produces and feeds on separatist assimilation. Therefore, as people who want to develop and live a truly Jewish communal existence we feel an extra degree of alienation from the present system and its culture.

Having determined that change of the present system is essential for not only our liberation, but that of the other oppressed peoples, both within and without this country, we are faced with the question of how we should work for such change. There are three basic ways of working for change: reform from within, resistance against, and the creation of alternatives. Before discussing why we have chosen to emphasize the third we should state that all three ways must be utilized in various mixtures. In determining the particular mixture each person must weigh what he/she wants to accomplish, the forces he/she can muster and those he/she must work against, and what fits in with his/her nature—the last is particularly important if one is interested in a revolutionary process centering about human values. We feel uncomfortable when working within and yet unfulfilled when merely resisting or even organizing others to do so; we feel the need to create an alternative and to work on the development of a communal culture that will fulfill our needs as people while also posing a challenge to the existing order. Aside from our personal reasons for emphasizing the third method, we feel there is a serious problem connected with both reform and resistance. In both cases, the frame of reference is the existing system, so that the individual is lead to define himself within its terms. Moreover, the pressures are very strong in the direction of pushing people to act and think like those they are struggling with or against. Therefore, the tendency to rely on the techniques of aggressiveness, trickiness and dishonesty becomes very strong and difficult to resist. To be trapped in the existing value system would not only be harmful to the individual but might also be harmful to the visions he/she is working for.

Working on the development of an alternative also has many problems which we shall allude to later on. However, its attractiveness stems from, among other elements, the unity of the process and the goal. The vision is a new community where members will be able to work and live together in order for each to develop fully as unique human beings, and which will join with other similar communities in the development of a new, richer pluralistic culture/civilization. In order to accomplish this we will have to live and work in an evolving communal framework; hence, the vision becomes an integral part of the process.

An essential part of our vision is the goal of personal, group, and societal liberation. There are four stages of liberation: three that refer to the removal of restraints and one that refers to the challenges of being truly human. The three negative stages are freedom from physical, material, and psychological oppression. Most of white America (except for children and adolescents) do not suffer physical repression, but Black

Americans and peoples of the Third World still do. Material repression in the sense of not having the prerequisites of survival is rare here, but dependence on the system is a form of oppression that is very much with us. Nearly all of us suffer feelings of guilt, loneliness, inadequacy, etc. that prevent us from fully facing ourselves and asserting control of our lives. The struggle for social change must continue to direct its energies towards the removal of the forms of oppression and repression still practiced by the system.

At the same time we feel the need to begin working on ways to deal with the fourth stage of liberation: the positive challenge of being a full human being. A human being contains within himself vast potential that can be tapped only when he understands himself, is at one with himself, his natural environment and his fellowman. The process of self-realization, or manifestation of the particular aspect of the Divine Presence, can occur only in the context of a dynamic harmony between the elements of each person, Man and Nature. This simple idea is what we would like to work towards.

II

We would like to establish a community that would be dedicated toward the development of a new culture that would address itself positively to the problems discussed in the introduction. As such, it would be an experience during which the members would attempt to relate to themselves, each other, the larger society, and the environment in a wholistic, organic manner. The dominant motif would be the establishment of a community based on the values of cooperation, sharing, and love that would work toward individual development within a communal context. The purpose is to develop an expanding sense of consciousness for the individuals and the community that would provide the base for a new culture.

Another important aspect of the community would be its focus on, or at least awareness of, the development of a Jewish culture. For the reasons previously discussed, we feel that Judaism can best be experienced and expanded in a communal setting because only there could its values be actualized. Just as the old Halacha provided the basis for the organic nature of the Jewish culture, so a new Halacha could direct itself to the problems of a new Jewish culture. We use the term Halacha because of its unique role in sanctifying each aspect of one's existence so that they could all relate as an integral and natural whole. Therefore, we see the community as a place where the evolutionary process of developing the new Halacha could begin. If this process were only minimally successful the results would be extremely beneficial to newly emergent cultures here and to the world Jewish community of which we feel an integral part.

Before embarking on a short description of the present vision, we should address the question of the community's relation and relevance to the external society. First, we view it as a living creative force for the establishment of alternative modes of living and cultures. It will, hopefully, by itself, and as a part of the continually expanding new culture, not only offer an alternative but provide evidence that people can live differently and more humanly. Under the theory of counter-institution building, the creation of a viable alternative will produce tension within the existing system to either change or collapse.

Second, we hope that this community will grow out of and expand on an integral relationship with several urban collectives located in different urban areas. We anticipate that many of the founding members will come from existing collectives and that newer members will come through the collectives. The establishment of the urban collectives is seen as an integral part of the process of developing the new community because of their importance in providing a living communal experience as well as potential recruits. The problems and process dealing with the urban collectives will be the subject of a separate position paper, but it should be noted at this stage, that their establishment and growth is considered vital for the success of the new community.

Third, through the various aspects of communal life to be described we hope to develop and maintain strong ties with groups in the cities and others in the country working on similar problems. In addition, a special emphasis will be made on maintaining contact with the Jewish community and especially those parts of it open to experimentation and growth.

We are finally ready to sketch in parts of our present vision of life in the community. Central to all activities is the notion of the development of a community that encourages integrated, wholistic, organic life-styles. From the vantage point of values, the emphasis will be on the development of the individual as an integrated person able to relate his intellectual, physical, spiritual aspects in a celebration of life. All activities will be pursued and evaluated in terms of their ability to deal with aspects of the human personality in an integrating manner. . . .

The one area of individual development we are most familiar with, the intellectual, is also the one we feel most needs new directions. The separatism from those aspects of life that we consider relevant is greatest in the abstracted realm of academia that we were all forced to submit to. In spite of the many highly negative experiences associated with the educational system we still feel that no community, let alone a Jewish one, would be whole without a learning component. However, if we are to have such a component it must be an integral part of the community in terms of its subject matter, its method of instruction, and the relationship between the participants. Hopefully, the entire community would develop, at least partly, as a learning community where everyone would partake of a continuing educational process aimed at promoting self-development. As an intermediate step we could establish an Institute that would serve as a center for learning about the development of new communities, the expansion of the new culture and the development of strong Jewish studies programs. The Institute would be open to people from without the community who would spend a few months living in the community and studying at the

Institute, establishing links with existing universities as a possible step in the process. In addition to the educational aspects, the Institute could serve as the focus of a retreat center and a place for alienated young people to turn to in order to work on some of their problems within the total context of the community. . . .

XV

FABRANGEN: A COMING TOGETHER

George E. Johnson

Fabrangen is an attempt to reach back into the Jewish tradition to reconnect the unnurtured sons and daughters, the untaught students, with the inspiration of the true Prophets, the beauty of an organically developed 3500-year peoplehood, the power of belief in the Unity of God, in order to work for the establishment of a wholistic Jewish community in America.

Fabrangen is a unique experiment. Begun in February of 1971, it has been open to all, the alienated, the troubled, the lost, but also the seekers and the searchers. It has been a meeting place, a focal point for reestablishing living connections among people in the Washington area, with each other, with Jewish culture, and with God. By open we mean not only free of charge, but free in spirit. Institutions and bureaucracies have a way of crushing people; Fabrangen holds out few barriers to participation, to a sense of being totally welcome, to a sense that people are listening and hearing what is burdening our hearts and souls.

Fabrangen is also direct. Participation can be as real as it is open. The *Kabbalat Shabbat* and communal Friday-night meal, as well as other religious and cultural celebrations attempt to involve everyone, whether old friend or newcomer, in traditional and original *nigunim*, readings from *Tehillim*, modern Jewish poets, essays, and *hassidic* legends. The format is flexible enough to permit spontaneous contributions from source material or from the heart. The key element is *kavannah*, the holiness of the intent or spirit with which

185

each offering of the self is made. Prayer is giving. Love is giving. Love and prayer bind individuals of diverse pasts and futures together in a boundless present.

The spirit of Shabbat envelops the Fabrangen, not only through the *Kabbalat Shabbat*, which is followed by an evening service and sometimes by folk singing and Israeli dancing, but also through the Saturday-morning Torah study and discussion, afternoon picnics and relaxation, *Havdalah*, and on into the week.

In its first eight months, Fabrangen has offered a full and varied program aimed at developing a sense of the wholistic nature of Jewish civilization. Community celebrations have brought between fifty and a hundred people together for such events as a Purim party with an original modern-day adaptation of the story of Esther, two Passover Seders, an all-night study session before Shavuot in the tradition of Moses preparing himself for the receiving of the Law, a contemporary High Holy Days service—for both the solemnity and the joy of the Jewish experience. Fabrangen reaches out and touches young Jews who have not been touched before.

However, good spirit and fellowship are only a beginning, a way of breaking down the interpersonal and personal barriers to realization of a conscious Jewish identity. If Jewish culture is to have meaning, then knowledge of it becomes a pressing need. The Fabrangen Summer Institute of Judaic Studies involved ninety persons in study of Hebrew, Yiddish, Bible, Mishnah, Jewish rituals, Yiddish literature, Jewish art forms, the Siddur, and History of East European Jewry. This development was preceded by individually arranged Hebrew instruction and seminars taught by Fabrangen community members. Beginning in October, an extended Institute will commence, focusing on twentieth-century Jewish thought, and the issues facing American Jews today—such as the sociology and politics of the Jewish community, the meaning of *kashrut*, the Sabbath, etc. for modern Jews. Currently under way is a seminar on Buber, weekly meetings to discuss the questions of man's existence as expressed in such varied works as *I and Thou, Paths in Utopia, Tales of the Hassidic*

Masters, and *Moses: the Revelation and the Covenant.* A workshop in silkscreening is continuing, emphasizing the manner of artistic perception and involving interpretation of Jewish themes. During the past months, workshops in sculpture, film-making, candlemaking, Jewish clothesmaking, and experiments in composition of new Jewish music have been developed by members of the Fabrangen community. Several Fabrangen members are planning to produce a recording of Music of the Fabrangen in the near future.

A Jewish alternative creative and productive work camp is being planned for the summer of 1972. The camp would be open to teenagers. Its closest model is the Israeli kibbutz, but the camp will focus on the need to create a wholistic Jewish community of celebration, social action, and consumption needs, and inspiring projects on social and political problems facing Jews in America today. The camp would create each summer new useful realities: a new building, film, posters, a book, food crop, etc. . . . .

In addition to its more educational, program-oriented activites, Fabrangen has had more open-ended and unstructured activities in an attempt to meet the varied needs of young Jews in the downtown area: a Thursday drop-in center with the aid of a young social worker from the Jewish Social Service Agency; draft counseling on an individual basis; personal and psychological counseling. Draft counseling was formerly done by a paid staff person, available on an everyday basis. Counseling activities will continue on a volunteer basis, and with part-time staff if funds are available. Cooperation among the varied downtown counseling agencies is important to make young Jews aware that there is a Jewish place where they can go for help. Various publicity efforts have in the past come from budgeted funds, and will continue as resources permit. In addition, a Saturday night "coffee house"—with live and often spontaneous local musical entertainment, improvisational theatre, movies such as *The Bespoke Overcoat, Goldstein, Chagall, The Red Balloon, Le Poulet,* as well as original films—has been open for people to drop in and meet others in the Fabrangen building at 1627

21st St., N.W.

The Fabrangen has not only been a bridge between young Jews and their tradition, but also between Jews and non-Jews in the downtown area. Shabbat services, coffee houses, and other activities are open to all, and have attracted a significant number of non-Jews who are drawn to the spirit and vitality of Jewish life found at the Fabrangen.

Fabrangen has a communitarian atmosphere in structure as well as program. Members participate in all aspects of Fabrangen management, from everyday chores to policy decisions. The Fabrangen community meets monthly to make general policy and determine programs. Implementation of programs is coordinated on a day-to-day basis by a six-person steering committee, which rotates every two months, assisted by small committees responsible for particular activities. Members contribute to the expenses of running Fabrangen, but, for the present at least, rely on outside funding to supplement its resources.

There are many entrances into Jewish life and community which Fabrangen has opened to young people, and people of all ages for that matter, in the metropolitan Washington area. It has often been the host for, and inspiration to, visiting Jewish groups and individuals from other cities. The doorways must be widened and deepened if Fabrangen is to be true its name, which connotes celebration, learning, and piety, and means literally, "bringing together."

PART FIVE

THE *HAVURAH* AS COMMUNITY

XVI

THE NEED FOR COMMUNITY
IN SYNAGOGUE LIFE

Leonard J. Fein

Through all of our work, no single conclusion registers so strongly as our sense that there is, among the people we have come to know, a powerful, perhaps even desperate, longing for community, a longing that is, apparently, not adequately addressed by any of the relevant institutions in most people's lives.

The need for community is not something people speak of easily. Most of us cope with our circumstances, take pleasure from the diverse symbols of our success, and recognize only a vague, though often pervasive, malaise, which we are reluctant either to analyze or to articulate. In our own experience, people did not pour out poignant stories of loneliness. Such stories as were told came out in fragments, in bits and pieces of evidence that became a story only in retrospect. Our sense of the matter is that the need for community is so strong, and the prospect of community so weak, that people are reluctant to acknowledge the need, knowing, or believing, that it is not likely to be satisfied. Moreover, it is a sign of weakness, and hence of lack of success, to speak aloud of need. In the workshops that were developed for this project—that is, in a carefully designed and

Leonard J. Fein is Professor of Politics and Social Policy, Florence Heller Graduate School for Advanced Studies in Social Welfare, Brandeis University, and Director of the Benjamin S. Hornstein Program in Jewish Communal Service at Brandeis.

professionally directed process, in which hope emerges slowly, in which support and encouragement are offered freely—people do begin to talk about their own sense of human deprivation. And even then, not all do. Some, to be sure, are silent because they do not share the experience; others say nothing because they have so long been accustomed to segmented and superficial relationships that they can scarcely imagine the possibility of something different.

But the need is not less great for its being largely inarticulate. In the desperate search for warmth, many people are attracted to cultish, often bizarre groups that appear to offer some hope of intimacy. Still more, especially within the adult generation, simply accept the desperation, viewing it either as a necessary cost of modern times, or as a reflection of personal incapacity. Whether the "solution" is frenetic cultism or quiet loneliness, large numbers of people never experience the warmth, the shared emotion, the sense of support, which community provides.

The need of which we speak here is obviously not specific to Jews, although it may be more keenly felt by those whose own memories go back to the life-style of the organic fold-society which characterized the immigrant generation. It is not, in any case, a "Jewish" need, one whose satisfaction depends upon some agency or institution within the Jewish community. People who are prompted to seek more intimate, more open, more organic relationships may look to Jewish institutions for a response, or they may look elsewhere. Where they choose to look, if, indeed, they choose to look at all, depends in part on their tastes and predilections but depends even more on where they sense the greatest likelihood of response.

In a moment, I will have something to say about Reform Judaism's capacity to respond. Here, my focus is with the individual, and the point that wants making is that from the perspective of the individual Reform Jews, the Reform temple appears an unlikely site for the effort to create community. Our survey data show that most people are not disappointed in their temple; the demands and expectations they have of the temple are too minimal for them to experience disappointment, even when they experience alienation. The temple is assigned certain limited functions, notably with respect to the young, and it is judged in terms of its performance of these functions. The large majority of our respondents report very few close friends among their fellow temple members; over a third hold that the temple is a relatively unimportant institution in their lives; most attend the temple quite infrequently. The most important reasons our respondents give for joining a particular temple are its religious school and rabbi; among the least important is that their friends or neighbors are members. And in our workshops, over and over people spoke of joining, without belonging; they spoke of the "new member" problem, of the common lack of interest in making new members feel welcome; they spoke of the fact that the temple seems the "property" of a small handful of its most active members; they spoke of their own sense of non-partnership in the temple.

To complaints such as these, there was usually a response that active membership was always welcome, that those who were infrequent visitors to the temple could hardly expect to find it a home, rather than merely a place to visit. More often than not, however, even the most active temple members among our participants were not prepared to argue that the temple was a warm and welcoming place; there was much to do, but even for those who did much, not much to feel. In fact, the word "cold" was not an uncommon description of the feel of the temple. Like Charles Silberman's classroom, the temple is a joyless place; the house of worship is not a home, except to a tiny few.

At a time and with people for whom the experience of affective community is not natural, how does one set about creating it? Except as a temporary phenomenon, community happens when people share important experiences with one another, of which the most important is the experience of personal growth. But if the temple is not seen as a place where experience is shared, is seen instead as a place where a limited number of services are consumed, then it appears an unlikely place for community to be pursued. And our data show that the primary expectation people have of their temple is that it will provide certain services, such as education, and a place to be on the high holidays, and a rabbi in time of personal need. Beyond these, people expect little; expecting little, that is what they get.

Further, the people we have dealt with call themselves Jews, and their Judaism matters to them. But they are vastly uncertain, in the main, regarding what calling oneself a Jew or caring about Judaism means or is supposed to mean; meanings seem rarely discussed, at least in ways that help. Consequently, the interest in meanings is repressed, sometimes lost entirely. And when, as in our experience, it is expressed, and the quest for meanings resumed, the paths that most people travel are unfamiliar, the maps they once were given of little use.

What makes the ideological ambiguity tolerable, as it is for most people, is the fact that it is not very salient. Most adult Jews of this generation have rich enough a set of Jewish memories that they can act out their Jewishness in a framework of memory and instinct, even where theory is wanting. For younger Jews, whose memories are less ample and whose instincts are more austere, the matter may be very different.

We need, it seems to me, to be concerned not only with a general lack of capacity to deal with Judaism as serious intellectual inquiry, but also with the apparent lack of adequate opportunities for Judaism as expressive, even sensory, experience. Several of our experiential techniques dealt with early memories of Jewish experience, and the richness of those memories was in stark, and threatening, contrast to the present experiences our participants report. In a different context, I have spoken of "an atrophy of Jewish idiom." That concept is confirmed by our temple experience. Even the most highly motivated of the participants report a peculiar inability to match their motives to their lives within the temple. If the most likely translation of Jewish commitment and interest is an invitation to serve on a temple committee, an imbalance between interest and opportunity exists. Yet that is precisely what we heard, and heard with disturbing frequency.

Some people, of course, try to go it alone, creating in their own homes, and, less often, within the temple, a corner that reflects their concern with Judaism, and not only with Jewish organization. More people, it seems, do not know where to begin, or are self-conscious about trying. It is perfectly possible to spend an extremely active Jewish life, going from meeting to meeting, from board to board, dealing with pressing matters of Jewish moment, without ever participating in a substantive Jewish experience, without ever relating oneself directly to the tradition, to the artifacts, to the sensations and the understandings that are the ostensible purpose of all the meetings and of all the boards.

There is, quite obviously, a limit to how long one can sustain a Judaism that cannot be expressed, whether because one does not know how to express it, or because the opportunity to express it is wanting, or because one is too busy with organizational needs to find time for expression. In one way or another, most of the people we met informed us that they had exceeded the limit, that they were themselves dissatisfied by the poverty of their Jewish experience. This was not an easy matter for many to acknowledge. Many of our participants were very active members of their temples, as well as of other Jewish organizations. For them to confess that something was wanting from their lives as Jews was no small thing. It was made still more difficult by the sense that most people had that little could be done about it, that the effort to create new capacities and new opportunities was not likely to succeed. Yet, withal, we report here not a wish of our own, but a clear conclusion of the five professionals who met with one or another of the temple groups. There was much holding back, and there were some who held back throughout; most came to speak of these matters, and, when they did, were often powerfully reassured that they were not alone in their concern. Indeed, it was precisely in this regard that the major support systems which the group fostered were initiated.

Yet, on the basis of our experience, I am not pessimistic about Reform Jews. Having said all that I have thus far said, this may appear a somewhat suprising conclusion, but, again, it is our unanimous judgment. We encountered far to many people of high motive and serious purpose to warrant a gloomy prognosis. To the degree to which motive and purpose normally tend to be suppressed, we believe, and our experience has shown, that intelligent professional intervention can encourage their expression, and can initiate the development of support systems which will forestall disappointment. Put differently: It is perfectly possible to initiate a revolution of rising Judaic aspirations. The question that arises is whether such a revolution is not bound to be, in the end, an experience in rising frustrations as well. The answer to this question begins with the provisions of interpersonal support, which we think can be generated. But the ultimate answer, for most people, depends upon institutional capacities.

The Reform Temple. In the preceding discussion, I noted three major needs of Reform Jews—the need for community, the need for ideological foothold on Judaism, and the need for more direct Judaic experience. It is true that most people do not expend a great deal of energy in meeting these several needs, and, indeed, are often not anxious—or even able —to speak of them without considerable encouragement. Once they receive the encouragement, they speak volubly, and eloquently, and one of the things they say, quite decisively, is that the temple is not especially helpful in showing them the way.

The most glaring inadequacy of the temple is precisely in the area of greatest need of the congregant, the need for community. I have already reported that we were repeatedly told that new members are not made to feel welcome, and that old members relate to one another only superficially. Indeed, our own experience confirms this testimony, since, quite commonly, participants in our workshops would express surprise that others shared, or differed, with their own central beliefs about Judaism; although they had been worshipping or serving on committees together, sometimes for many years, issues such as these had rarely, if ever, been discussed.

Put most simply: The experience of temple membership is only rarely an experience in community.

There are, as I see it, at least two major reasons why this should be so. The first is that few people, even among those who may actively pursue community, turn to the temple to find it. Our survey data, it will be recalled, show quite clearly that the temple is not based on close friendship among its members, nor, apparently, does it foster such friendship. The temple is, instead, a purveyor of services, the most important of which have to do with young people.

Most people, as I have said, do not invest great energy in the pursuit of community. If they sense its absence, they adjust to its absence, for most would scarcely know where to begin to look for it, or how. Thus it is not the case—and I believe this point to be critical—that the temple is seen as less promising a site for community to happen in than some other institution or agency. The gap is not filled by "competitors"; in the main, it is not filled at all.

How, then, does one create a temple that is congenial to community, to which its members turn for more important purposes than now attract them? The way to create community is not to set about to create community. The concept of community implies an organic relationship, rather than a contractual relationship. Let no committees be created that will "have charge" of fostering community; organic relationships grow out of organic experiences, or they do not grow.

In my judgment, the single best way for the temple to turn towards community would be for it to provide its members richer opportunities in the other two problem areas I identified earlier, the area of intellectual, or cognitive, Judaism, and the area of experiential, or affective, Judaism. The process of sharing in intellectual and emotional growth is also, and inevitably, a process in community-building. Few, if any, people will respond if the temple announces as its goal for the next year the creating of a spirit of community; more will respond, and the spirit will follow, if more plausible, and more directly manageable goals, are announced.

That is a judgment which is based on our general professional experience, as well as on the specific experience of the workshops. It would be a mistake to exaggerate the significance of the workshops over the long haul; three weekends, or two, out of a person's time will have only marginal consequences for most, especially where there is no concerted follow-up activity that is encouraged within the temple. But it would also be a mistake to minimize their importance as the first step along the path to community, even though the creation of community was never the explicit goal. But when people come together in open search, and share in one another's search, the seeds of community are planted; if nurtured, they will grow.

The search in which our participants joined was a search for Jewish meanings and for Jewish experiences. And that is exactly the search I propose be extended to include larger numbers, over a longer period of time.

I view this as a central point. In the frenetic pursuit of community which some adults and many of the young seem now to be embarked upon, the rewards, such as they are, are typically ephemeral. The decision to "find" community is like the decision to fall in love; deciding doesn't make it so. Nor have the diverse matchmakers of community done much better; after the initial thrill, the real work begins, but by then the matchmaker is gone. Yet for Jews, as Jews, the problem should be simpler. The way into the affective living community, the community of shared emotion, shared experience, and shared support, that is needed may well be through more intensive exploration of the meanings of the historic, religious, sociological community that already exists. Jews are, after all, not strangers to one another; the task for them is not so much to create community as to extend its scope and to deepen its significance.

Now it might well be argued that the search for Jewish meanings and for Jewish experiences is precisely the search to which temples have traditionally been devoted, and which most members have traditionally been reluctant to join as active participants. If, as we have found, the temple is a peripheral institution to many of its members, perhaps that is because they want it kept at the periphery, and would resist its efforts to become more central.

But it is also possible that the temple, by coming to devote so large a part of its attention and the attention of its members to organizational ends, has trained its members to think of it as essentially an organization, and a set of services, rather than a set of interactions and experiences. We have found it possible to generate both interactions and experiences which quite diverse groups of people have, in large measure, found rewarding. While it is always somewhat hazardous to generalize from experimental results, the test of whether our experiments are, in fact, applicable on a larger and more institutionalized scale is easy enough to conduct.

What is wanted, I believe, is not so much a sudden transformation, as a gradual process of development of mutual confidence and testing of new roles. If the temple announces that it is anxious to promote interaction as well as to provide service, the announcement is likely to be greeted with initial skepticism, even by those who already acknowledge the desirability of interaction. Others will simply be perplexed, uncertain what this new departure is all about. And if people approach the temple as a home of interaction and humanity, those who have traditionally set the tone for the temple will find, with all the good will in the world, that this new demand is not easily met. Special skills may be required, skills not normally available, and exceptional tolerance, as people stumble to find a way, will surely be required. The process of reaching out is a fragile process; in the short run, it is surely safer to avoid it. In the short run, indeed, the temple is safer where it is, at the periphery. But the short run is very short, and, if the price of safety is irrelevance, that may be too high a price to pay even for a moment.

Temples, in their organizational parts, are sometimes fearful that to seek to deepen meanings and to broaden scope, to demand more of their members and of themselves as institutions, would drive people away. Large numbers of people, after all, seem to want no more (perhaps even less) than is currently offered; will a still more ambitious program attract, or further alienate? It is my judgment that people tailor their ambitions to fit their estimate of possibility. We cannot be sure that the potential constituency for a more intensive (i.e., more intimate, more inquisitive, more expressive) Judaism includes the large majority of present temple members, but I am convinced on the basis of our work, that there is at the very least a constituency of substantial size. That constituency, it appears to me, is not so much interested in "more" as it is interested in "different," in the development of congregational styles that touch them and challenge them in ways they do not now feel either touched or challenged. I suspect, moreover, that were that constituency to be encouraged, were its needs to find creative response, others, in large numbers, would begin to revise their expectations upward, and would begin to make the kinds of demands of their institutions—and of themselves—which alone can issue in genuine vitality.

XVII

AN ACADEMIC HAVURAH

Daniel J. Elazar

The *havurah* is now being considered not only as an additional means of Jewish involvement, as it was in Tannaitic times, but even as an alternative to prevailing forms of Jewish religious affiliation, particularly for those who are dissatisfied with the institutions currently available.

As explained by Jakob Petuchowski, one of the leading proponents of the *havurah* idea today, the ancient *havurah* as an institution had its roots in the desire of the Pharisees to devise a means above and beyond the ordinary ones for small groups of Jews, committed as individuals, to observe the precepts of ritual law more rigorously. The original *havurah* movement seems to have disappeared because the standards of observance which it encouraged were embraced by the entire Jewish world and became the standard of practice in Jewish life. Yet, as Petuchowski points out (*The Reconstructionist,* December 16, 1960), the idea of separate *havurot* had a value of its own as a means for close interpersonal fellowship within the organized Jewish community. The institution of *hevra* lived on within the Jewish communal framework as a means whereby like-minded people could unite for specific intellectual and religious pursuits. Such groups as the *hevrah shass* (for study of Talmud) and *hevrah kadishah* (burial society) were examples of this form of fellowship among Jews

Daniel Elazar is Professor of Political Science and Director of the Center for the Study of Federalism at Temple University.

in the recent past.

Petuchowski envisions the reintroduction of the *havurah* as a local and immediately personal means of meeting the challenge of perpetuating the ideas and function of the Jewish People as a "holy community" while coping with the distractions of modern life. Since there has as yet been little success in reconstituting the larger Jewish community in a religious sense, it is hoped that the creation of small voluntary groups of individually committed Jews will serve to attack "the basic problem, which permits of no solution on either the international or the 'coast-to-coast' level" but which "can be solved, and must be solved, on the *local* level" (Petuchowski's emphasis).

Another leading proponent of the revived *havurah* idea, Jacob Neusner, sees the *havurah* both as a means for reconstructing contemporary Jewish life "out of its own stone and mortar," and as a means for at least partially overcoming the universal isolation of individuals that he conceives to be the product of our age. Neusner has discussed the *havurah* idea in two articles in *The Reconstructionist* and in at least two other journals as well. Like Petuchowski, he views the modern *havurah* as operative either within the American congregation, or as a congregation in its own right. Thus the *havurah* is conceived by both to be a revolutionary device, in that it provides a new alternative for Jewish affiliation in the area of organized religion (an area where choice has been limited in American-Jewish life), an alternative that embodies a higher set of goals than are normally required by Jewish religious institutions.

In this writer's opinion, provision for such an alternative is an important step in the right direction. In fact, one of the most promising aspects of the *havurah* idea is that it provides a means of religious affiliation for those Jews who, for one reason or another, do not find their religious needs met in the synagogue as it is presently constituted. Affiliation with the Jewish community at the lowest level is no longer difficult. Even if one avoids joining Jewish organizations, the near-universal desire to contribute to the rebuilding of Israel and the relief of Jewish affliction (or the near-universal pressure to contribute exerted by most of our communal organizations) has brought with it at least minimal affiliation for all even moderately interested Jews through the annual Federation campaign. This means of affiliation is indeed important, since it is already the basis for organizing organic communities.

Partly for the same reasons that Federation campaigns have succeeded, an increasing number of Jews are affiliating with Jewish institutions beyond that level more or less to their satisfaction. However, a small but very significant percentage of those Jews who are sincerely concerned with Jewish life, and who have affiliated at the communal level, are looking for ways to affiliate with Jewish institutions (particularly in a religious way) on a more personal level than is possible in most synagogues today. For those who want more than a simple synagogue affiliation as well as for those who cannot find their place in the contemporary synagogue, the *havurah* may provide an alternative institution.

Yet the *havurah* would be fulfilling only part of its function if it were simply to be developed as a synagogue-surrogate. Indeed, it might serve only to weaken the synagogue without contributing to the elevation of the Jewish community. The *havurah* must imply some form of commitment that will enrich Jewish existence, in the ways that the proponents of the idea have indicated. I use the word "imply" advisedly. It may not (and perhaps even should not) be necessary formally to covenant this commitment, as has suggested. Indeed, by its very nature as more than just a "group," the *havurah* itself may have to evolve organically (unlike study groups, synagogues, or other formalized institutions which must be formally organized, often from the outside). The example that follows is a case in point.

In 1958, two couples (the men were then graduate students at the University of Illinois in Champaign-Urbana, Ill., and with widely differing backgrounds), decided to get together (not "meet") every *Shabbat* afternoon to study. Within three years, the expanded group that developed from that original *hevra* had come to constitute a *havurah* at least in a rudimentary way.

From the original two, the *havurah* grew to include a total of seven couples, though, because of the high rate of mobility endemic to the academic world, no more than four couples were active local participants at any one time. These six couples included advanced graduate students and faculty members from fields as diverse as the biological sciences, the humanities, law, and the social sciences. One couple came from (and has since returned to) Israel. The other couples were all Americans, half from the East Coast and the other half from the Middle West. The Jewish backgrounds of the participants ranged from extensive to very weak. Including the Israelis, five spoke Hebrew, four been in Israel, three had continued their Jewish education on the college level. On the other hand, three had virtually no Jewish education before entering college, and the other four had the type of minimal Jewish education necessary for *bar mitzvah* or the equivalent. The initial religious orientations in the *havurah* ranged from orthodox to secularist to apathetic.

Some of the *havurah* came to the group with a habit of Jewish study which they wanted to continue on a regular basis in Champaign-Urbana. Some came to the *havurah* with a growing commitment to Judaism as a way of life and an immediate interest in finding a personal pattern of Jewish life for themselves and their young children. Others came to the group with only the dimmest hints of Jewish consciousness, the bare minimum that, coupled with a personal interest in being with the members of the *havurah*, was needed to bring them to the group. In no case was friendship in itself enough to bring people into the *havurah*. Several otherwise "eligible" friends of the members did not enter the *havurah* either because of lack of interest or absence of commitment to the *havurah's* ideas.

The members' first intentions had been to form a "study group." It immediately became apparent that the weekly *Shabbat* gathering was not just a "study group" but a more meaningful gathering of four friends observing *Shabbat* together in a manner entirely befitting the day. (It should be noted that, at the time, none of the four was particularly interested in attending formal religious services, though both couples maintained "Jewish homes" in the real sense of the expression).

During the first year, the two couples focused their study on selections from the Bible. Though the more formal "study" aspect of the *hevra* was not as successful as they had hoped, the two couples deepened their own relationship by working on certain questions of Jewish living and observance together. This factor in itself more or less determined the future direction of the *hevra*. Once the bond that held the *hevra* together was based on this commitment to a Jewish way of life (rather than on a desire to study alone), the *hevra* was forced into two implicit general positions (neither of which has ever been directly discussed by the members). 1) The group's study had to be a religious act rather than a purely intellectual one, since it was realized that a combined religious-intellectual interest rather than a purely intellectual one lay behind the members' desire to study in the first place. This meant that new members for the group could not be easily recruited, since a level of religious commitment to Jewish life was necessary for participation. 2) The personal nature of the members' relationships to each other also operated to limit the possibilities for new people to join the *hevra*. While close personal friendship was not a necessary precondition for participation, the potentiality for such friendship (i.e. compatibility in some undetermined form) was necessary.

These two factors affected the *havurah's* membership patterns considerably, though the criteria mentioned above were never formally applied. Even their operation was tacit rather than overt in character. New people were invited to get together (there was no "joining" as such) from time to time and, while the above criteria were never discussed, they seemed to govern the invitations. Occasionally people (usually friends of most of the members) seeking a *study* group and no more came to our get-togethers. They returned, perhaps once or twice, but then bowed out of their own accord, having no doubt sensed the difference between a *havurah* and what they were seeking.

The difference between a *havurah* and a study group was made particularly apparent to this writer in the Champaign-Urbana community itself. For several years I conducted a study group in Jewish history, (sponsored by the local Hadassah chapter but open to, and including men and women from every section of the Jewish community). This group was based on the Jewish attachments of its members but was actually bound together by their common interest in Jewish studies alone. Its members sought their primary and interpersonal satisfactions elsewhere (though in keeping with Jewish tradition, there was undoubtedly a religious motive behind their interest). As a study group, it was quite successful. It had no pretensions to being anything more. Unlike the members of the *havurah*, the participants were not committed (either explicitly or implicitly) to further develop their own personal relationships to Jewish life or to each other through the study group.

After the first year, the *hevra* members decided to spend their study time examining modern questions in Jewish life. It was decided to study Mordecai Kaplan's *The Meaning of God in Modern Jewish Religion*. This text, Dr. Kaplan's *midrash* on the Jewish calendar, was eminently suitable for the type of Jewish study desired by the *havurah*. By blending contemporary modes of analysis with the traditional midrashic patterns of Jewish thought, this book is more than a serious inquiry into questions of Jewish belief and practices. It is, in itself, an introduction to the modes of Jewish thought. The year was a good one. The text stimulated considerable thought and discussion, and the entire scope of the *hevra* was deepened. Perhaps this was the point where the *hevra* became a *havurah*.

The transformation was indicated by the development of subsidiary activities within the *havurah*. Three of the men with better Jewish backgrounds developed a Kabbalah study group that also met weekly. The women developed less formal shared activities, based on their own concerns as Jewish homemakers.

The *havurah's* activities have continued to revolve around *Shabbat study*. While this study was modern in general approach, it was highly traditional in its fundamental orientation to the continuous study of the constants in Jewish tradition as expressed in Jewish texts. Thus the weekly Torah readings and the annual sequence of holy days and festivals served as the central points upon which its studies were based. The fact that this approach evolved only semi-consciously may be an indication of the inherent value of these traditional foci in Jewish life, even for those not rooted in the closed society which nurtured these foci.

In sum, the central function of the *havurah* was to provide a highly personal means for a small number of young couples to regularly meet for what are essentially religious purposes— the study of Jewish tradition out of commitment as well as interest. Though they had no explicit goals, it would seem that their actual goals were implicit in this central function.

If this *havurah* can be taken as an example, it seems clear that the fundamental distinction between a *havurah* and a study group (or any other small group operating in contemporary Jewish life) lies in the former's particular religious character. I should emphasize that in Jewish tradition, where study of the tradition is considered to be a form of worship, any study group that concerns itself with Jewish sources is essentially engaged in a religious activity. The *havurah* differs mainly in that it carries within it the basis for non-bureaucratized religious convocation rooted in a face-to-face community of friends (though one should not overdo the degree of friendship necessary for the creation and maintenance of a successful *havurah*). This non-professional atmosphere is unique in the contemporary Jewish world, which, like the contemporary world in general, is organized on the basis of specialization and bureaucratization even in its most sacred aspects. Indeed, the lay character of the *havurah* should be one of its main attractions for both synagogue affiliates and those unable to find a place in the synagogue. For those who desire a level of direct and intimate participation in Jewish life necessarily absent from contemporary Jewish institutions, the *havurah* may provide the appropriate vehicle.

If the *havurah* were to become a means for people to remove themselves from the Jewish community, it would have to be considered a failure from a Jewish point of view. The essence of the *havurah's* Jewishness lies in its dual purpose of serving the personal needs of its members and at the same time in some way serving the great needs of Jewish life today, the need "to rebuild the city with its own bricks and mortar." This latter task is a peculiarly local one. The American Jewish community provides innumerable examples of how this task cannot be undertaken by a a national office (though the right type of national organization can assist in the task, just as the wrong kind can do it harm). The members of Champaign-Urbana *havurah* tacitly accepted this principle. After the creation of the *havurah*, its members began to serve the local Jewish community in a wide range of capacities. They served as board members and active workers in the local Federated Jewish Charities and other community-wide activities; as leaders of a University married couples group and in the Jewish faculty discussion group; as officers in Hadassah and Bnai Brith; as Jewish teachers and study group leaders. Indeed, there is no activity in the local community in which some *havurah* members were not involved. If a full count were made, it would almost certainly show the highest per capita level of participation in Jewish communal activities of any organized segment of the local Jewish community (second would come the Hadassah study group, which was founded and led by members of the *havurah*).

Without delving into the elusive question of cause and effect, it seems clear that communal activity is a function of *havurah* membership. This is particularly clear since only two of the *havurah* members had a substantial record of community activity prior to becoming part of the *havurah*. It may be that personal commitment, fostered on an intensely local basis, can lead to the desire for active participation in the community at large. At the same time, it may provide the necessary support to overcome the frustrations almost inevitably attendant on community activity. Thus it seems that the development of *havurot* may have consequences for the level of activity in the Jewish community at large as well. If this is the case, the *havurah* idea may really have the potentiality for reaching Jews as individuals, while at the same time rebuilding the city of Jewish life with its own bricks and mortar.

Postscript

The Champaign-Urbana *havurah* came to an end in 1964 with the departure of the last of its members from the community to other academic positions. Nevertheless, the impact of the *havurah* has continued to be felt in Jewish life. The Israeli couple returned to Israel to assume positions in academic and professional circles there where they are active participants in the Orthodox community of their city. Another couple has since made *aliyah* and are teaching at one of Israel's universities where the husband—an eminent student of American Jewish life—is participating in the development of an exciting new program of Jewish studies. Two couples moved to California where one took the lead in founding a day school and established another *havurah*, and the other a *havurah*-congregation in a college town that had never had organized Jewish institutions. (In 1971, he "retired" from the presidency of the congregation.) Another couple were active in founding the first synagogue in Oak Ridge, Tennessee. The author and his wife have been involved in various facets of Jewish life in two major cities since leaving Champaign-Urbana, in one of which they formed another *havurah*.

None of the *havurah* members was or is professionally involved in Jewish affairs. Whatever roles they have played, they played as *baale batim*—householders who serve the community voluntarily. If the sum of their communal activity has been extraordinary, so, too, has been their ability to reproduce *havurot* wherever they have gone. It seems that the two go hand-in-hand.

XVIII

A SATISFYING FORM OF
JEWISH EXPERIENCE

George Driesen

Several years ago, Maurice Samuel argued in a lecture at the Jewish Theological Seminary that the Jewish people are currently undergoing a metamorphosis. The changes taking place within the Jewish body politic are so fundamental, he suggested, that tomorrow's Judaism (if there will be one) may not be recognizably "Jewish," if the referent of that term is a form of religious and cultural life familiar to our grandparents. Indeed, the foci of Jewish unity, the Law, prayer, ritual observance, and a set of assumptions about God, appear to be dissolving under the impact of the resurrection of the State of Israel, the acceptance of American Jews as full-fledged participants in Gentile society, and radical changes in the fundamental beliefs underlying our actions. In the face of such challenges, perpetuating old forms simply because they are "authentically Jewish" is a hopeless strategy, Samuel argued. To survive as a distinct entity, the Jewish people must develop new modes of expression which effectively respond to the needs of today's Jews. Indeed, he said, if we are going to survive, the seeds of these new forms must already be planted in our midst, though over-shadowed by the dominant institutions of our own day, just as the rabbinic academies existed but were overshadowed by the Temple ritual and political life of Israel in the first century.

Samuel said that none of us could dexcribe the Judaism

Mr. Driesen is an attorney in Washington, D.C.

211

which would emerge from the travails of our own time.
Indeed, he was pessimistic about the possibility that the
current metamorphosis would be successful. He refused to
guess what new forms of Jewish life might be taking root in
our midst, though he thought that the Hebrew-speaking
summer camp might conceivably be one of them. Only the
recognition that the Jewish people had undergone equally
radical metamorphoses in the past—upon the destruction of
thd first and second Temples, and upon the initial settlement
of Eretz Canaan—gave grounds for hope that Jews would
recognize one another as such in the future.

Viewing Jewish history in that perspective, one naturally
examines carefully any new form, no matter how unfamiliar,
in which today's Jews seek to relate to their past—especially if
that form excites the enthusiasm of previously uncommitted
Jews. One such modern experiment with the materials of
Jewish experience is the *havurah*. Discussed in *Reconstructionist* and elsewhere, the *havurah* is an informal, small
association of Jews who come together periodically to
encounter themselves and each other as Jews through reading
and discussion, and through ceremonies affirming their
common beliefs and values. This article describes such a
havurah in Washington, D.C. Surprisingly, this group was
born and has flourished in an institutional vacuum, unaffiliated with any other Jewish institution and, until recently,
entirely unaware that other *havurot* existed. The Group calls
itself the "Bible Study Group." Its origin, its activities, and
the strength of its hold on its members afford some reason to
believe that the *havurah*, despite its relative unimportance
among Jewish institutions today, may be one of the seeds of
the new, metamorphosed Judaism of the future.

The Bible Study Group was founded in the fall of 1962 by
four Washington, D.C., attorneys and their wives, all in their
late twenties. Unaffiliated with the local Jewish community,
these couples' only contact with Jewish life was through Rosh
HaShanah and Yom Kippur services which they had attended
together for two years. After Yom Kippur services they met at
one of their homes to break the fast—which not all of them

observed. In 1962, during a critical discussion of the Yom
Kippur services just concluded, one of the group suggested
that they meet regularly to discuss some Jewish subject. They
quickly agreed that a systematic, book by book study of the
Bible would best meet their needs, because several were
unfamiliar with the Bible, and because they hoped to gain a
deeper understanding of contemporary Jewish life by studying
its seminal document. Twelve others soon joined the
enterprise, which became known as the "Bible Study Group."
It has met regularly on alternate Friday nights.

The young people who founded the Study Group all had
spent most of their lives in school, and one was then working
for an advanced degree. They shared an alert curiosity and a
common bond of respect for intellectual attainment, but their
religious backgrounds and views were diverse. One member
had studied Hebrew, Bible, Jewish history, and Talmud,
though not in depth; another had a strong interest in biblical
history and archaeology; and a third had a wide acquaintance
with the growing body of Jewish books in English. Although a
few had had no formal religious training, most had attended
synagogue schools as children and a few had had some contact
with Reconstructionism. The group included one or two
atheists who thought questions concerning the meaning or
existence of God "sophomoric" and a few members who
confidently asserted the existence of a Creator or interpreted
the word "God" in such a fashion that they could claim belief
in Him; but most were uncertain where they stood.

The Group adhered to its original Bible study format for two
years. In preparation for the discussions, each member read
the assigned portion (usually one book of the Bible) in the
translation of his choice. Most also read secondary sources,
among them Anderson (*Understanding the Old Testament*),
Noth, Rashi, and Albright.

The discussions ranged widely. The morality of some of the
biblical characters was challenged, textual problems were
debated, especially beautiful passages were read aloud, and
the Bible's historical setting, insofar as it could be pieced
together, was reconstructed with the aid of secondary sources.

Occasionally, the Group grappled with the implications of biblical events for contemporary problems, sometimes over spirited objections that such discussions distracted the Group from achieving its principal objective, understanding the Bible in its own terms. Then, too, the accuracy of biblical history and the commentator's explanations of troublesome portions of the text were vigorously debated.

The discussions changed the views of some of the participants. One near-fundamentalist began to accept the proposition that some parts of the Bible were allegorical and the likelihood that our text reflects a "layering" of several sources. At the same time, others who had freely accepted some commentators' radical revisions of the text discovered that it often made more sense as written.

After two years, the Group completed the Bible and faced the difficult choice of a new topic. Various alternatives were proposed: read the Bible again (no one argued that one reading was sufficient); begin a survey of Jewish post-biblical history; read some of the classical Jewish thinkers; devote a number of sessions to important Jewish institutions and problems, Shabbat, prayer, the synagogue, and so forth.

The Group made no clear-cut choice. First, it decided to attempt a survey of Jewish history, using Leo Schwarz's *Great Ages and Ideas of the Jewish People* as a text. But that effort was abandoned when the chosen book proved too facile and, in certain instances, too chauvinistic. After two sessions on the New Testament and the rise of Christianity, the Group discussed the Shabbat, Heschel's *The Sabbath* and Kaplan's *The Meaning of God in Modern Jewish Religion* providing the textual background. Since then, the Group has chosen materials at random. *Rome and Jerusalem*, selections from the writings of Josephus' *Jewish War* and *Antiquities* edited by Nahum Glatzer, excerpts from Philo in *Three Jewish Philosophers*, Samuel's *The Gentleman and the Jew*, Hannah Arendt's *The Origins of Totalitarianism*, and Buber's *I And Thou* exemplify the Group's recent discussion topics. At present, some members of the group are urging that it return to its original format of Bible reading and discussion. Others

wish to study contemporary Jewish problems and philosophers. This conflict has not been resolved.

The Group's efforts have not been restricted to reading and
discussion. When the *Yamim Noraim* approached in 1963, a
few members decided to conduct an experimental service at
the close of Yom Kippur, which opened with a "conventional" discussion meeting devoted to the Book of Job and the play
J.B. These texts posed a dilemma most appropriate for Yom
Kippur: the relationship, if any, between suffering and sin. Job
is perplexing, especially to those whose principal contact with
Jewish thought is earlier books of the Bible. For Job seems to
say that there is no relationship between an individual's
conduct and his fate. So does the extermination of European
Jewry, fresh in the Group's mind after reading Hannah
Arendt's *Eichmann*. By contrast, the earlier biblical books,
the Prophets, and the teaching of Yom Kippur exemplified in
the *U'n'tanah Tokef* prayer all seem to say that suffering is
the product of sin.

Following the discussion, the participants conducted a
Neilah service, built around a few traditional prayers and
excerpts from the Reconstructionist High Holy Day Prayer
Book chosen to highlight the prior discussion, to recall those
Jewish experiences which had come to life for the participants
through their year's study, and to reflect a consensus of the
members' hopes and convictions. The group conducted
similar Yom Kippur services in 1964 and 1965.

The Group's study of the Shabbat in 1965 stimulated the
members to conduct an experimental Shabbat service and to
join in eating a traditional festive meal. The service included
an original poem, a solo recital of excerpts from the *Shir
HaShirim*, two rabbinical responsa, and prayers selected from
the traditional and Reconstructionist prayer books. Following
the service, the Group made Kiddush, ate a traditional
Shabbat meal, sang Shabbat songs, danced Israeli folk dances,
and talked about Jewish life and contemporary politics—all
embodying in action the ideas about the Shabbat's potential
for modern Jews which had emerged during their discussions.

Because of the brevity of the services, the freedom to select only the most poignant materials, and the intimacy generated by the experiences and ideas the participants have shared, the Group's experimental services have thus far been highly successful. Some members felt the first Yom Kippur services were the most moving they had ever attended, and a few wept during the reading of "The Resurrection," David Polish's angry poem commemorating the European holocaust published in the Reconstructionist High Holy Day Prayer Book. The impact of the services was greatly enhanced by their relation to the Group's studies and discussion.

Finally the Group has occasionally helped celebrate *simhot* in the lives of its members. One couple invited the members to a *Pidyon Ha-Ben* upon the birth of their first child, and the Group has sponsored Hanukkah parties for both children and adults.

The membership of the Bible Study Group is typical of a substantial number of young American Jews: thoughtful, articulate, highly trained and moving freely in a segment of American society where ethnic differences are recognized, but not as barriers. Despite that freedom, they retain an affirmative sense of Jewish identity. They regard the experience of the Jewish people as their own, and recognize that having had Jewish ancestors significantly shaped their own personalitites and values, partly through formal training but mostly by having acquired certain habits and thought patterns which the experience of the Jewish people has imbedded in Jewish families over the course of many generations. Consequently, these Jews associate compassion for the underprivileged, hatred of injustice, respect for learning, close family ties, and a sense of being partly an "outsider" with the fact of being Jewish, and expect to find these attitudes in themselves and in other Jews. Respecting these traits, they are confident that a deepening of their understanding of the experience of their own people would be rewarding. But they find little satisfaction in membership in conventional synagogues, and, if they join at all, they do so reluctantly, often for the sake of their children. Most members of the Bible Study Group, for example, have remained aloof from local synagogues.

The problem is partly belief. The synagogue's principal adult activity is prayer. And some of these young people are atheists and doubters who are made uncomfortable by the contradiction implicit in their attendance at services, although they occasionally participate as an act of family or group loyalty. Those who believe God exists know that He does not answer prayers, and regard repetitive praise of Him as pointless. Equally important traditional prayers assume philosophical convictions which these Jews doubt or reject, occasionally reflect ideas which they consider unethical, and rarely hallow challenged values which they struggle to achieve in their own lives or which underlie their political and social convictions. The result is that these Jews are frequently indifferent to the synagogue's primary function, prayer.

Coupled with the problem of belief is revulsion at some secular activities which have been engrafted onto the contemporary synagogue: card parties, fashion shows, dances, repeated fund drives, "brotherhoods," etc. Then, too, synagogues have established programs and well-entrenched leaders—usually of an older generation. The Jews we are discussing, like the Bible Study Group members, are young, their tastes and needs are decidedly unorthodox, and they prefer groups in which they can help lead to those where they must follow. Small wonder that few find synagogue membership satisfying and that many do not join at all.

Young people dissatisfied with conventional synagogues for these reasons, but, nevertheless, unwilling to jettison their Jewish heritage, are beginning to organize or join *havurot*, some sponsored by synagogues, others by the Reconstructionist Federation and some, presumably, like the Bible Study Group, unaffiliated. Just recently, for example, a new Washington congregation organized two *havurot*, becoming the second in the Washington area to do so. A third congregation is considering sponsoring such a group, another *havurah*, affiliated with the Reconstructionist Federation has been meeting regularly in Washington for several years. Many younger people have expressed strong interest in joining study groups like these, but have been prevented from organizing new groups by the lack of an essential nucleus of relatively well-informed Jews, such as the Bible Study Group attracted at the outset. The formation of the Bible Study Group without professional stimulus or support demonstrates the *havurah*'s potential in microcosm. It shows that young people who seek the *havurah* experience do so not out of a sense of obligation to the past, and not for the sake of future generations, but for themselves. That motivation imparts vigor to an enterprise which neither nostalgia nor belief in the "mission" of the Jews can generate.

There are several reasons why the *havurah* is particularly well suited to the segment of American Jewry I have described. For one thing, these Jews relish learning and spirited discussion *per se,* and those are the *havurah*'s principal activities. For another, they are caught in a perplexing contradiction which can be explored, perhaps even resolved, in a *havurah*. Accepting themselves as Jews, they nevertheless reject much of what they regard—sometimes wrongly—as the Jewish faith. Through study, they deepen their understanding of Judaism and through discussion they clarify their own religious convictions. But that clarification is not automatic. There is always a danger that study may serve as an escape from thought, a danger heightened by the scholarly preference for understanding a document or philosophical viewpoint "in its own terms," and by the corresponding temptation to avoid questioning its truth or relevance. Nevertheless, contradictions between faith and identity are unavoidable, and the *havurah* provides a constructive setting in which to face them.

Clarification of belief is valuable in its own right, but in the *havurah* a frank recognition of changed beliefs can stimulate a search for new ways of making the celebration of Jewish holidays more meaningful—as it has in the Bible Study Group. That recognition uncovers the need to supplement, if not supplant, conventional services, a need which cannot be met in most synagogues. Those who now go regularly to synagogue testify by being there their satisfaction with the *status quo* and are likely to resist innovation. Furthermore, experiments require preparation by the participants and are unlikely to prove fruitful where the group involved is large and heterogeneous. But the *havurah* is small, its members are accustomed to preparing for meetings, and their intellectual bent both sharpens their need for innovation and increases their acceptance of it. Although some readings and innovations developed by *havurot* and suitable for larger groups may be transplanted to synagogues, perhaps to those sponsoring *havurot*, the principal beneficiaries of these experiments will probably remain the *havurah* members themselves.

Does all this demonstrate that the *havurah* is one of the seeds of a new Judaism? Not necessarily. The *havurah* idea is too new and the numbers involved too small to make such a claim. But experience to date does show that these groups can play an exciting and fruitful role in the lives of a vital segment of the American Jewish community, which has so far largely remained aloof from the "religious revival" of the last decade. The close fit between the tastes and talents of these Jews and the *havurah* program could lead to a multiplication of *havurot* among them. Conceivably, some *havurot* may expand or join with others to support professional staffs and physical facilities to service a new type of Jewish institution emphasizing adult education and innovation in Jewish observance, thus putting the *havurah* idea to work on a larger scale. If either or both of these developments occur, the *havurah* will indeed turn out to have been one of the seeds of a new Judaism. In the interim, these groups offer a satisfying form of Jewish experience which their members find nowhere else, and that is no small accomplishment.

XIX

A PROPOSAL FOR THE UNSTRUCTURED SYNAGOGUE

Everett Gendler

When Havurat Shalom Community Seminary was established three years ago, its founders felt a keen sense of the crisis both in the United States at large and within the Jewish community in particular. The draft, Vietnam, racial and economic injustice, and personal disorientation were evident to all. These issues persist today in perhaps aggravated form, while the deterioration of cities and the massive environmental threat join the list of urgencies. As for the Jewish scene, there was little within organized Jewish religious life in the U.S. which adequately related the resources of the tradition to the problems faced at the time; and that has not changed significantly during these three years.

Havurat Shalom has provided an important alternative for some concerned Jews of the college and post-college age group, but it has not addressed itself to the religious needs of many other Jews, including those with young children. Neither has it been particularly satisfying for Jews with a social activist bent; nor has it related to comparable religious experiments in non-Jewish segments of our society. In short, Havurat Shalom, for all its accomplishments and value, has not concerned itself with the needs of many Jews whose present alternatives seem either to be established synagogues or non-affiliation, with consequent religious isolation. Are there other conceivable alternatives?

Personally, I do not write off the synagogue as a potential resource, but there are some basic problems with the

221

institution in its present form which make it an unlikely agency for religious involvement of a kind appropriate to the coming age.

The present synagogue depends on a full-time professional staff whose income needs are constantly rising. The present synagogue also presupposes a sizable building which, however modest, is still costly to construct, finance, and maintain. Together, these factors tend to make the synagogue captive to an affluent life-style which is ecologically untenable, economically unjustifiable, and religiously questionable. Even a slight economic recession threatens its solvency, and it has a built-in tendency (like all institutions) to become self-preoccupied, financially and institutionally.

In addition, for economic reasons, it must grow to a size which precludes the very intimacy and warmth which people rightly seek from religious involvement.

The religious professionals, especially the rabbi, both enjoy and suffer from being the primary focus of the institutionalized religious activity. On the one hand, the rabbi enjoys great personal gratification from his creative work with services, teaching, preaching, counselling, and pastoral functions. On the other hand, his hierarchical position is a burden as well, making enormous demands on his time and emotions, leaving little time for his family, and tending to routinize his contact with people.

As for the congregant, his own opportunities for personal gratification through such significant religious activities as planning and leading services are few. However talented, however learned, the structure tends to place him in passive relation to the religious life of the synagogue, with few opportunities to share his personal gifts of religious sensibility.

The religious education which students receive often bears little relation to their homes or lives outside the synagogue. They often find little meaning in the instruction; they retain little; the burden of additional formal class hours added to overly demanding school days pressures them further, and their indifference to Jewish learning quickly becomes active resistance and hostility.

Synagogues are almost never selective in membership. Financial needs combine with a commendable spirit of hospitality to make the synagogue open to all who can afford it. This means in practice, however, that each synagogue tends to have such a mixture of people in it that, attempting to meet the needs of all in this quite random grouping, there develops a distressing uniformity among the institutions. Given the rich individual diversity among Jews today, it is sad that particular synagogues do not represent particular emphases and outlooks so that those so inclined might find fuller satisfaction of religious expression in them. Furthermore, in this situation each rabbi must moderate many of his own particular gifts and tendencies in order to be as "fair" as he can be to all involved. This, too, contributes to a lack of distinctiveness in the institutions, and what the rabbi pays in loss of genuine selfhood is hard to calculate.

What I have mentioned should be sufficient to suggest that the plight of the synagogue today is not basically due to egotism, greed, or personal inadequacy, but rather results from characteristics of the institution as we know it at present. . . .

Given the present situation in the United States and in its Jewish community, what significant alternatives to the present synagogue structure might be imagined? There are already some in the process of emerging, with the model of the Jews for Urban Justice especially suggestive. However, this model presupposes a communal life-style which most of us are either unable or unwilling to adopt at this time; or else it requires a physical relocation which again many of us are not able or willing to make. Our own search, then, should be for an alternative which could help us grow toward changes in our life-styles without demanding, as the starting point, an impossible and immediate break with where we are now.

Such a model should be modest in its use of resources, minimize regular travel, be intimate yet not insulated from the larger society, be respectful of all the people involved in it, and utilize the capacities of all. It should relate to the traditions of Judaism but to other traditions as well, and therefore be a possible agency for whatever religious development and change may be appropriate at this period of history. It should also offer maximum possibilities for distinctiveness and spontaneity of expression. In yet other terms, it should offer us some support for our own lives while helping us direct ourselves to other lives as well.

What, then, might such an alternative be like?

Formally, YESH B'RERA? would be a buildingless network of regionally grouped nuclei which would meet regularly in homes of the members for various functions. For example, let us assume that there are three to twelve families in a given area of the city, the suburbs, or the countryside who feel that they share certain religious/societal/communal interests. These families would arrange to meet on a weekly basis. There could be considerable individual variation, but one possible cycle might be the following: One week a Shabbat evening potluck supper at one home, with the hosts assuming special responsibility for the religious atmosphere, table ceremonies, singing, a home service, etc. Other weeks, Shabbat morning services in someone's home (or lawn or at a park) which, meeting at different times of day, might produce quite different moods. ("The raiment of morning is not the raiment of evening.") Still another week, the group might meet for a sunset *Havdalah* service with yet a different mood and focus. . . .

We might also find ourselves collecting and sharing with one another meditative material, selecting appropriate expressive music, using artistic talents to design pages for loose leaf prayer books, writing new material, etc.

Combined with this would be a program of religious-cultural-social learning centered primarily in homes and related directly to the weekly coming together of the entire group. After exploring in a preliminary way some of the religious sensibilities and inclinations of members of the group, both adults and children—N.B.: adults first; no cop-out via "it's only for the kids"—a relevant program of activities for learning would clearly suggest itself both for the children and for the adults, and this could be assisted in several ways.

First of all, we should hope to have a regular weekly session for children of each group, with an innovative curriculum which could be assisted, led, or taught by parents of the group, students from Havurat Shalom, or students from other colleges in the area. The rabbi would be one resource person for leaders of the various learning groups, and the imaginings of all of us might provide interesting stimuli for our children's expressive learning activities (though, in all likelihood, the children would soon provide a good bit of their own curriculum).

Secondly, in order to avoid the segregation of religious education from the rest of life, a sharing of resources with one another could help the religious material flow in and out of the children's experiences easily and naturally, becoming part of the texture of life rather than an element isolated from it. . . . What I have in mind are records of Hebrew, Israeli children's, and Holiday songs which, played at home among other records, quickly become part of the children's natural frame of reference; simple but colorful Hebrew letter projects out of felt or wood, with flannel boards; some charming, easy, and bright Israeli children's books. Shared at story hour before bedtime, or at other times during the day, these will help desegregate the "Jewish" and the "religious" from the rest of life.

Thirdly, for those who feel unsure of their own resources in these areas, support and instruction should be provided. After knowing what we're after and why, we can become very specific in ways of sharing such material and experiences naturally and comfortably with our children. It's important to remember, after all, that children are delighted to learn *with* as well as *from* adults, and that not everything has to be done immediately. It's also important to remember that it's not a matter of sitting down and summoning the kids to order. If the music is right, the sounds will themselves invite attention and interest; the same applies to colors, shapes, objects, movements, and occasions.

As for the adults, besides the discoveries about ourselves

which we shall be making from our involvement in the religious education of our children, there ought to be another kind of relating among ourselves. This will surely vary from nucleus to nucleus, but could be seen as an exploration which draws upon intellectual resources without being intellectually bound. Thus, to share feelings, problems, and concerns of a personal kind, and to follow these wherever they might lead, could be aided by our various learnings and competences as well as by elements of our own and other traditions. To determine a course, a study, or an exploration by internal promptings and personal concerns rather than by external classifications of subject matter would be our point of departure.

One other formal element should be mentioned: periodic gatherings when the various nuclei could share concerns and celebrate together. These gatherings might take place at camp or retreat facilities in the Boston area, and could be either for a Shabbat or for an entire weekend. The timing might be related either to special Sabbaths, holidays, new or full moons, or to occasions in the growth cycle of either vegetation or humans. . . .

XX

FROM THE DENVER *HAVUROT*

Compiled by Ruth Jezer Teitelbaum

Note: The Colorado Reconstructionist Federation, now consisting of three *havurot* of approximately fifteen families each, came into existence in 1967. Affiliated with the Federation of Reconstructionist Congregations and Fellowships, the Denver groups meet regularly for discussions, worship, and study; they hold summer and midwinter institutes, have a program in social action, and otherwise work out a program of Jewish activities involving the members directly and personally in the attainment of the purposes of the group.

They evidently realize in one form the proposal for the unstructured synagogue advanced in the foregoing article by Rabbi Gendler. Documents from the Denver *havurot* include excerpts from the Constitution of the Colorado Jewish Reconstructionist Federation, a newspaper report on an educational program, the agenda for discussion at two Friday evening workshop discussions, and excerpts from a self-evaluation questionnaire prepared by the Goals Committee of the Colorado Federation. These and other documents were assembled by Mrs. Teitelbaum shortly before her death; had she been spared, they would have formed the basis for an essay on the Denver experience in Jewish fellowship.]

1. Excerpts from the Constitution of the Colorado Jewish Reconstructionist Federation

I. Organization

    A. Name—The name of this organization shall be The Colorado Jewish Reconstructionist Federation.

    B. Membership—The Federation shall consist of all present and future Reconstructionist Havurot in Colorado.

II. Purpose of Federation

    A. To promote Reconstructionism in Colorado.

    B. To coordinate and implement joint activities of all member Havurot.

    C. To represent the Reconstructionist Movement in the total community.

    D. To represent the Colorado Reconstructionist Federation within the National Reconstructionist Movement.

III. Eligibility

    A. The Council of the Federation shall determine standards of eligibility for membership of Havurot in the Federation. . . .

IV. Matters Requiring Havura Approval

    A. The following matters shall be referred to the Havurot for decision in accordance with Section B of this article:

        1. Questions of public religious position and observance.

        2. Financial assessments of individual members or Havurot above the annual dues set by the Council.

        3. Any activity which requires for its implementation the involvement of a majority of the individual members of the Havurot.

        4. Issues explicitly involving the public posture of the Reconstructionist Movement.

    B. Manner of deciding aforementioned referred matters:

        1. Each Havura shall have one vote which shall be based on instructions by that Havura.

        2. If on first vote unanimous agreement is obtained

from all member Havurot, the matter shall be carried.

3. If a unanimous vote cannot be obtained and a 'member Havura desires further consideration, then the matter shall be referred back to each Havura for further discussion.

4. On second consideration of a referred matter the question shall pass if no more than one Havura votes *no.*

5. On referred matters that have passed on second consideration by vote of the Council, prior to implementation of the decision of the Council, the dissenting Havura shall have the right to request the Council to call a meeting of the general membership of the Federation to discuss the question. The matter shall be passed if approved by a 2/3 vote of the individual members present and voting.

2. An Educational Program (From the *Rocky Mountain News,* December 30, 1967.)

Nearly 50 Jewish youngsters in the Denver area took a "Flight to Israel" this week, part of an imaginative and creative attempt to teach them about that country.

The youngsters, ranging from kindergarteners through eighth graders, are offspring of members of the three Denver Reconstructionist Federation groups in the Denver area.

Mrs. Betty Lande, who co-ordinated the ambitious activities of some 30 adults involved in the day's activities, said the cooperation of many members of the community and of the Jewish congregations made the event successful.

BMH Congregation donated the use of school facilities at 550 S. Monaco St., and other groups furnished various materials, including airline tickets used as invitations to the day's program.

The invitations were so realistic that several of the younger children were anticipating an actual flight to Israel.

"The imaginary day started off with a 'take-off' by jet, accompanied by actual jet plane sounds on tape recording,"

Mrs. Land explained. "We had all the sound effects, pilots, stewardess, etc."

An "in-flight movie" gave the youngsters a pictorial view of Israel, the land they would be visiting for the day.

"We wanted to give the children both the facts and the feeling of life in Israel," Mrs. Lande added. "We wanted them to know the people, hear the sound of the Hebrew language, listen to and sing the music and take part in the dances of Israel. We were particularly interested in the emotional aspects. An action-oriented experience is what we were after."

The children were divided into three groups according to age and each group took part on their own level of experience and ability.

Dedication of the Reconstructionist group was seen in the fact that many of the fathers took the day off to help out.

The groups drew huge maps, starting with "pre-June 6" maps and updating them according to the results of the Israeli-Arab war; they put on various skits to help them understand the geography, economy and history of Israel; dolls were used to illustrate both the history of the nation and the people who came there to found the state.

"An afternoon in the kibbutz" was a popular activity as the children tried to live the life of children in these famous Israeli work settlements. Slide pictures took them on a tour of Israel's cities.

"Each group, according to their ability to understand, considered what Israel means to them as American Jews," Mrs. Lande explained.

The questions for which the groups were seeking answers included: "Why was there a need for Israel? What does Israel look like? Where did the people come from? What do the Israelis look like? What are some of Israel's problems?"

"The program certainly was successful as far as the children were concerned," Mrs. Lande said.

"They were very enthusiastic. We will evaluate the program and if we believe it turned out well it might lead to other similar programs for the children."

3. Two Friday Evening Workshops

A. Humanistic Implications in Ethics and Values

Directions: Change the following statements until *all* members of your workshop agree with the wording.

1. The Ten Commandments are the Jews' basic source of ethics and values and are as valid today as they ever were.

2. In some aspects of life there may be room for "ethical relativity," but when it comes to "pre-marital" sex standards or "adultery" there is only one correct position. . . .

3. Honesty is one value that is clearcut and does not become clouded by "relative" situations—you're either honest or you're not.

4. Giving charity is a moral action even if the motivation for giving is a response to group or social pressure.

5. If someone doesn't want to utilize his talents and abilities, that is his business alone, and none of ours.

6. The decision to smoke or not is based on an individual's personal needs.

7. Man's commitment to action on a moral principle supersedes personal or family sacrifice.

8. One problem with "Humanistic" ethics is that it gives people a good excuse to do what they want, rather than what they know they should.

9. We have a moral right to hate Germans because of what they did to the Jewish people.

B. Humanistic Implications in Interpersonal and Inter-group Relations

1. How does the varying commitment by individuals to a group affect the operation of the group?

2. Before public action in controversial areas can be taken by a *Havurah*, should unanimity be necessary?

3. Do we feel truly free to express our feelings, concerns, criticisms, and suggestions within and between our groups?

4. What should be the role of the Havurah and/or the Federation in the area of social action?

4. Goals of the Colorado Reconstructionist Federation (Excerpts from a Questionnaire, November 26, 1969.)

. . . . Continuously during the life of any movement or organization, it is imperative that we all critically review our goals, objectives, and in particular, the degree to which our current activities and organizational format accomplish our personal objectives. In order to make such an evaluation for the Colorado Reconstructionist Federation and all its member Havurahs and their members, it is extremely important that everyone complete this questionnaire. . . .

The primary purpose of this questionnaire is to obtain information from a variety of sources which will then be summarized and compiled, both in a statistical manner and in some areas in a subjective manner, and present it both to the Colorado Reconstructionists Federation and to each individual Havurah for informational purposes. Hopefully, the response to this questionnaire will help clarify the areas where there is a consensus of objectives within our group and also help give us direction concerning the best approach to accomplishing those objectives. . . .

1. The following are paired samples of possible Federation and Havurah activities. For each pair, please circle the activity or characteristic that you feel is most important.

Federation:
Formal/Informal

Consensus/Majority
Roberts' Rules/Informal
Delegate Assembly/Town Meeting
Governing Body/Coordinating Body
Doing Something/Planning to Do Something
Colorado Federation/National Federation
Committees Decide What They Can Do/Federation Sets
Policy for Committee
Most Important Group I belong to/Another Group I
belong To
A Very Important Group I belong To/Another Group I
belong To

Havurah:
Informal/Formal
Majority/Consensus
Havurah/Federation
Business/Study
Activity/Business
Activity/Study
Getting Something Done/Working Out Best Way for
Doing Something

Participate in Decision Making/Delegate Decision Making
Most Important Group I Belong To/Another Group I
Belong To.

A Very Important Group I Belong To/Another Group I
Belong To

2. The following are possible activities that the local Reconstructionist movement could participate in. Please rank in the order that you think are most important.
    1. Education for children
    2. Religious services
    3. Weekend institute

4. Taking a stand on important social issues
5. Activities that try to improve the Denver Jewish Community
6. Orientation activities for interested people
7. Education for adults
8. Holiday observances

3. The following are attitudes that may have attracted you to Reconstructionism. Please rate as very important, important, or not important to you.

1. God concept
2. Jewish Humanism
3. Concern for implementing the democratic process in the Jewish Community
4. Concern for implementing the democratic process in our lives
5. A pragmatic Jewish philosophy
6. Fellowship
7. A place to meet people
8. A group in which each person can be involved in shaping the direction of the group
9. A dissatisfaction with existing institutions in the Jewish Community
10. To help reconstruct the Jewish Community
11. A group in which we can participate as Jews for ourselves and our children
12. A place where I feel I can belong in the Jewish Community

4. Please rank, in the order that you think are the most important, the activities that you personally would want to participate in.

1. Membership orientation meeting
2. Study meeting
3. Social action meeting
4. Holiday gathering
5. Religious service
6. Retreat

7. Planning childrens' education program
8. Meeting to evaluate the structure of the Denver Jewish Community. . . .

5. Rank in order of importance *to you* the following goals of education.
1. Jewish survival
2. Positive attitude toward Judaism
3. Naturalistic approach to religion
4. Humanism
5. Development of the individual to one's fullest potential
6. Synagogue skills
7. Develop a sense of identification with the Jewish people
8. Making tradition relevant
9. Others

PART SIX

CONCLUSION

XXI

HAVURAT SHALOM:
A PERSONAL ACCOUNT

Bill Novak

I. ORIGINS

The recent appearance on the American scene of a variety of new Jewish groups, many of which describe themselves by the term *havurah*, represents the most intense form and expression of the budding Jewish counterculture. Despite the fairly widespread publicity that has been accorded these groups—which, for the most part, they have sought to avoid—their number is far less than is commonly supposed. Early in well-known, a wide variety of new Jewish forms and projects in existence, only a handful of young American Jews are actively involved in a serious quest for Jewish community. More recently, they have been joined by several groups of families in eastern suburban localities. The first of the new attempts to build a Jewish community, in chronology and probably in influence, was Havurat Shalom Community, which began in 1968 in Cambridge, Mass., and is currently located in nearby Somerville. Its sister group, the Havurah in New York City, began a year later.

More recently, two other groups have become well known, and although neither calls itself a *havurah*, both the Fabrengen Community in Washington and the House of Love and Prayer in San Francisco are original and important attempts to create new forms of communal Jewish living. Smaller, less intense groups using the name *havurah* can now be found in such places as Ann Arbor, Ithaca, Cleveland, and in several other college centers, while the Reconstructionist movement has for many years used this term to describe cells of Jews who meet together regularly for study and worship. It must be understood that *havurah*, the Hebrew term for fellowship, is neither a new word nor is it the property of any one person or group, and is therefore used freely by a variety of rather different entities. My purpose here is to describe one of them, Havurat Shalom, which will hereafter be referred to as the Havurah.

The sequence of events and the social context which produced various new Jewish forms, including the *havurot*, a variety of publications (over fifty have been started since 1967, and most of them continue to publish), and numerous political and cultural concerns, have been discussed in detail elsewhere.* Such phenomena as the traditional third-generation's response to that which, in many cases, had belonged to their grandparents, and was then ignored by *their* children, as well as the much commented upon change in the civil rights movement from a goal of universal integration to Black Nationalism, which in turn set the stage for other ethnic and minority groups, including Jews, to assert their own cultures and interests—all this is by now fairly obvious. So too is the vital role played by Israel, and the 1967 war in particular, and the subsequent experience of young Jews who felt betrayed by the New Left's new-found hostility toward Israel.

But another social context has been less well understood. It has to do with what Charles Reich attempted to describe in *The Greening of America* (New York, 1971), a much maligned but nonetheless useful account of the differences between the generations, or what Philip Slater has written about in *The*

---

*See my "The Making of a Jewish Counter Culture," *Response* #7 (Spring-Summer, 1970); "The Greening of American Jewry," *Judaism* (Spring, 1971); "On Relevance, and Beyond," *Judaism* (Summer, 1971); and such publications as *Response*, *Genesis Two* (Boston), *The Jewish Radical* (Berkeley), and dozens of others. *See also* the movement's first two books: Alan Mintz and James Sleeper (ed.), *The New Jews* (New York, 1971), and Arthur Waskow, *The Bush is Burning!* (New York, 1971).

Pursuit of Loneliness (Boston, 1970), a portrait of a frightened and fragmented nation. Both of these works are concerned with the problem of modern alienation and the break-up of the human community as a result of technology and modernizations. More importantly, both works describe various solutions which have been undertaken in the effort to regain community. As both authors are aware, many young Americans are no longer concerned with a revolution conceived of in purely physical, or political terms, as was popular in the middle and late 1960's, but are instead coming to realize, as the Beatles put it, that "the movement you need is on your shoulders." In other words, they are saying and understanding that a "revolution" need not necessarily mean the physical transformation of a society, but might also signify the improvement of its collective spirit and soul. This can only come about through *individual* change and growth, through the realization that you can change the world by changing *your* world. It is probably not a coincidence that only a generation born into relative affluence could afford to turn its back on the traditional search for "security," and could instead decide to seek for itself "meaning." But whatever the explanation, it is evident that a new approach to society is being developed by the working out of a number of small, social experiments in communal living.

If a single concept lies at the heart of this new consciousness, it is the awareness that size is not a *measure* of success, but as often as not, serves as an *impediment* to significant human achievement. On the other hand, a fragmented, technocratic and complex society tends to isolate individuals into lonely, frightening situations. At the same time, however, the last twenty or thirty years in American and especially in Jewish life have seen the building up of large organizations, centralized institutions, and huge networks of power and capital. The reaction against corporate capitalism being taken to its logical limits is what Reich calls Consciousness III. Its most visible manifestation has been the coming together of small groups of people all over America especially, but not only, in communes. The Jewish movement, incidentally, has as yet produced *no* communes, although there have been several experiments in building communities. Above all, young Jews, and in some cases their parents as well, have come to understand that alienation and loneliness in society cannot be effectively resisted by large, impersonal organizations, which intensify rather than alleviate the problems, but instead by small, intimate groups and communities of no more than three or four dozen individuals.

The rhetoric of the late 1960's, of the tearing down of walls and the smashing of institutions, generally produced more heat than light. And although it was not taken seriously by the vast majority of the young, there was nevertheless a widespread notion that what appeared to be bad in society had to be physically, even forcibly, altered. A more benevolent attitude has come into acceptance, however; one that is less self-destructive and more positive in its approach. It is an idea which says, in effect, that institutions which seem to be useless, or even negative in their effects on society ought not be torn down, destroyed or even occupied, but instead should be simply bypassed. If there is a stone wall in your way, it is far easier and more productive to walk around it, by changing your own course, than to attempt to knock it down. And, it has been discovered, that in the course of walking around it you may see things you never noticed before. So we have witnessed the appearance of a variety of counter-institutions, and a host of new attempts to create more personal, more humane, more democratic and ultimately more experiential forms of living.

In terms of the Jewish situation, things are slightly more complicated. Those who wanted a community that was in some sense overtly Jewish were obviously interested not only in the ideal of community, but in certain other Jewish ideals as well: the study of traditional texts, the creation of a religious life-style, a desire to improve the Jewish condition, and so forth. It was almost inevitable that the new forms of Jewish community, in addition to being small and autonomous, would have to represent an organic integration of the various functions normally served by such existing institutions as synagogues, Hebrew Schools, colleges and seminaries, libraries, and cultural centers.

In their desire to respond to the conditions of the time in some specifically Jewish way, the founders of these new communities naturally turned their attention to alternative kinds of Jewish communities. The most obvious example was, of course, the *shtetl* of Eastern Europe. However, this particular model represented not a particular community of consent, but a way of life for all Jews within its confines. A model experienced by many of the founders of both the Boston and New York *havurot* was the Camp Ramah experience. Until the *havurot*, there was never a successful translation of the Ramah summer experience into an urban environment. Not that Ramah was established as a criterion for the ideal Jewish community; there were many criticisms of Ramah on the part of its staff members, most of whom left Ramah within a year or two of joining the *havurot*. Zalman Schachter's proposal for a community called *B'nai Or*, which had appeared in *Judaism* in 1964, served as a further incentive, especially for those who tended to favor a rural setting for their community.

In the formation of the New York Havurah in particular, another model was seriously examined: the particular effort to create a community on the part of a few individuals in the first century who created a form also known as *havurah*. It was Jacob Neusner who brought this ancient experience to the attention of those who were, in some sense, to duplicate it. In his seminal study of Judaism and its social setting in the first century,* Neusner describes a group known as *havurah*, which had two distinct versions. One, known as the Qumran group, represented an escape to the wilderness, an abandonment of normative, corrupt society. Neusner calls this group "revolutionary Utopianism." The other option, which the author terms "Social Utopianism," was the direction taken by

---

*Jacob Neusner, *Fellowship in Judaism, The First Century and Today* (London, 1963).

some of the Pharisees in Jerusalem who, following the dictum of Hillel, "Don't separate yourself from the community . . ." (*Avot*, 2:5), retained a basically urban community, but one which practiced an exclusivity which was ritual rather than geographic.

Today's *havurot*, it must be said, do not in any way claim to represent an authentic version of that ancient form, despite the interest on the part of many members in this and other early social experiments. Both the Boston and New York groups, for instance, might easily have located themselves in a rural setting, but in both cases it was decided that it was more important to remain in physical proximity to the Jewish and general communities, even if one did not choose to deal with either on a daily basis. But if the modern *havurot* do not resemble the Qumran group, neither are they very much like the Jerusalem Pharisees, at least in their major concerns. For as Neusner describes the latter, their chief emphasis appears to have been in the realm of ritual preparation:

> The particular emphasis on ritual purity and tithing indicates that the Havurah was fundamentally a society for strict observance of laws of ritual cleanliness and holy offerings. This was, indeed, all it might have been. Membership in the association could be achieved only through adherence to a pattern of actions which demonstrated devotion to neglected commandments and traditions of Judaism. In urban society deeds alone truly marked the man, rather than any commitment of faith or intellect. The social relations in the city, brief and random at best, could not manifest any profound virtue of mind or heart. They could, however, serve as a tentative measure of a man's willingness to serve God in ways held particularly significant. The fellowships were open to hypocrites, it is true, and the Gospels and Rabbinic sources give evidence that a faith expressed only through deeds might represent in the end only a meaningless pattern of naked gestures. Such a perplexity troubled the Pharisaic fellows and their heirs. *

Fellowship in Judaism, pp. 18–19.

In this respect, too, the modern *havurot* are markedly different. While in no sense abandoning Jewish ritual life as it currently stands, they have attempted to invest with meaning many aspects of the ritual which might, in time, have become merely routine gestures. Of course, not all of Jewish ritual or observance can be explained in rational terms, and the members of the *havurot* are struggling with the realization that religion is a proclamation to the world that the realm of the rational has distinct limitations. (This is one reason, for example, that many young Jews who have been influenced by the writings of Mordecai Kaplan have nevertheless not found themselves able to join the movement he created.) At the same time, none of the *havurot* has gone out of its way to uncover little-known or obscure rituals, although the patterns of observance are treated with a great deal of respect, and are accorded a large measure of beauty, care, and dignity.

So much for what the modern *havurot* are *not*; what are they? Realizing that the ancient forms would not provide fully adequate models for the contemporary situation, Neusner decided to turn his attention to the issue of building Jewish communities in modern society. By combining traditional Jewish themes with an appreciation of modern problems, he devised an understanding of what Jewish fellowship ought, perhaps, to represent in our own time:

> It is an effort among individuals to create a community of people who share with one another the most precious possession, namely life, and choose to seek the fraternity of others among whom life . may be sanctified. It is, quite specifically, not merely an effort to serve some cause, though good causes may be well served indeed, but a commitment of one soul to another, and of all to God. It is therefore not a purely social group, but a *way* some men may take together, united for strength along the road. *

---

* Jacob Neusner, *Judaism in the Secular Age* (New York, 1970), pp. 85–86.

In an age when ritual purity no longer carries the force it once had, Neusner's description of the basis for Jewish religious community is most appealing. In addition, he suggests several broad categories of concern which might serve to characterize a modern *havurah*: the effort and cultivated ability to engage in prayer; a program of study, centered around, but not limited to, traditional Jewish texts; a sense, which is acted upon, of the demands made by Judaism on individuals and groups in the areas of compassion and social welfare; a sharing together of the life-cycles of the community, its members, and the Jewish and natural calendars; and (this less emphatically), a keeping of records which document in some form the experience and growth of the community. It is because this last category has been largely ignored by Havurat Shalom (for understandable reasons) that this description is at once less fully accurate and more important than it deserves to be. While not intended in any sense to be a history of the *Havurah*, what follows will attempt to take into account both historical and personal perspectives, although the latter, of course, will constitute the dominant viewpoint throughout.

II.   THE RELIGIOUS DIMENSION

Few words have become so distorted and confused in modern English usage as those having to do with man's spiritual search, and his desire to communicate more honestly and more intimately with other men, and with the non-human forces at work in the universe. About three years ago, several of us who were then involved in building the New York *Havurah* were invited to Cleveland to speak with a group of potentially interested adults. The group consisted for the most part of young parents who, like ourselves, had become restless and cynical toward synagogue-based life and activities. We spoke to them about our plan to establish a small, intense, religious community, but it soon became clear that they were not understanding our ideas. For to their generation, only ten years older than our own, the word "religious" was so threatening, so completely bound up in its associations with dogma, fundamentalism, and organization, that true dialogue around that particular concept was virtually impossible.

The individuals who formed Havurat Shalom also used the term "religious" unashamedly. This did not mean that they necessarily held in common a shared theology, or that they agreed about the nature and relative importance of Jewish observance. Likewise, the problem of a belief in God, while never easy, did not have to be *resolved* before one could speak meaningfully of religious acts, or attempt to create a religious society. "Religious" was more attitudinal than theological; it described a tone rather than a content.

The God-is-Dead controversy had come and gone, affecting Jews primarily in terms of the debate over the God of history, especially in light of the Holocaust. But in the late 1960's another element of religious life became publicly observable, as the activist strands of American society experienced a resurgence of symbolic form, and appreciation of the power of religious ritual, a commitment that the society had to move beyond a politics that was essentially strategic and horizontal. What took place, in the words of one participant, was that

> . . . it became clear that something remarkable was happening among young Americans. Religion had become not only an arena of insurgency, but a *form* of insurgency. . . . People like Allen Ginsberg were trying to exorcise the Pentagon as well as besiege it. People like the Bread and Puppet Theater were handing home-baked bread around between the actors and the audience. People like an Episcopal Bishop were holding Mass among bleeding, crying students at Grant Park during the Chicago upheaval. People like Dan Berrigan were celebrating a new religious ceremony: burning the records of the Selective Service System. Precisely on the Left, where for a century the automatic dogma had been that religion was the opiate of the people, religion had turned from a narcotic to an awakener. My

own inward experiences during the spring of 1968 were not idiosyncratic: I was sharing them with scores of thousands of other Americans. Including young Jews. *

Along these lines, it is important to note that the initiating event of the New York *havurah*, the moment that made the need for such a group precisely clear, was the highly successful and emotionally moving sanctuary afforded to Burton Weiss, a draft resister. In the chapel of the Jewish Theological Seminary, Weiss remained in the company of friends, teachers, and well-wishers until the federal marshals came to take him away.

The religious development of Havurat Shalom followed very different lines. One reason for this was the high degree of political awareness in Manhattan, which contrasted with the less hectic pace of New England. More important, however, was the fact that the personalities in the two groups were very different. And although Albert Axelrad, Everett Gendler and other highly politicized figures have been involved in varying degrees with the *Havurah*, the normative religious sense which has emerged has been almost totally inward-directed. From time to time, the issue of religious activism is raised in the *Havurah*, but as things now stand, there is little overt political awareness or interest. For those of us who see the Berrigans as models of ideal religious personalities, this has been a source of great disappointment. Indeed, several former members have left the *Havurah* because of the group's complete lack of interest in anything but the most inconsequential political engagements.

With so many people in the *Havurah* divorced, as they were, from the American political scene, there was also little in modern Jewish life that could be incorporated into their own religious growth. During the first year or two, therefore, there was a good deal of talk about religious communities in other traditions, while the fascination with Eastern religions which seized so many young Americans in the 1960's was

*Arthur Waskow, *The Bush is Burning!* pp. 14-15.

also evident in the *Havurah*, as was the psychological residue of the most serious aspects of the drug culture, and of psychedelics in particular.

To its credit, the *Havurah* resisted the temptation to chart a course of religious observance or belief for its members to follow; as a result there was a good deal of divergence and variance, especially during the earliest stages. Arthur Green, the dominant religious personality in the *Havurah*, sought to describe the general religious situation at the end of the first year:

> As things have worked out there does seem to be a particular Havurat Shalom style that is developing. . . . We are generally a heterodox (as distinct from Orthodox) community. This means there are those here who question even the most basic articles of traditional Jewish faith. While we run a pretty full gamut with regard to observance, even the most traditional in observance generally are such for personal existential reasons rather than out of absolute theological commitment. In general, I would say that theological issues as such are not central concerns of most of our students. Most seem to be more concerned with faith as experience, not with faith as ideology. There has developed here a type of concern for the inner life and for the relationship between the religious and personal growth to a degree that is not characteristic of Jewish institutional life, perhaps outside Lubavitch and Bobov.*

While theological concerns, even today, are not central to all the members, they are an important component of the religious interests and practices of the group. The most important theological influences are Chassidic and mystical, although of late a group in the *Havurah* has—only half-jokingly—established itself as *misnagdim* (rationalists, and of Chassidism).

What the *Havurah* has attempted to create, it seems to me,

*From a letter sent by Green to friends of *Havurat Shalom* at the end of the first year—June 6, 1969.

is a religious style that is at once both traditional and liberal. It is generally agreed that the denominations and factions in modern Jewish life are of little help to the individual Jew in search of religious commitment, unless he happens to be Orthodox. The *Havurah* has attempted, even before formulating its own religious ideology (as someday it must), to develop a sort of religious laboratory where certain tests can be run and recorded. This is not to suggest that the *Havurah's* religious life is for the most part experimental; it is not, except in the sense that the *Havurah* frequently finds itself on new ground. Until now, most forms of liberal Judaism have been decidedly *untraditional*. The *Havurah*, on the other hand, has attempted for the most part to preserve the traditional liturgy, calendar, and ritual of Jewish life.

A prime goal of the *Havurah* has always been the *integration* of religious sensibilities with the rest of life. For one thing, it was hoped that an appreciation of religion would have to go beyond liturgy or ritual, but without bypassing either along the way. Religion, it was felt, must be part of the *Havurah's* basic character, rather than a characteristic. It was not, therefore, something that could be relegated to a certain time of the week, or a special occasion. Nor was religion to be confused with observance, although the tendency in modern Jewish life to confuse the two is strong indeed.

How, then, does a community remain organically religious without defining religiosity in terms of observance? This has been an extremely difficult task, although a broadened understanding of religion has certainly made it easier. A fellowship community, living and acting together in a sincere and honest way, with regard to what is proper, fair, and beneficial to all segments of the community cannot help but be religiously sensitive. When, like the *Havurah*, it pays special attention to the place of liturgy and ritual, and defines even its academic program in primarily religious terms, the matter becomes less complex. The *Havurah*, according to an early document,

strives to transcend the divisions in American Jewry, inviting and welcoming the participation of both traditional Jews and those who are non-traditional in their patterns of religious observance. Members of the community will be encouraged to familiarize themselves with the full range of traditional Jewish forms of religious expression, while at the same time having the freedom to seek new ways and to give expression to that spirit which the tradition has sought to embody.*

By being open to the religious possibilities of all facets of Jewish expression in America, the *Havurah* has attempted to blend the traditional forms of Orthodoxy, the intellectual rigor of Conservative Judaism, the frank liberalization of the Reform movement, the historical and cultural sense of Reconstructionism, and the passion and, hopefully, some of the intensity of Chassidism.

The problem of creativity and spontaneity within a set structure of religious observance is a complex issue, but one which has gradually been resolved over the years in the *Havurah*. The first year or two saw a great concern with what was then seen as religious creativity. Particularly in the liturgy, but in other aspects of the religious sphere as well, there were numerous attempts to be different, innovative, somehow new on almost every occasion. Committees would be established, and a variety of readings, recordings, and themes were introduced into various parts of the services with the hope that this would lead to a deeper spiritual understanding and awareness. These projects were often successful, but the *Havurah* gradually abandoned this approach in favor of a simpler, more traditional service. For one thing, it is impossible to be continually creative, nor could the direction of a service be realistically determined by more than one person at a time. There were other factors as well:

From a spiritual point of view, I think we reached the point where we realized that we were burdened by a combination of

*From the brochure, A *Still Small Voice*, 1969.

modes of expression that simply did not sit well with one
another: a good poetry reading, a good concert and a good
dovnen just cannot be mingled to produce anything other than
a staccato hodge-podge. The choice was for *davening:* poetry
was largely eliminated and music became group singing, with
or without words. Outside readings are today sometimes used
as an introduction to the service or as part of a comment on the
Torah reading, but the main body of Shacharit employs the
Siddur alone.*

Most of the religious issues and observances center around
the most important aspect of the *Havurah* cycle: Shabbat. Just
as the *Havurah* is the center, the focal point, of the lives of its
members, so the Shabbat is the central point of the *Havurah.*
It is a weekly regulator, giving an order and a pattern to the
days. The progression of the Torah reading moves us steadily
forward, while the repetition of the continuing ritual reminds
us of the unchanging nature of things. In addition, Shabbat
provides an opportunity for a heightened awareness of the
natural world, of the weather, of time, providing the
participants to be more fully human, to incorporate, as it
were, the *neshama yeterah,* the extra soul which descends
with Shabbat.

Shabbat at the *Havurah* begins, in effect, with the Thursday
night activities. Generally, there will be a communal meal,
with a program or a meeting afterward. There is a subtle sense
of urgency, which can be seen in the hasty preparations before
we go to our homes Thursday night. Who is going to clean up
on Friday? Who will buy the *challah* (if time permits, some
people will bake their own)? Then there is the unspoken
weekly ritual, where at least half of the *Havurah* can usually
be found late Thursday night in one of the Cambridge
supermarkets.

Friday is a time for chores, running errands, for cleaning up,
some studying perhaps, for guests coming or for going out of
town for the weekend. During the warm weather, the service

From the June 6 letter of Arthur Green.

will begin at sundown, but the schedules of some *haverim* are such that we begin at six o'clock during the winter. Unlike Saturday morning, when the *Havurah* is jolly and crowded with guests, Friday night is a small, intimate and generally subdued experience. While there may be three or four guests present, the majority of the people are *haverim* themselves, which makes the service on Friday night the single occasion of the *havurah's* exclusive, private moment each week. The House is mostly darkened, the prayer room lit by candles. Like all *havurah* services, this one is held with the participants, including the *chazzan* seated on cushions on the floor. There is no separation of sexes, no fixed seating, and no rigid shape to the roughly circular pattern of people in the room.

But in spite of its fairly informal setting, the service itself is traditional. Except for an occasional page announcement if there are guests, the service is entirely in Hebrew. Before it starts, and as people enter the room, we may sing a *niggun*, or meditate in complete silence. The *chazzan* will determine the form; he may decide to read a chapter of *Shir haShirim* (The Song of Songs) before the actual liturgical service begins. The service—especially the opening Psalms of the Friday-night liturgy—is slow and deliberate. There is a low-keyed, restful, almost sad mood which nobody can explain. The service ends as it began, with a *niggun*, but it is now Shabbat, and the world is somehow different from what it was an hour earlier. We greet each other warmly and go off in small groups to the homes of various *haverim* for dinner. Some of us, especially those who are unmarried, will eat together in the House. The meal will be leisurely, full and spiced with good conversation and tuneful, joyous singing.

The next morning is a different world altogether. There may be as many as fifty or seventy guests, in addition to the twenty or so *haverim* in attendance. Here too the service is largely in Hebrew, although many more liberties are taken, at the discretion of the *chazzan*, as to the specific format of the liturgy. The opening section of the liturgy is generally replaced by a period of music, or meditation, or sometimes both—a sort of prolonged preparation. The traditional *Shacharit* (morning service) follows, intact but with much singing. Then there is a Torah reading, in which one chapter or so of the week's portion will be chanted. Somebody, usually Art Green, will have prepared a short talk or lesson on the portion, and there will often be a discussion. There is no *Musaf* (additional service); the Torah reading and lesson is followed by a final *niggun* or two, and the service ends. There will be a kiddush of some wine and cookies for our guests, who will generally stay around for up to an hour talking to each other, for there is a sort of community made up of people *around* but not *in* the *Havurah*. Inevitably there will be somebody, here for the first time, who wants to know what the *Havurah is*, anyway, as though it could be easily explained!

This is followed by lunch, in the same style as the night before. If there is any time for an afternoon walk, or a talk, or a game of chess after lunch, any of these things may and do happen. In the winter, there is only an hour or so between lunch and *seudah shelishit* (the traditional third Shabbat meal), when most of the *Havurah* will return at dusk. More symbolic than substantive, the meal will usually consist of a glass of wine, something to *nosh*, a story, perhaps and inevitably the staple of the *Havurah*'s diet: more *nigunnim* (woe to him who doesn't like to sing!). Sometimes there will be a talk, or a reading, but usually there are no words spoken. Havdalah is short, unelaborate, and suddenly another week begins. Then it is off to the movies, or back home to prepare tomorrow's Hebrew-school class, or, frequently, both.

The *Havurah*'s religious awareness is of course not limited to Shabbat. There is a great desire to reinvest with new meaning and dignity various observances, like *birkat hamazon* (the grace after meals), or the idea of a daily, morning service. There is a profound concern with the *spirit* of the law, and a frustration with those elements of the Jewish people whose religious concerns seem to leave little room for form, meaning, and asthetics. Kashrut, Shabbat, the holidays, are observed in earnest, if not strictness; in love, if not devotion.

From time to time the *Havurah* will go away en masse for a weekend, usually to celebrate a holiday or a wedding. There is a tradition of holding retreats on Shavuot and Succot especially. For the most part the retreats take place in a rural setting, and are generally held on weekends. Shavuot and particularly Succot are so much tied up with the natural cycle as well as the interests and needs of a community like the *Havurah* that this practice of going away together at these times has become very important.

The retreat inevitably becomes a chance for spiritual renewal for the *Havurah* as a group, and for the members as individuals. It is a chance to get closer to nature, to explore new territory together, (both figuratively and literally), to take more time than is generally available even on Shabbat to learn together, to sing, to walk, dance and just simply to live communally for more than a few hours at a time, and without the friendly but sometimes obtrusive eyes of well-meaning visitors.

III.   STUDYING IN THE HAVURAH

The casual visitor to Havurat Shalom is more likely than not to be present at a service, on Shabbat or perhaps on a holiday. At these times, the *Havurah* takes on the appearance of an alternative synagogue, and it is often difficult for non-members to imagine that on regular weekdays the *Havurah* is alive with a whole other set of concerns and activities. The chief activity in the *Havurah*, within the broader goals of creating a religious community, has been and remains the ongoing commitment to and participation in higher Jewish learning. Havurat Shalom was in fact first conceived of as a *yeshivah*, or, at the very least, a new kind of Seminary (it is chartered in the state of Massachusetts under the name Havurat Shalom Community Seminary), and while that particular aspect of *Havurah* life has—perhaps tem-

porarily—been set aside, it is certainly possible that the
Havurah, or perhaps one section in it, may yet be able to
develop a new kind of program specifically geared to
rabbinical training.

A significant number of people who currently are or have
been involved with the *Havurah* were previously students at
the Jewish Theological Seminary, and of that number, at least
half were ordained as rabbis. Yet the greatest impetus in the
creation and early development of the *Havurah* came
precisely from those men who had themselves received
ordination, and who looked back on their own Seminary
training with great reservations and highly ambivalent,
generally frustrated memories. The reasons are not difficult to
appreciate. At the Seminary, it was often felt that a lack of
real (not to mention religious) community served to render
the studies too academic, too removed from the concerns of
(religious) life, while a too-rigid system served to prevent an
integration of religious study with personal growth. Those
whose Jewish learning took place on the college campus were
often no less disenchanted, for there the courses in Judaica are
frequently seen as academic esoterica, while the lack of
community, or even fellowship, within the Academy is,
unfortunately, well known.

It was understood from the beginning that the activities—if
not the spirit—of the *Havurah* would be centered about
studying. This studying would be qualitatively-different from
what most of the *haverim* had experienced up until that point
in their lives. For one thing, the *Havurah* was to have no
"required courses," no subject or group of subjects which
everybody *had* to learn. At the same time, however, it was
recognized that no formal degree would be offered to those
who completed these studies, although the possibility of the
Havurah's eventually granting academic degrees at some
future time has always remained. There was to be no system
of credits, no administration, no central authority other than
a coordinator whose sole responsibility would be to see to it
that the classes were indeed operating without major
problems. But the program itself, the actual content of the

courses, as well as their spirit and direction would depend totally upon the natural intellectual and religious curiosities of the students and teachers. When the *Havurah* first began, there was a clear distinction between those two roles, which, when combined with the group's egalitarian tendencies, gave rise to a host of problems. More recently, the *Havurah* has developed to the point where the differences between teachers and students are all but erased, as a person who teaches one class will usually be a student in two or three others.

The egalitarian ideal of the *Havurah's* approach to education is frequently misunderstood, and is often thought of, quite incorrectly, as a case of the blind leading the blind. One reason this has not taken place is that the *Havurah* has been relatively fortunate in that among its members have been people qualified and willing to teach in a variety of capacities. As Barry Holtz was to explain,

> . . . our desire to learn from all our members, our recognition that "student" members can also be teachers, does not mean that we are not involved with serious study led by competent people, but rather that we try to encourage all members of the *havurah* to share with the group the disciplines of study they have been able to command.*

To a large degree, these hopes were fulfilled, and were strong in their impact on the group as a whole, at least to the point where Stephen Lerner could react to the *Havurah's* learning enterprise in these terms:

> To this writer, the most remarkable revelation is that the students are clearly contented. Whereas students all over the country express widespread dissatisfaction with institutions of higher learning, both Jewish and secular, the members of the *havurah* actually like their courses.**

*From a letter published in *Response 9* (Winter 1970-71), p. 14.
**Stephen Lerner, "The Havurot," *Response 8* (Fall, 1970), p. 21. This article appeared originally in *Conservative Judaism* (Spring, 1970).

What distinguishes the *haverim* from students in most colleges and seminaries is that they are *members* rather than merely students, and, in studying, are fulfilling their own needs and interests, not those prescribed for them by an institution. Not that this has left the *Havurah's* study program without problems. The *Havurah's* relaxed atmosphere has made rigorous, scholarly work more the exception than the rule, while graduate schools and other competitive ventures reduce the amount of time and energy devoted to studying at the Havurah.

What has occurred at the Havurah is that the process of studying has, quite unintentionally, developed into something akin to what has been proposed by Ivan Illich, the Catholic priest turned social visionary, in his recent and fascinating volume *De-Schooling Society* (New York, 1971). Illich proposes that education be taken out of the schools and put instead, with no protective cover, into local communities, in the form of matching up students and teachers for private and small-group study and exploration. The way the Havurah determines its curriculum is a case in point. There is a meeting usually held in June of each year, where the Havurah takes a sort of poll to determine the kinds of courses which should be offered when the group comes together after the summer break. Quite simply, we go around the room, and each person suggests two or three areas which he would like to work on in the Havurah. If two or more people hit upon something in common, then *automatically* (if they so desire) there is a course. Similarly, when members of a course decide for any reason that the group ought not meet any more, it ceases. The members of each particular course make all of the decisions that affect them: what should be studied, how it should be studied, what readings and resources ought to be used, whether it is necessary to consult somebody outside of the Havurah for guidance, how often the class should meet, and so on. The members of the Havurah would for the most part find themselves in agreement with Illich that the formal operation of organized schools has in fact served more as an impediment to education than as a means of access:

> Schools are designed on the assumption that there is a secret to everything in life; that the quality of life depends on knowing that secret; that secrets can be known only in orderly successions, and that only teachers can properly reveal these secrets. An individual with a schooled mind conceives of the world as a pyramid of classified packages accessible only to those who carry the proper tag. New educational institutions would break apart this pyramid. Their purpose must be to facilitate access for the learner; or allow him to look into the windows of the control room or the parliament, if he cannot get in by the door. Moreover, such new institutions should be channels to which the learner would have access without credentials or pedigree—public spaces in which peers and elders outside his immediate horizon would become available.*

In spite of certain similarities to Illich's proposed model, however, the Havurah is not a public place of learning, but a basically closed system for the communal program of studying. There are mixed feelings about having the study program limited to *haverim,* and a special adult study institute was established a year ago. Made up for the most part of young adults and college students in the greater Boston area, this program is a series of evening courses in Judaica, on various levels, taught by Havurah members. The participants in each class are invited to join some of the *Havurah's* activities, and it is hoped that eventually some of the classes will be able to go on occasional weekend retreats together, along with several *Havurah* members. Adult Study courses have included Hassidism, Jewish Philosophy, Hebrew and Yiddish literature, Jewish mysticism, and Bible.

One of the existing conditions which led to the formation of the *Havurah* in the first place was the dissatisfaction on the

*De-Schooling Society, p. 76.

part of many college students with courses in which a professor would enter the lecture hall, talk for an hour, and leave until the following week. The *Havurah's* purpose has been to greatly reduce the amount of fragmentation caused by the standard categorizations of teachers and students. This is not to suggest that nobody knows more than anybody else, or that nobody can guide, and nobody can learn from that guidance. Obviously such attitudes would lead to a waste of everybody's time and energy. The concern is that certain traditional *roles* in education, when carried to their logical extreme, can be harmful not only to learning itself, but to the type of community the *Havurah* wishes to become:

> As a community of people who study and worship together, we want our actions and our speech to be characterized by the openness that makes true meetings possible. . . . All this means that we must be wary of anything that would set up artificial barriers between us as people. We do not wish to *be* students and teachers but to learn and to teach. All members of the community thus share in the responsibility for planning and executing courses, reading programs, and research projects which speak to their own religious needs. In this way, we hope to insure the organic connection between study and worship, and to prevent the imposition of pre-established relationship modes upon us. Creating an educational model without a conventional authority structure cannot be for us merely a far-off pedagogical objective; it is a necessity if a community of religious study is to exist.*

Courses of study in the Havurah have covered a variety of subjects. For the most part, the classes are limited to subjects of Jewish concern, because other types of learning are more easily available at some of the nearby colleges. A current and fascinating exception is a course in character typology, led by a member of the group who is a psychologist. But for the most part, the emphasis has generally been on the study of primary

---

*From the original *Prospectus*.

sources, in the original Hebrew (or Aramaic), and has included such subjects and texts as Genesis, Prophets, Psalms, Song of Songs, Talmud (usually by topics), Shulchan Aruch, Zohar, liturgy, Agnon, Yiddish literature, Nachman of Bratzlav, Hassidism, and first-century Judaism. In addition, haverim have been able to make use of the Judaica department at Brandeis University, and have been able to study with such scholars as Alexander Altmann, Nachum Glatzer, Nachum Sarna, and more recently, Michael Fishbane, who had previously been a teaching member of the Havurah. In addition, the nearby Harvard Divinity School, with its superb library facilities, has always been convenient and helpful.

Some observers are surprised to learn that study in the Havurah is not, in any normal sense, goal-directed. There is no attempt here to achieve an easy "relevance"; on the other hand, there is also no wish to store information for future "use" in the sense of graduate training for a career:

> . . . we do not view the Havurat Shalom experience as primarily one of professional preparation. Many of us have experienced dissatisfaction with the existing structures of higher Jewish education, arising from their highly professional orientation and from their quantitative view of knowledge of texts as a standard for religious growth. . . . [O]ur aim . . . is not the training of religious professionals, but the education of religious personalities on the basis of a personal encounter with the sources of Judaism.

For better or worse, studying in the *Havurah* is not limited to the *Havurah's* own courses. Most members have at one time or another worked on their own projects, or group projects, often having to do with writing, editing, or translating. Others have been busy reading and researching. In addition, many members of the *Havurah* are involved in teaching in some of the local Hebrew High schools. Communally, the entire *Havurah* will often study together at a retreat, sometimes with specially invited guests, usually with teachers from the *Havurah*. There is an attempt—at this point not yet successful—to establish one course in the *Havurah* which would involve everybody in the group. But, in general, it is difficult and somewhat artificial to isolate the process of studying, since it is organically attached to everything else, and, despite its primary importance, is only one aspect of the religious character of Havurat Shalom.

IV.   HAVURAT SHALOM AS COMMUNITY

We are always accounting for the state of our souls. We are always answering the telephone and explaining things. We are always repeating ourselves to each new person who walks in the door and wants to know what happened today.
> —Joel Rosenberg
> *(Response 9*, p. 69)

We are not, however, a wide-open community. To be meaningful in our lives, the group, we feel, must remain small; and it is clear that the *havurah* as now constituted is geared to a certain age group with a certain social situation. However, I don't think we can be blamed for trying to establish the kind of group that best fits our particular needs as long as we retain a sense of responsibility to the "outside" world.
> —Barry Holtz
> *(Response 9*, p. 13)

There is a strong tension in any new community surrounding the question of outsiders. The irony behind Joel Rosenberg's understandable lament is that the very fact he bemoans has been so crucial in the self-awareness process of life in the *Havurah*. For it is only after enough people have walked in the door, written letters of inquiry, made telephone calls, and asked questions that one begins to feel, slowly but concretely, what until then was only sensed. And while this constant explaining is surely not adequate proof of community, it is, in the best sense, a good indicator of it.

A group of people growing together often cannot see itself grow, for there is nothing against which to measure that growth. On almost any level, day-to-day progress is difficult to record, and since a community is certainly a day-to-day experience, it frequently requires an outside factor to help formulate its own self-image. A case in point was the visit to the *Havurah* of Harvey Cox and a group of his students late in 1971. This particular group of visitors was also involved in creating a religious community at the Old Cambridge Baptist Church. They joined us at the *Havurah* for a communal meal, and afterward both groups met together in the living-room. We gradually came to understand by their questions that, in their eyes, we already were a religious community. Even more important than their questions, however, was the fact that we had to answer them not only in front of their group, but in front of our own as well. It was this public accounting of the state of our community which taught us, as perhaps nothing else could have, that to some extent we had already achieved at least the minimal level of community.

Of course we are talking here of a community that is highly artificial, as are most new communities, in that the members have come here from a variety of other places for the sake of the *Havurah* itself. Naturally, each person brings with him a slightly different conception, and unique dream, of what kind of community ought to be developed. In the first two years especially, there were many long and sometimes bitter discussions about the nature of the community that was to be formed. In the second year, when the number of people in the *Havurah* had swelled to forty, there were several splits and within three months the community was reduced to half its former size. Some of those who left had felt that the *Havurah* was not sufficiently intense in its communality. For others, the lack of political awareness and activity made this kind of community simply inappropriate for their own needs. Still others wanted a more rigid degree of Jewish observance.

With a little hindsight, it is all too easy to realize what went wrong. It rests upon a mistake which is probably made by many new communities. *Before it starts, a new community* must take as much time as is necessary to decide upon certain fundamental questions. Had the Havurah talked over certain issues for the first six months *prior* to its actual beginning, some of the problems of the second year might have been avoided. Still the group did manage to deal with these issues, although there were some serious wounds, which are not yet forgotten, even if most of them have healed over the course of time.*

When the *Havurah* first began, nobody knew what the group would come to resemble. To this day, there are various tendencies and opinions within the group, although for the most part a certain stability is in evidence. In 1968, when things began, there were very few models, and none of them were very much like any of the options that seemed appropriate to the new *Havurah*. More recently, hundreds of

---

*New communities would do well to pay heed to a little booklet circulated in the Commune movement, and published by Alternatives! Foundation in San Francisco. Untitled, the booklet was written by a Canadian commune, and makes the following suggestion:

These basic agreements are the most important. They must be real *agreements*. Don't give in on an important issue to preserve community harmony at this point: there will be plenty of opportunity for that later. Write the agreements down so you won't forget them. Talk about them as long as the subject is interesting to you. It's during these months that you will decide if you can live with your brothers. Make specific agreements about: (1) money: where it will come from and where it will go; (2) child rearing: how permissive or how authoritarian to be, schooling, etc., (3) sex: how much to limit it, strict monogamy or complete freedom, or what stage in between? (4) living situation: separate houses, dormitories, etc.; (5) possessions: what to be held in common, what as private property; (6) work responsibilities: who does what part of maintenance tasks, how many hours a day to work, etc.; (7) visitor policy: how open to be, how important is privacy? (You will have lots of visitors); (8) drugs: policy on use, cautionary measures; (9) neighbor policy: how to relate to the greater community; (10) decision-making policy: who, specifically, is responsible to make what decisions, at which times? will you vote, get consensus, delegate leaders to decide which issues that arise? (11) how will your eating/cooking/dining arrangement be structured, if at all? (12) how about pets? (13) how about outside political involvement of the group and/or individual members?

While the Havurah is not a commune, about half of these items have become issues in some form or another, and we would have done well to have anticipated some of them.

communes and small communities have sprung up in
America, particularly in the southwest, and while the
commune movement has never directly affected the *Havu-*
rah, there have been certain common problems. Religiously,
the available models were all non-Jewish; monasteries, and
other forms of religious brotherhood were within easy access,
but these were obviously different from the *Havurah*, which
was, among other things, an urban center of learning and, it
was hoped, of spirituality as well.

"Friendship," observes Neusner, "never transcends individual friends; fellowship must begin with such transcendence."* It was clear from the outset that within the *Havurah*
there would be varying degrees of closeness and intimacy. Not
everybody, it was understood, could possibly be on intimate
grounds with everybody else. Still, there was (and remains) a
basic reluctance to see in the concept of *havurah* a suggestion
of *only* fellowship, because the connotations of and desires for
real friendship are naturally very strong. There is a temptation, also, arising perhaps out of the neo-utopianism of the
late 1960's, to create a kind of idealized community where
each person is responsible, loving, and kind toward each other
person. On some levels, that *is* possible; there are certain
kinds of love that are probably easier than friendship. But
even this takes time and effort. Again, Neusner:

> Fellowship has no substance. It is not a social continuum. It
> manifests no existence independent from that of its communi-
> cants. Fellowship is a dimension of time: one cannot say
> fellowship is, but rather, fellowship happens. It is created and
> re-created from moment to moment when certain elements,
> namely, radically isolated individuals, coalesce to create it.
> The catalyst of fellowship needs to be discovered and defined.
> The components of fellowship are individuals coming together
> out of radical self-involvement and isolation from one another,
> to pursue a purpose that transcends their own individual
> lives.**

*Fellowship in Judaism, 71.
* *Ibid., 73.

Neusner's reference to a process of "transcendence" which occurs in a fellowship-community need not imply any detraction from the importance of the individual. The *Havurah*, happily, is not the kind of society where the individual is continually being asked to sacrifice his identity and his needs "for the good of the group." The group itself is served, it is commonly held, by the fulfillment of its individual *haverim*. Naturally there must be, and is, a certain amount of flexibility to enable this to occur; compromise is also an important factor. Perhaps it is the small size of the *Havurah* which has prevented authority from becoming destructive whenever it is exercised. The "authority," when it is specific, is no more than the power of access, invested in a rotating chairmanship. Decisions are made at group meetings, by consensus.

At the core of the *Havurah* is the realization that the group itself has no existence, despite its public image, apart from that of its members. Inasmuch as a group naturally tends to become a sort of authority, the *Havurah* has developed, fortunately, an authority of enablement, as distinct from the well-known alternative, the authority of prevention. This is an authority that seeks not to control individual charges, but to enrich their lives. In other words, the framework is never permitted to be more than a shell for the content. To be sure, the *Havurah* has found it expedient, if not essential, to have a house, a bank account, a series of meetings during the year, and an allocation of responsibilities. But at no time is the form allowed to dictate the content; that pattern must constantly be fought, and reversed.

This can best be illustrated by an annual ritual in the *Havurah* that is so subtle and low-keyed that its profound importance is almost obscured. After a communal meal, or at a meeting, somebody will decide to make a count of the number of people who intend to remain in the *Havurah* after the summer. For the most part, members stay in the group unless they leave Boston, or withdraw from the *Havurah* for a specific reason. The procedure is never acted out in exactly these terms, and sometimes it is not said at all, but merely understood by all those who are present: *It is not taken for granted each spring that the Havurah will necessarily resume operation in the fall.* Of ·course, it is by this time almost assumed, and certainly hoped, that this will be the case. *But it does not have to happen.* The essence of the *Havurah* as a counter-institution is precisely this fact: that there is no authority higher than that of the members. The form cannot outlive the content by a single moment. This is, I think, the fundamental difference between groups like the *Havurot*, and the larger and better-known organizations in American Jewish life. However effective the *havurah* may appear to be as a form, it is always less important than the lives that control it.

This is not to imply that there is no sense of politics, of the sharing of power, *within* the *Havurah*. That would be naive and of course untrue, for *every* social grouping has within it various forces and dynamics of power. Authority within the *Havurah* is remarkably well balanced; there is no dead weight. There is rarely a formal vote, however, and the process of consensus does occasionally cover up real differences. But the most exciting aspect of the regular meetings is the *patience* which is everywhere in evidence. The *haverim* have somehow learned how to *listen* to each other, and that alone is half the battle. The *Havurah* can be somewhat effective because it has managed to isolate power, which resides in the group, from responsibility, which is almost always an individual matter, used by members at their own discretion. Finally, there is, by now, a certain trust which enables individuals in the group to proceed on their own, and not always feel they must return to the group for further instructions at every point along the way.

Although this was not true in the first two years, there is now a division of labor and responsibilities, assigned by the coordinator on a volunteer basis each fall. Somebody must be in charge of the retreats, of the study program, of the services, the adult studies, and various other aspects of the *Havurah's* program. In addition, there will be letters to answer, guests who will ask to stay with us at various times, communal meals to arrange for, and a variety of small but essential physical chores. These, including the meals, the weekly clean-up, the buying of challah, the arranging of wine for *kiddush* and provisions for the *seudah shelishit,* are all shared by the group on a rotating basis.

During the third year, there was a growing but undetected problem that had to do, in my own opinion, with a certain crisis of comfortability. Unlike the first two years, the meetings had been surprisingly pleasant and effective, the programs were always successful, the services were good. At the same time, there seemed to a certain mechanical feeling, a distance among the members themselves. At a time of no conflict, there is also no chance for release, and for confrontation. Small frustrations inevitably build up, and if not expressed, can lead to frustrations and to coldness in the community. After a great deal of discussion, and much healthy caution, it was decided that at the end of the year there would be an encounter session for those members of the *Havurah* who wished to participate. Most, in the end, did join in, and for three days we worked, with a professional trainer, at uncovering deeper levels of honesty among ourselves. What emerged in these sessions is obviously too private to be shared outside the *Havurah,* but at least one lesson became apparent that could be learned by many different kinds of social groups. It is a simple lesson, but one so easily forgotten that it bears repeating, and, still better, demonstration. In any community, people inevitably tend to see themselves in certain respects as different from the community. They will make certain assumptions based on the premise that certain characteristics are common "to everybody else." It is only when people's private thoughts and fears can be exposed to the entire group that the group can realize that such fears are, more likely than not, common to everybody. In the encounter session, the members of the *Havurah* learned that the problem of forming close relationships within the group itself is common to everybody, as is the desire to become more involved in the community's various activities.

In view of the encounter group, which was—despite some serious problems—judged to be helpful, the *Havurah* decided that such a safety-valve ought to be used more than once a year, and could, if used more frequently, prevent the building up of feelings past the point of safety. There has been, so far in the fourth year, a small encounter session once a month, and while there is some doubt as to the effectiveness of these sessions, the important thing is that the forthrightness that had to be learned in the initial three-day experience can be more easily applied to the daily life of the community.

The most regular form of the community meeting is not the actual meeting but the communal meal. The person in charge will arrange for everybody to bring something: a main course, a vegetable, a grain, bread, desert, salad, a beverage, and is also responsible for the tone of a particular meal. After the meal, which, incidentally, is always vegetarian, there will generally be a program of some sort, or a meeting. Often a guest will come and lead a session. Recent visitors have included Allen Grossman, professor and poet, who spoke on religious poetry; Adin Steinzaltz, the Jerusalem Talmudist and mystic; Maurice Stein, on the faculty of Brandeis, who is developing a form of deprofessionalized counseling; Everett Fox, a colleague of ours who is doing a new translation of the Bible; several Israeli *kibbutz* intellectuals, including Muki Tzur and Avraham Shapira; Jacob Neusner, who led a discussion about the religious nature of study, and many others. From time to time, members of the *Havurah* will make a presentation to the rest of the group, in an attempt to share some personal thoughts, or research, of various forms of creation. This may also take place on a retreat, or sometimes at *seudah shlishit* as well.

Because of the great stress upon the inner-directions and the community itself, it is often charged that the *Havurah* has no concern for the outside community. It has been said, for instance, that the *Havurah* is fragmenting the Jewish community instead of strengthening it, as though the Jewish community were and has been a monolithic entity. In addition, it is wrong to assume that by devoting their energies to communal activities, the members are somehow "robbing" the rest of the Jewish world. The *Havurah* was, after all, established by dissidents who had already given up on the Jewish "establishment," and who would not be interested in directing their energies in those areas. In the same manner, the absence of political activism in the *Havurah* often leads critics to assume that there is no concern for the rest of the Jewish people. That is to ignore the fact that most of the members are deeply involved in teaching and leading high school students, and are working on many individual projects involving such issues as federation priorities, publishing, Hillel work, lecturing, Soviet Jewry, and many other concerns. Still, it is unfortunate that the *Havurah* has not managed to develop any kind of moral leadership for the rest of young Boston Jewry. Of course, this is not one of its purposes, but one wishes it were.

The *Havurah*, as has been pointed out, is a sort of temporary setting. It may indeed develop into a community which serves the needs of adult members for the rest of their lives, but this is unlikely. Society is in such a state of transition that it is impossible to know what the next years will bring. People are always asking us questions, saying "That's fine for now, but what about the future?" It's hard enough making something that's fine for now, after all. A generation that grew up alongside the threat of atomic war cannot think of the future in the same terms as its parents. One could certainly speculate on possible scenarios. A group in Israel composed of former Havurat Shalom people could be a realistic picture in 1975; so could a different kind of group in the woods of New Hampshire. The immediate objective at hand, however, is not to map out the future so much as to keep the community going, and to seek out new members to replace those who will, for various reasons, be leaving after this year. Beyond that it is impossible to predict.